FACE VALUES

Vernon Coleman is the author of *The Medicine Men, Paper Doctors, Everything You Want To Know About Ageing, Stress Control, The Home Pharmacy,* and *Aspirin or Ambulance.*

He has written three novels as Edward Vernon, and writes two weekly columns, one of which is syndicated to newspapers around the world. He is a Fellow of the Royal Society of Medicine and a member of the Desperate Dan Pie Eaters Club.

Dr Coleman was born in 1946, and has been a general practitioner long enough to acquire totally illegible handwriting.

Dr Miriam Stoppard has published a number of books on health and is well known as a result of her frequent appearances on television and radio and her articles in newspapers and magazines.

Dr Vernon Coleman
with Margaret Coleman

FACE VALUES

How the Beauty Industry affects you

Foreword by Miriam Stoppard

Pan Original
Pan Books London and Sydney

First published 1981 by Pan Books Ltd,
Cavaye Place, London SW10 9PG
2nd printing 1982
© Vernon Coleman 1981
ISBN 0 330 26506 7
Printed and bound in Great Britain by
Richard Clay (The Chaucer Press) Ltd, Bungay, Suffolk

to X
the chromosome that makes the difference

CONTENTS

PART TWO
THE PROFESSIONALS

PART THREE
CLASSIFIED SECTION

FOREWORD

I love cosmetics. I love the plethora of products that allows me to paint, disguise, camouflage, accentuate and define. Dr Vernon Coleman does not seem to like them quite as much. But then that's not surprising as he has less frequent recourse to them than I. But on the cosmetics industry (and that would include manufacturers and hangers-on, hangers-on being defined as beauticians, cosmeticians, beauty writers etc.) we are in accord. It goes something like this; 'I'm with you on the cosmetics, it's the cosmetics industry I can't stand.'

Ever since I learned about the physiology of the skin, hair and nails as a medical student I have been condemned to this love-hate relationship with the cosmetics industry. So many of the claims are exorbitant, so much of the language is pseudoscientific, so much of the packaging is blatantly seductive or falsely clinical that it takes no more than common sense to question the basic premise behind the pizazz. 'New product X will make you look younger, longer.' Younger than what? Whatever you're using now? All the other products on the market? The hanging comparisons give the game away. Because, of course, to show that any cosmetic could make you look younger, longer, the perpetrator of the claim would need to examine the skin of several hundred women several times a year for ten to fifteen years according to objective measurable criteria, *with product X one side of the face and a rival product on the other,* research which no manufacturer has to my knowledge undertaken.

Dr Coleman and I share concern that the 'depth of dishonesty and amount of secrecy which still exists in many dark corners . . .' of the cosmetics industry has not been scrutinized by critical consumer bodies. What astonishes me is that the consumer herself has not been able to see through the transparency of the advertising claims and the profiteering of the glossy wrappers.

Any reader of Dr Coleman's book will find herself disenchanted with much that goes on in the beauty world. Much careful research has gone into the compilation of what Every Woman Ought to know About Cosmetics Before Spending a Penny on Them. In his introduction, Dr Coleman admits that his book can be described as tough and knocking. And so it is in the right places. Myths are exploded, confusions are clarified and jargon is decoded. Quite rightly, in my opinion, Dr Coleman concludes that no special ingredient, be it Vitamin A,B,C,D,E, or F, collagen, hormones, avocado oil or cucumber juice can do more for the skin than a moisturising cream. Oh, and in passing the shortcomings of those are listed too. As are those of the beauty editors, peremptorily described as the 'eunuchs of the cosmetics industry', beauty experts who talk nonsense and pseudoscientific rubbish, and beauticians themselves who in Dr Coleman's view are simply not trained, and whose advice he considers commercial and worrying in its omissions.

For the woman who asks: Who am I to believe? What should I use? This book will act as a helpful guide through a morass of conflicting claims, myths and legends. To a doctor, much of cos-metology seems to be witchcraft. In his glossary of terms, Dr Coleman resolutely clears away the mists and in doing so gives some very sound advice:

If all is going well, don't interfere – eye drops have no place in healthy eyes. Choose good simple unperfumed products – exotic ingredients are unproven and only push up the price.

The ultimate test of our congruency came when I turned to read what Dr Coleman had written about cellulite, which I've described as a fake complaint. There is a multi-million-pound business sup-ported by hundreds of clinics and countless treatments dedicated to the abolition of what is no more than a normal variant of fat deposition. Dr Coleman's book passes the tests: he concludes, 'From the evidence I've been able to find I'm certainly not con-vinced that cellulite exists at all.'

INTRODUCTION

I readily confess that until I began to write this book I had no idea of the number of magazine inches devoted to beauty care, nor did I realize just how many books have been published by beauty experts of one sort or another. When I first began my research I went into a bookshop in London to look for a few introductory titles and came out with armfuls of books. A visit to a newsagent's left me staggering under the weight of a selection of women's magazines carrying beauty pages.

I suppose in a way I should not have been quite so surprised as I was by this quantity of literature: after all half the population is female, and I have increasingly come to realize that the vast majority of women wear at least some make-up. Men simply haven't realized this because they never see the women with whom they don't share bathrooms in their naked faces.

It is a curiously unnerving discovery, but it shouldn't be thought that all this art is employed entirely to dupe and mystify men, since women clearly enjoy making themselves up as much for each other and themselves as for men. Most women have a routine whereby they apply a minimum of disguise every morning – either foundation, mascara or lipstick – and without it they feel unhappy. It can work as a mood-changer. For instance, part of the enjoyable anticipation of a party or an evening out is reflected in more time spent creating more elaborate effects with face paint, while at the other extreme when a woman is feeling low she may go out and buy a new lipstick or eye-shadow, or have a haircut to cheer herself up.

Doubtless men would enjoy using cosmetics too, if society approved and their equivalent bathroom time weren't spent removing their beards. At various periods in the past men have been quite as artfully decorated, and male punks today must enjoy using make-up as much for the same reasons women do as for the sake of shocking the conservative elements in society.

We all admire good skin and bone structure, but few of us have them; even fashion models apparently have flaws they are neurotic about. Make-up is a device which enables women to enhance their good features and cover up those which are unfashionable or unattractive. It can allow fair heads to complete with brunettes with eyelashes that emphasize their eyes; it can provide the girl without hollow cheeks with at least the semblance of them; it can cover up teenage acne, signs of worry, ill-health and age to some degree. In all, it helps women feel less vulnerable – something we all try to hide in various ways.

Several experiments have been carried out by psychologists on the subject of attraction and how looks affect the way we perceive one another. What these have shown is that if we enjoy someone's looks we are more likely to attribute them with all sorts of other qualities: intelligence; charm; sympathy; confidence. Make-up will therefore indirectly create the impression that a woman possesses these qualities. Men seek the same façades in other ways – by their choice of cars and clothes. Probably they have less of a feeling of vulnerability anyway. It will be interesting to see whether more men take to make-up as the Women's Movement grows and more women leave theirs off.

At any rate women do not have problems finding out how to experiment with styles and alter their faces to make themselves more attractive to others – magazines and beauty books exist in plenty. My aim here is to try to ensure that this need so many women have is not exploited by the cosmetics industry to the point where women are persuaded to waste a lot of money on useless or even damaging products when the simplest solutions will perform the same function. For as I read through all the material I was astonished to find that many of the so-called beauty experts seemed to understand remarkably little about the scientific bases upon which the cosmetics industry is based. The advice contained in book after book and column after column proved to be founded not on any attempt to assess the available products but simply on the publicity material produced by companies marketing specific products.

As a naive and innocent observer I found the information and advice that is available confusing and unhelpful. I felt sure that any casual book or magazine reader must be similarly bewildered for the simple reason that much of the promotional material for cosmetic products seems to be based on scientific evidence that is summarized but never explained in any detail.

As I read on and found myself daily more and more confused about the advantages of toothpastes with fluoride, hair shampoos with conditioner, skin creams with vitamin E and so on and so on, I began to realize just why Kyle Cathie, my editor at Pan, had suggested I write this book. I confess that at first I'd completely underestimated the extent of the pseudoscientific world which has grown up around modern cosmetics and toiletries. I found my ignorance a boon for had I begun with any preconceived notions and prejudices, an objective analysis of the available products would have been far more difficult to produce.

This is perhaps an apt point at which to introduce a short note about myself. As a medical practitioner I have some basic understanding of the human body and I know where to find out things I don't know. More importantly I have in the past ten years written a great deal about the pharmaceutical industry and I have learnt something about the tricks and deceits used by manufacturers to overpromote their products. These two qualifications have hopefully enabled me to write a fresh, honest and straightforward analysis of the cosmetics industry which I trust will be of use to all those who buy and use these products. I must here add that my third important qualification is that I have been able to work with my wife Margaret who, as a consumer of a vast variety of these products, has been able to guide and help my explorations in this alien commercial world.

Having detailed my qualifications let me explain how I've set about writing this book. I quickly became aware that there are a great many myths and misconceptions in the cosmetics industry and my first and main aim was obviously to get some facts on which to base my advice. To do that I've read hundreds of books and magazines and journal articles and I've written hundreds of letters and spoken to countless people. Like a child I've asked Why? Why? Why? and demanded Prove it, Prove it, Prove it, until the people who have helped me must have been heartily sick of my persistence. I thank those who have been patient with me but I do not apologize. I don't think that the book could have been written in any other way.

As I collected material I slowly began to realize that the cosmetics industry makes the drug industry look positively honest, open and uncomplicated. The depth of dishonesty in some parts of the cosmetics industry appalled me. It seems to me that this industry has for too long been ignored by critical consumer representatives.

The amount of secrecy which still exists in many dark corners of the industry made realistic scientific assessments of some products impossible. Where that was the case I have resorted to estimates about the values of specific groups of products rather than individual cosmetics. In some ways this has probably made this book more and not less valuable, since products come and go remarkably quickly so that brand names are often forgotten before dust has settled on the advertising material.

Inevitably there are parts of this book which can be described as 'tough' and 'knocking'. The first part of the book in particular contains some harsh comments about the industry. This material is not, however, included simply to satisfy my personal desire to publicly savage pseudoscientific verbiage, but because I firmly believe that by understanding the working of the cosmetics industry more people will be able to judge the products available according to their quality rather than the skills of the copywriters.

But that is just one part of the book. There are also many pages devoted to providing positive and simple answers to simple, often asked questions such as 'what causes brittle nails?' and 'what is the best way to prevent dry skin developing?' Sometimes the answers to these questions involve professional medical or surgical help as well as simple cosmetic assistance, and where this is the case I have described the help available.

Finally, I would like to invite readers who have information or advice which they feel might be useful to future readers to write to me care of the publishers.

PART ONE
THE COSMETICS
INDUSTRY

INTRODUCTORY EXPLANATIONS

AN ESSENTIAL DEFINITION

In a statutory instrument entitled 'The Cosmetic Products Regulations 1978' the Secretary of State defined a cosmetic product as 'any substance or preparation intended to be applied to any part of the external surfaces of the human body (that is to say the epidermis, hair system, nails, lips and external genital organs) or to the teeth or buccal mucosa wholly or mainly for the purpose of cleaning, perfuming or protecting them or keeping them in good condition or changing their appearance or combating body odour or perspiration except where such cleaning, perfuming, protecting, keeping, changing or combating is wholly for the purpose of treating or preventing disease'.

Now reading official prose is never easy, but I think that this particular short definition is an extremely important one since it contributes to the confusion caused by the fact that there are a great many products on sale today which cannot be clearly defined as cosmetics or medicines – products which exist in the extensive no man's land between the two camps.

The sort of products I'm talking about are those such as nourishing skin creams, rejuvenating oils and hair conditioners. The cosmetic counters in chemists' and stores are piled high with such products for which there are said to be medicinal as well as cosmetic indications.

There are many manufacturers who exploit this overlap between beauty preparations and over-the-counter medicines and who take advantage of the fears, needs and anxieties of potential customers, promoting their wares as though they had been prepared by leading researchers using all the technology available to modern medical scientists. They know well that there are a great many potential customers who will pay extra for a product which is said to have qualities other than purely cosmetic ones.

The official definition which I quoted earlier plays right into their hands since it puts those products which have or which are said to have only partly medicinal qualities into the same group as products which are purely cosmetic. This allows manufacturers to promote their cosmetic products as having medicinal qualities without their being subject to the regulations which govern the manufacturing, marketing and sale of medicines.

In my view it is the word 'mainly' which is the key word in the official definition. To reduce the opportunity for manufacturers to promote cosmetics in this way I would like to see all products said to have medicinal qualities dealt with as medicines, with only those which are made and sold as purely cosmetic products being labelled cosmetic. This isn't just a pedantic argument: the controls which govern the manufacture, promotion and availability of medicines are different from those which govern cosmetics, and the looseness of the official definition allows cosmetic manufacturers far too much freedom.

I believe that if a company promotes and presents a product as having medicinal qualities of any kind then it should be prepared to have that product judged on the same grounds as other medicines are judged. And that is exactly what I have done in this book. Those products which are advertised purely as cosmetics are assessed as cosmetics. But those products advertised as having therapeutic qualities have been assessed more strictly. —

Manufacturers may squeal a little but it seems to me to be quite fair that if they want to sell their products on medicinal grounds they should expect to have them judged in the same way that medicinal products are judged.

HISTORICAL PREJUDICES

The use of cosmetics has developed over many thousands of years and has been influenced by a great variety of factors. Primitive men, smearing their faces with crude vegetable dyes in attempts to frighten off their enemies, may have been influenced by watching birds and animals changing colour when threatened by predators. Egyptians added perfumed oils to their baths to keep their bodies clean and sweet smelling. Assyrians painted their eyelids with blue or green dyes to provide themselves with some protection against the midday sun.

The most important single influence on the use of cosmetics has, however, been something simpler and more basic. The women of Rome didn't go to the trouble of lengthening their eyebrows with soot-stained sticks because they wanted to protect their eyes or frighten intruders, but because they knew that it would make them look more attractive.

Sex may have always been the most important natural influence on the production and use of cosmetics, but during the last few centuries other more contrived influences have played a part.

During the Renaissance artistic and scientific developments affected just about every aspect of life, and the production and use of cosmetics were no exception. Indeed the world of cosmetics was influenced both by art and by science with the use of cosmetics growing under the control of fashion designers and artists, while the production of cosmetics was developed through the skills of alchemists. Sex was still the basic driving force in the use of cosmetics, but their preparation had become a science and their application an art.

Things progressed so far that attempts were made to control the use of cosmetics. In 1770 a Bill was introduced into the English Parliament which was designed to control the use of cosmetic products. The Bill ordered that 'all women, of whatever rank, profession or degree, whether virgins, maids or widows, that shall from and after such Act impose upon, seduce, and betray into matrimony any of his Majesty's subjects by the scents, paints, cosmetic washes, artificial teeth, false hair, Spanish wool, iron stays, hoops, high heeled shoes and bolstered hips, shall incur the penalty of the law now in force against witchcraft and like misdemeanours, and that the marriage upon conviction shall be null and void'.

But the desire to be attractive to the opposite sex is a greater driving force than legal necessities and the Bill had no effect on the sale or use of cosmetics. Indeed the demand for these products grew so rapidly that an industry developed to satisfy it.

That industry was greatly influenced by the prejudices of the art and the science which had helped lead to its formation. For example, it has always been acknowledged that the fashion industry guards its latest theories and styles with jealousy. But it is a fact that mediaeval scientific philosophies emphasised the closer relationship between mystery, magic and secrecy. The seventeenth-century scientist knew well that secrecy both heightened the value of a product and reduced the risk of any outsider successfully crying 'fraud'.

It is therefore perhaps not surprising that modern cosmetic companies, owing such debts to post-Renaissance fashion and scientific endeavour, should still struggle to keep secret the composition of the products they sell. It is, after all, difficult to discard prejudices which are so well established.

THE INDUSTRY TODAY

It is hard to estimate the total value of the international cosmetics and toiletries market, although *Cosmetics International*, a twice-monthly report on world cosmetic markets, reports that Unilever claimed that in 1979 worldwide sales of toilet preparations alone exceeded £10,000 million. It is perhaps enough simply to say that one cosmetics company alone, Avon, had net sales of 2.38 billion dollars in 1979. That is something like one thousand million pounds a year, and the company concerned started less than a century ago with one product and one sales representative.

If sorting out the amount of money involved in the industry is difficult, trying to estimate the number of companies and the number of products they make seemed at first to be downright impossible. I'm sure that even Sherlock Holmes would have found his opium consumption rising to unacceptable levels if he had ever tried to work out precisely how the world's many cosmetic companies are related to one another. One company will prepare synthetic additives for another and yet have a subsidiary buying vegetable oils from an associate company of one to which it sells minerals. The incestuous tangle seems never-ending.

However, once one has some inkling of how the industry is organized and how cosmetics are made and marketed, such complex relationships begin to appear quite explicable and even inevitable.

I have no intention of trying to describe in fine detail exactly how the industry is organized, but a brief explanation of how cosmetics are made will undoubtedly help set the scene. Let me therefore begin by saying that the cosmetics industry can be divided into three main parts.

First, there is the part of the industry which produces and markets the raw materials from which cosmetics and toiletries are made.

Many of these companies are small and privately owned, some are subsidiaries of larger international organizations. Companies in this category will offer for sale hundreds of different bases and extracts with which it is possible to prepare finished products. From a supplier of raw products a manufacturer can buy anything from angelica root to wormwood.

Second, there is the part of the industry which actually turns raw materials into finished cosmetic products. Some of the companies in this category are again subsidiaries of larger companies or members of a holding company. But there are many private organizations which do nothing but manufacture finished cosmetics for companies which will later market those products under their own brand names. Kolmar, for example, will develop, manufacture and pack products for customers who simply and solely involve themselves in marketing, promotion and distribution. In one recent year alone Kolmar made 130 million lipsticks for companies around the world and altogether they are responsible for the manufacture of 400 cosmetic ranges. E. R. Holloway Ltd of Sudbury in Suffolk make *Tu* and *Evette* for Woolworth's, *Natur* for Sainsbury's and *Eleanor Moore* for British Home Stores.

This method of manufacturing cosmetics suits the industry particularly well since there can be no other industry which has to change its products so regularly. A cosmetic that stays on sale for more than a few years becomes something of a celebrity and Kolmar have forecast that in the future a cosmetic product's market life will be even shorter as the marketing search for something new intensifies.

By arranging for a manufacturer with massive production facilities to make a single batch of one product, a marketing company can safeguard itself against a future fall in the market. If the company had to set up a complex production line to manufacture, say, a new lipstick, it would be in severe trouble if sales of that brand of lipstick fell. If it attempted to manufacture the lipstick with a small production outfit unit costs would be prohibitively high. Indeed, this style of manufacture lends itself to new fashions since a marketing company can easily change a product, name or package if it is ordering a new run of 5,000 or 50,000 lipsticks. Only the most popular lines will be re-ordered.

Third, but just as important as the companies in the first two categories, are the companies which market the finished cosmetics.

Again companies in this category may or may not be linked to companies which deal in raw materials or which manufacture finished cosmetics. A company which sells cosmetics may either have its products made specially for it or it may buy a mass-produced cosmetic and then sell that product under its own name and with a special label. There are in addition companies which market products imported from other countries.

Finally, it is important to remember that companies in any one of these three groups may be associated with other companies which may have nothing to do with the manufacture or sale of cosmetics. For example, the Unilever group of companies includes those which produce famous toiletries and cosmetics such as *Parfums Roberre*, *Twink Home Perm*, *Harmony* hair colourants, *Sunsilk* shampoo, *Pears Transparent Soap* and *Signal*, *SR* and *Close-up* toothpastes, alongside Birds Eye Foods, Walls Ice Creams, Lipton Teas, John West Foods, Batchelors Foods and Mac Fisheries. It almost seems superfluous to point out that the company also makes *Persil*, *Square Deal Surf*, *Drive*, *Radiant*, *Omo*, *Lux Flakes* and *Stergene Liquid* for clothes washing and other soaps which are sold under the names of *Sunlight*, *Lifebuoy*, *Shield*, *Lux*, *Knight's Castile* and *Astral*. I only began to realize the full extent of the involvement of major companies in the cosmetics industry when I wrote to ICI for information and received a letter back from Goya.

The unique way in which the cosmetics industry is made up suits its particular purposes very well. The proof of that fact is, of course, in the profits. The ICC Business Ratio Report on *The Toiletries and Cosmetics Industry*, published in 1979, shows that UK manufacturers' total sales and profits have both risen in recent years. A study of *Cosmetics International* and *Cosmetic World News* shows that this trend is not confined to the British cosmetics industry, and those companies which manufacture cosmetics and other products often show a healthier profit in their cosmetics sector than elsewhere. Moët Hennessy, for example, who also make champagne and brandy report that recently cosmetics accounted for 29 per cent of their total sales while they made up 33 per cent of their total profits.

The major success story in the cosmetics industry must be Avon with which I started this section. Today Avon have nearly one and a quarter million representatives around the world, and although the annual report for 1979 reports that net profit margins fell from

11.2 per cent in 1978 to 10.5 per cent in 1979 I doubt if anyone would claim that the company doesn't make a good living from its business. It recently acquired Tiffany and Co. as a wholly owned subsidiary. Total sales have risen every single year for at least a decade, and today the company has over 700 products.

The average life of each product can be judged from the fact that the company produces 200 new products each year.

PRODUCTION PROBLEMS

PRODUCT PLANNING

There isn't much brand loyalty in the world of cosmetics and toiletries. Customers tend to try new products which appeal to them and to readily abandon products, which they've already tried and used, as tastes and fashions change. It's a fact that the cosmetics industry makes a large chunk of its profits out of the half-empty bottles lying at the back of dressing-table drawers.

One reason for this lack of loyalty is the simple fact that there are few obviously superior products on sale. Cosmetics usually sell on their marketing merits rather than on any intrinsic values, and so a new marketing strategy or a new promotional campaign can easily capture a share of the existing market. People buy dreams and images rather than products.

It is to keep up with these ever changing tastes that most major companies produce so many new products and work so hard at recapturing their own share of the market as each new fashion comes and goes. I should perhaps explain that by fashion I don't just mean dress style and colour; there are subtler fashions to be accommodated too. For example, as I write this there is a growth in the more expensive part of the cosmetics market and, although there is a recession in other industries, this part of the cosmetics world appears to be booming. It seems that when times are hard women are more prepared to spend money on luxury items. Fashions are made by financiers as often as by dress designers.

As well as following trends and fashions formed outside the industry, marketing men also confess that they are not above leaping on to bandwagons set in motion by their competitors. A new products director speaking at a meeting of American marketing directors admitted that it is not as important for a company to innovate as it is for its representatives to spot winning ideas and to then imitate them successfully. This marketing man explained that the trick is not simply to copy the right new product with the right image but to be the first to do so. This eagerness to imitate a winning product explains the proliferation of perfumes designed for liberated ladies which followed the success of *Charlie* when it was launched by Revlon a few years ago.

Product planning is undoubtedly a vital task with the cosmetics industry. The man who decides what products are to be made must be sure that his marketing scientists have listened to all whispers and rumours and must take into account all known and expected dreams and fashions. Then, when he's decided what products his company needs to produce, he hands over a brief to his company's scientists, for before anything else can happen a chemical formulation has to be prepared.

FORMULATION

Cosmetics may be introduced according to needs established by market research and their use may well be an art, but there is little doubt that cosmetics manufacture is a science. The chemists who actually decide what constituents will go into cosmetics and toiletries have between them compiled an enormous library of information about the various ways in which products can be successfully formulated, and although it may well be a fact that the greater part of the cost of a finished cosmetic is allocated to advertising and promoting the product there is, nevertheless, a considerable amount of expenditure, both in financial and temporal terms, on the development of each product. According to the *Manufacturing Chemist and Aerosol News* the cosmetics and toiletries industry in the United Kingdom spends almost £100 million a year on raw materials alone.

Even an apparently simple product such as lipstick will have been the subject of a great deal of scientific study during its preparation and manufacture. For example, the *Journal of the Society of Cosmetic Chemists* recently published a scientific paper entitled 'Evaluation of mechanical stresses set up in lipstick during application' while the *International Journal of Cosmetic Science* published a paper entitled 'Moulding techniques in lipstick manufacture: a comparative evaluation'.

These papers were intended to help cosmetic scientists ensure that lipsticks did not break when used, and although the technical content of the papers does not really concern us I mention their existence simply to give you some idea of the work involved in the formulation of many apparently simple products. Together, these two papers consist of thirty-seven pages of closely argued material and one of the papers alone has no less than twenty-one references listed at its end.

Marketing requirements often result in the emergence of new technical problems and some of these are well illustrated by the history of the lipstick as described by Mr T. J. Elliot of Beecham Products in an article published in the journal *Cosmetics and Perfumery*. Mr Elliot points out that the classical lipstick formula of a mixture of castor oil, candelilla wax, carnauba wax and beeswax, together with an organic pigment, became unacceptable when fashions led to a demand for paler lipsticks. The traditional mixture did not adhere well enough, and so low viscosity oils such as isopropyl myristate had to be introduced. Unfortunately, these oils caused sweating on the lipsticks and also made the products more liable to break. More changes had to be made in the production process. Then, when glossy lipsticks became fashionable the scientific changes which had to be made created a durability problem. The glossy lipsticks simply didn't last and sometimes needed re-applying after a mere thirty minutes.

That particular technical problem proved so insuperable that it resulted in many women abandoning lipsticks altogether, and when other technical problems resulted in different coloured lipsticks ending up looking the same colour when they had been on the lips only for a matter of minutes, other women gave up buying so many different shades of lipstick. Marketing needs may well create technical problems, but there is no doubt that on many occasions technical difficulties have produced marketing problems. It is the job of the cosmetic chemists responsible for formulating new products to try to anticipate and avoid technical problems as well as to satisfy marketing requirements.

APPLICATION TECHNIQUES –
AEROSOLS AND ROLL-ONS
Once a need for a specific product has been identified and a formula created to satisfy that need, a decision has to be made about the best way to package the product. By that I don't just mean that

the advertising people have to decide what picture to draw on the wrapper, but that technical and marketing experts have to get together to discuss the various possible ways in which the finished product can actually be applied by the consumer.

Very often the way that a finished product is packaged will have a vitally important effect on its eventual success, and since the package can, in the case of an aerosol for example, cost ten times as much as the contents, a decision about packaging is obviously important on all grounds.

I've discussed elsewhere (see p. 27) the different qualities and uses of creams, ointments, gels and so on and here I'm going to confine myself to a brief discussion of aerosols, pump sprays and roll-ons, since these three types of applicator are currently among the most fashionable.

Aerosols were first introduced in 1946 when they were used to project insecticides into the atmosphere. Today there are 200 different registered uses for aerosols and the 2,500 aerosol brands on the British market together sell a total of 500 million cans. Astonishingly, that means that each man, woman and child in Britain will get through about ten aerosols in the next twelve months. From hair spray to foot spray and from shaving soap to deodorant there doesn't seem to be much in the cosmetics and toiletries world that isn't available in an aerosol spray.

The major differences between an aerosol and a pump spray are that a pump spray can be refilled and it fires a metered dose by finger pressure whereas an aerosol uses an internal propellant such as compressed gas to fire the can's contents. A pump has the advantage that it simply fires the product and not the product plus a propellant. In addition, it is far easier to fire a fixed dose with a pump than with an aerosol spray, while aerosols have the disadvantage of leaving a fine cloud of particles in the air after use – a disadvantage that many people with respiratory diseases find quite serious. Aerosol sprays cause a chilling sensation if sprayed on to the body and they cannot be refilled at home as pumps can.

Because a pump doesn't contain a propellant it will usually be lighter than an aerosol and will often contain more of the actual product. Finally, there is the undoubted fact that under some circumstances propellants can be dangerous – both to the individual and to the community at large. Dangers to the individual result from the fact that some people may be allergic to the propellants and dangers to the community result from the projection into the atmosphere of propellant gases. Since the annual world-wide production of aerosols now exceeds 6,000 million cans, the amount of propellant involved is quite significant.

Since both aerosols and pumps tend to be expensive to produce there isn't much to choose between the two on purely economic grounds. Both pumps and aerosols, however, are more expensive to produce than roll-on applicators.

It is its relatively low price which has helped to make the roll-on applicator so popular today, but in addition to the fact that they are much cheaper to produce than aerosols roll-on applicators are often less wasteful. If you're spraying a deodorant on to your body a good proportion of the product will end up on the wall. If you use a roll-on applicator most of the product ends up where you want it. In 1975 roll-on applicators had 27 per cent of the British deodorant and antiperspirant market but by 1979 their market share had risen to 45.9 per cent. The use of aerosol sprays to apply personal cosmetic and toiletry products has fallen slightly recently and all the signs seem to suggest that this trend will continue.

In the final analysis, of course, the selection of an aerosol or a roll-on or some other type of applicator is a personal matter, but in general, while some products, such as hair sprays, are obviously well suited for use in aerosol cans, other products, such as deodorants, are better bought and used in more direct forms. The discerning consumer will buy the product she wants in the form she wants it and will ignore the exhortations of the marketeers.

TRIALS AND TRIBULATIONS

The first step in the preparation of a new cosmetic product is to define the need. The second step is to decide exactly how the new product is going to be formulated. And the third step is to ensure that the product that has been made will be safe enough for general use. However great the need for a product and however complex the scientific formulation, the product will be unsaleable if it produces too many unpleasant side-effects.

Before I begin to describe some of the ways in which cosmetics are tested I want to discuss some of the general principles which govern the testing of these products. It is, of course, of primary importance that cosmetic products be prepared in such a way as to minimize the risk of any adverse reaction, since they are intended to be used mainly to beautify rather than to heal. When a product has genuine medicinal qualities and is expected to change the course of a disease process, uncomfortable side-effects are considered to be an acceptable risk and more severe and potentially damaging effects are considered unavoidable. A drug which has a positive effect on any physiological process must, by pharmacological definition, also have a potentially negative effect and the more important and potentially useful the drug, the more acceptable are the potential side-effects.

Cosmetics and toiletries, on the other hand, are used simply and solely to accentuate good points and disguise bad ones; they have no value other than the psychological one and consequently must be regarded with more suspicion when side-effects are expected. Both the British Regulations and the relevant EEC Directive hold that cosmetic products must not be liable to cause damage to human health when applied under normal conditions of use.

This philosophical concept is usually described as the benefit-risk ratio, and those in the cosmetics industry will sometimes argue that the official policy, which holds that since a consumer is healthy when a cosmetic product is first applied then she must still be healthy afterwards, and that the risk must be nil since the benefit is nil, is wrong. They argue that cosmetics *do* have benefits and that the improvement they make to the quality of the user's life makes some risk acceptable. Nevertheless, I think that any cosmetic scientist would argue that the risk should always be minimized.

So much for the philosophical aspect of cosmetic safety. I'll now get back to the practical ways in which the safety of these products is tested and the safeguards which are used.

To begin with, I think that it is only fair to point out that most manufacturers take considerable care to ensure that their products do not contain constituents likely to cause severe reactions. This is not an entirely philanthropic measure since all manufacturers are well aware that a product known to cause illness of any kind will soon fall out of favour, particularly since the side-effects likely to be produced are almost certainly going to involve the area of the body to which the cosmetic was applied. The woman who spends money on a skin cream is not going to be well pleased if she ends up with an unpleasant rash and the woman who wants her hair to look prettier isn't going to buy a product again if it makes her hair fall out.

The most effective type of test for any cosmetic product is for the product to be used by human beings for a long period of time, and those products which have a long history of safe usage and which have been established as safe have a distinct advantage over newer, less well tested products. However, no product can enjoy long-term use until it has first been adequately tested and approved for public sale.

To begin with, tests are usually performed on animals. Every year thousands of rabbits and other rodents are sacrificed in attempts to ensure that cosmetic products are relatively safe. Products which will come into contact with the skin are applied to the shaved bodies of rabbits while products which may affect the eyes are dropped in concentrated form into rabbits' eyes. Products which will be used in the mouth or vagina are tested in the vagina of a bitch. These tests do not, of course, guarantee that the products will be safe when used by human beings, since there is no guarantee that a chemical which does not have an adverse effect on a rabbit will be equally safe when used by human beings. The test only really works in the negative direction; in other words a constituent which has an adverse effect on a rabbit is unlikely to be used in a finished product intended for use by humans. Despite these disadvantages, however, it seems that animal testing is likely to be with us for the foreseeable future. People occasionally complain about the vast numbers of animals killed purely in an attempt to produce safer cosmetics, and organizations such as FRAME (Fund for the Replacement of Animals in Medical Experiments) publish a considerable amount of literature opposing such experiments, but there seems little real interest in the subject. Those who are genuinely opposed might like to know that they can buy products made with constituents not tested in this way from organizations such as Beauty Without Cruelty. This particular organization claims only to use ingredients which have been employed in the production of cosmetics for at least twenty-five years. Extra animal testing is, therefore, unnecessary.

Once animal tests have shown that a product isn't obviously likely to produce an excessive number of unacceptable reactions most companies perform tests to study the number of allergy reactions likely to be caused by the product. Patch testing on human volunteers is the usual method of testing a new product and most major companies do this routinely. The companies which specialize in selling hypoallergenic products do tend to be rather more fastidious than most other companies about this and may make a particular effort to ensure that their products do not contain known allergens. Once patch tests have been done without any unexpected results, volunteers are usually invited to use the finished cosmetic for a period of weeks and to report any side-effects, allergy reactions or other problems. At this stage most companies will also invite volunteers to report on the acceptability of the product in purely cosmetic terms.

The result of all this testing is that side-effects with cosmetics and toiletries are relatively rare.

MARKETING AND PROMOTION

INTRODUCTION

Packaging and promotion are more important in the sale of cosmetics than in just about any other industry. Millions of pounds are spent on launching products, and there is plenty of evidence that the money spent is rarely wasted. The manufacturers of *Mum* antiperspirant roll-on found that a new label design helped to produce a 13 per cent increase in sales and there are many manufacturers who have found that repackaging a product which hasn't been improved or altered in any way can completely change sales patterns.

The money spent on advertising programmes can reach astronomical proportions, and companies seem prepared to go to unbelievable lengths to prepare the right campaign. When Andrew Jergens Company wanted to promote *Gentle Touch* soap in America by using a rocking bath they found that the water kept splashing out of the bath. So they constructed a bathroom set which rocked while the bath remained stationary.

Advertising copywriters are not above using psychological tricks to sell the products that they are hired to promote, so in this part of the book I want to explain some of these tricks. If you as a consumer are going to become more critical and more careful about which products you choose to buy then you need to be aware of the tricks the ad-men use. If you know and understand how they intend to persuade you to buy what they want you to buy then you'll be far better equipped to study their claims as a critical consumer.

WHIMS AND FANCIES

The sale of cosmetics is influenced, and indeed governed, by many whims and fancies. The most obvious, the best established and perhaps the most influential is the world of fashion which, through its high priests, controls almost every aspect of the cosmetic world.

Many of the major fashion houses produce their own perfumes and cosmetics, of course. Pierre Cardin, Christian Dior, Yves Saint Laurent, Paco Rabanne, and Gucci are just some of the names associated both with clothes and cosmetics. Even those companies which aren't directly associated with the world of *haute couture* do all they can to associate themselves with that world, and when I looked at advertisements for perfumes from a handful of women's magazines which I picked up purely arbitrarily, I discovered that of a total of seventy-six advertisements only eleven failed to include a mention of Paris or a few words or phrases in French. An advertisement for the product *Opium* manages to confirm this link with precision. The advertisement shows a lady in what I can only describe as an ecstatic state and includes the headline 'Opium – pour celles qui s'adonnent à Yves Saint Laurent'. The manufacturers know very well that many of their customers would never be able to afford originals by top designers. Buying perfume is a way to establish a link with the beautiful world and the advertisements stress this association as often as possible.

The manufacturers (or their advertising agencies) naturally also realize that many cosmetics, and more particularly perfumes, are bought not by the potential user but by someone buying a gift. Four-fifths of all fragrance sales are said to occur during the Christmas season, and so it is hardly surprising that much of the packaging is designed to make individual products look attractive. In an interview in *Cosmetic World News*, the sales director of one company admitted that 'a large part of the price of gift cosmetics is absorbed by elaborate packaging' but even without that confession it wouldn't take a genius to realize that the man buying a Christmas present is probably paying more for the container than for the contents.

This dedication to packaging and presentation isn't confined by any means to the top end of the market. Mums and Dads looking for stocking fillers at Christmas are likely to find themselves choosing between *Desperate Dan Bubble Bath*, *Buzby* toiletries and such items as a bubble bath which changes colour when poured into the bath, an aerosol hand cream which crackles when rubbed between the hands and a space dust talcum powder. *Matey Bubble Bath* was promoted with a TV campaign costing £275,000.

The ability of the advertisers to create markets as well as to satisfy existing whims and fancies is perhaps best exemplified by the way in which the demand for male cosmetics has grown in recent years.

Not long ago most men regarded all cosmetics as feminine and unsuitable for the truly heterosexual male. Only the most outrageous man would buy and use a fragrance. Today the male market is said to be worth £70,000,000 a year and half-million-pound advertising programmes for male fragrances are not unknown. In America the sales of male cosmetics have reached even greater heights and the total market there is said to be worth nearly £1,000,000,000 with more than half that amount going on men's fragrances. There are pre-shaving soaps, aftershave lotions, body splashes, and special skin creams. Some of the fragrances sold for men are nearly identical to the ones sold to women, although the advertisements obviously disguise that fact.

Men's cosmetics are advertised both in women's magazines and in men's magazines although the advertisements do tend to vary. In the women's magazines (considered important in the sale of male cosmetics since many men start using fragrances only because their womenfolk buy them for them) the products are sometimes sold with a romantic angle. *Eau Sauvage* was, for example, advertised in *Cosmopolitan* with a picture of a man and a woman in each other's arms and the heading 'Togetherness with *Eau Sauvage*'. At least one product for men advertised in that same magazine is sold in a blatantly phallic container.

Many of the advertisements for men's fragrances, and in particular, those which are intended to appeal to men themselves, concentrate on providing the purchaser with reassurance that by buying a fragrance he isn't labelling himself as 'gay'. The *Playboy* fragrances for men are advertised with the line 'You can get away with it' and a photograph of a cool looking guy surrounded by women, clearly having a good time. An advertisement for *Chaps*, a men's cologne, contains the line '*Chaps* is a cologne a man can put on as naturally as a worn leather jacket or a pair of jeans'. While a product from Fabergé is actually called *Macho*. *Jovan Musk Oil* is sold in a box with a label which reads 'Musk oil for men. The provocative scent that instinctively calms and yet arouses your basic animal desires. And hers. In an aftershave/cologne. To take you a long way to where it's at. To the most pleasurable of conclusions.

Because it is powerful. Stimulating. Unbelievable. And yet, legal.'
The effect is perhaps spoilt by the line underneath which reads
'(Continued on back)'.

The market for male cosmetics seems certain to continue to grow,
and when the manufacturers think that they have achieved satura-
tion coverage and can no longer improve the size of that market I
have no doubt that they will think up some new fancy or fashion.

Fragrances for dogs, perhaps?

FEARS AND AMBITIONS

Advertisements for cosmetics and toiletries may seem deceptively
simple and some may look as though they were prepared by a gang
of mentally retarded chimpanzees, but it is important not to be
deceived by appearances. However simple and stupid they may
look advertisements are usually prepared by teams of highly paid
and intelligent people whose sole aim in life is to part you from
your money. They don't mind if you laugh at the advertisements
or even if you despise them, as long as you buy the product that
they are selling. It is important to remember this, for it is very easy
to underestimate the effect that advertisements are likely to have.

Some advertisements are remarkably straightforward, and there
are naturally a great many products which are marketed with the
aid of such well tried selling points as sex. Even those magazines
which claim to cater for the liberated woman usually contain a high
proportion of advertisements where the reader is promised a better
sex life or a more satisfying romantic attachment.

There are, for example, such lines as:

'*Eau D'Aviance*: the cool way to raise his temperature'
'*Amazone*: it's bold, fresh, French, spiky, assertive and asking
for trouble'
'*Love* was created by Coty'
'*Femme* by Rochas. Seductive, enticing, bewitching'
'*Intrigue*: a gift as sensual as woman herself'
'*Partage*: when it isn't a casual affair'
'*Miss Worth*: when he calls across oceans at 3 a.m. . . .'
'Men just can't help acting on *Impulse*'
'*Eye dew eye drops*: drive them wild with a quick flash'
'*Outdoor girl*: we talked all evening; suddenly he noticed my lips
and leaned towards me. . .'

Under the heading 'How does a woman decide whether to wear *Arpège Extrait* or *Arpège Eau de Toilette*?' there is a short story entitled 'Valerie's Wednesdays'. It goes like this:

'Valerie is a gentle, dreamy kind of woman. She loves music. And she also plays golf rather well. She uses a lot of *Arpège Extrait*, which is her favourite. Even when she's playing golf . . . or the piano . . . or just dreaming. Except on Wednesdays. That's her day for *Arpège Eau de Toilette*. How can you explain that? Usually, she likes to leave a tell-tale trail of fragrance behind her. But on Wednesdays, discretion takes over. Strange . . . but maybe, deep in her heart, there's a reason. . .'

Then there is *Jontue* – 'Sensual . . . but not too far from inno-cence'; while the advertisements for *Badedas* show a half-naked woman looking out of a window at a man. The headline reads 'Things happen after a *Badedas* bath'. Incidentally, *Badedas* con-tains extract of horse chestnuts, and those familiar with the short stories by the Marquis de Sade will remember that horse chestnuts are said to have a smell that only the experienced woman will recognize (see p. 155).

Sex isn't just used in the advertising copy. Many products are sold in containers which are, to say the very least, phallic in shape. Such products as *Mum*, *Bodymist* and *Right Guard Roll-On* fall into this category. Other products such as lipsticks are sold with the use of suggestive photographs. The classical picture shows a woman with wet, red, half-open lips holding a lipstick a few cen-timetres away from her mouth. Her eyes are usually half-closed in apparent ecstasy.

Money is another basic selling point, but whereas groceries and less exotic products are often sold on the basis of their quality, low price perfumes and cosmetics are often sold on the basis of their exclusivity and high price. Some are subtle, some are not.

The advertisements for a product by Hermès read 'To arrive by *Calèche* is a state of mind, a carriage ride on the boulevards of innocence. *Calèche*, the ultimate French perfume by Hermès. A very special way to arrive anywhere.' In contrast, the advertise-ments for *Joy* and *1000* perfumes are more straightforward. Their manufacturer, Jean Patou, simply claims that these are: 'The cos-tliest perfumes in the world'. At not much less than the price of gold they may well be right. Lancôme have also claimed to have produced one of the most expensive perfumes in the world while

Chanel and Rochas have both used the unusual trick of putting the higher price product in their range first. So Chanel describe their products as selling 'From £500 to about £10' while Rochas advertise their products as costing 'From £58 to £10.50'. *Azzaro Eau de Toilette* is simply described as 'a slightly more expensive eau de toilette' while *Vetiver de Puig* is said to be 'for the gifted man', and one advertisement I found read 'Of course, such distinction has its price and *Vetiver de Puig* is not for everyone. But, if it were, would you want to try it?'

The copywriters who produced these advertisements are clearly well aware of the fact that some people associate quality only with price and that sheer expense and exclusivity can make a product valuable. They also undoubtedly know that for many people there is kudos in giving or receiving a gift known to be extraordinarily expensive. It isn't so much the fact that the product is expensive which makes it valuable as a gift but the fact that the product is *known* to be expensive. Put more crudely the advertisement would read: 'Does he love you enough to buy you *XYZ* perfume?'

Sex and money are straightforward enough as selling points but there are obviously many far more subtle ways in which to promote a product. Advertising researchers go to great lengths to discover exactly what weaknesses and anxieties they can exploit and they spend a great deal of time and trouble investigating the needs, fears and special anxieties of possible potential customers. I rather suspect that more scientific activity goes into the selling of many products than goes into their manufacture. Psychiatrists and psychologists are hired to evaluate and estimate the conscious and subconscious preferences and prejudices of potential customers. Package colours are carefully selected for psychological reasons rather than aesthetic ones, and the trick has now become not simply to sell you a product but to sell you a need so that you keep on buying the product.

In a revealing book called *Confessions of an advertising man* David Ogilvy, the founder of the advertising agency Ogilvy, Benson and Mather, describes how he and his colleagues tried to find out which promises were most attractive to consumers. He describes how, when planning an advertising campaign for a new face cream from Helena Rubinstein, consumers were shown cards on which were printed various alternative promises. The promises ranged from 'Cleans deep into pores' and 'Prevents dryness' to

'Prevents skin from ageing' and 'Smooths out wrinkles'. The winning promise turned out to be 'Cleans deep into pores', and as a result of this particular piece of research the face cream they were selling was called *Deep Cleanser*.

Ogilvy also explains how important it is for advertising to appeal to the consumer's self-interest. To accommodate this requirement Ogilvy produced a headline for *Helena Rubenstein's Hormone Cream* which read: 'How women over 35 can look younger'. Ogilvy is quite right of course. Many people do worry about looking older and are prepared to buy products designed to delay the ageing process. *Palmolive* is advertised with the slogan 'Help keep your skin young looking' while Hymosa headline one of their advertisements with the question 'What is a beautiful woman?' and answer it themselves with the statement 'It's not a question of age'. You can almost hear the sigh of relief as women reach for the product.

The advertising men are not satisfied with simply catering to fears and anxieties which exist. They are not above creating new fears and then satisfying those fears themselves. For example, many companies now tell potential customers that they won't have to worry about body freshness again if they use such-and-such a product. The fact is, of course, that until they read the advertisement most people won't have even thought about their body freshness. They won't have suspected that their best friends have secrets they daren't share! But with this newly developed fear they will realize that the only way to deal with the problem is to buy the product. The companies selling products such as mouthwashes are moving into this area with great vigour. *Gold Spot* produce advertisements which show a picture of a mouth and the title: 'You talk and kiss with it. Keep it fresh'. While *Listerine Antiseptic Mouthwash* is advertised with a picture of a gorilla and the headline: 'Nice legs, shame about the breath'. Manufacturers of deodorants of all kinds use the same simple trick.

Flattery is commonly used by advertisers. Helancyl claim that 'if you don't feel a beautiful difference after three weeks of the regime *Helancyl* then clearly you were born beautiful'. If you think about it you'll see that they have cleverly used flattery to ensure that all their customers are satisfied. If the product doesn't work it is your fault for being too beautiful! Who is going to complain?

They are not just selling a beauty product – they are selling you confidence and a beautiful body.

Other manufacturers reassure customers about their value as mothers and wives and when selling such mundane products as soap will win brand loyalty by emphasizing the customers' value in the family and in society at large. They'll sell security and good value by giving products names such as *Evidence* and *Imperial Leather* and promise value with ambiguous slogans such as 'Our reputation means a great deal'. Some of the scientific tricks used are described in the next section of this book.

Most of the advertising strategies which I have described are, of course, aimed at women and they were evolved to satisfy the requirements of women happy to be treated as sex objects. The women's revolution threatened to destroy all this, and it looked for a while as though the gravy would get rather thin unless some astounding new strategy could be found.

It was found by Revlon, who in 1973 launched a product called *Charlie*, specifically intended to satisfy the growing number of independent young women who wanted to be treated as independent equals rather than as dolly birds. Cannily the copywriters realized that they would have to sell their products in such a way as to reassure the worried feminist about her feminity while at the same time acknowledging her individual status as a liberated lady.

They did it with astonishing success and not only did they keep what might have been a diminishing market, but by convincing women that perfumes shouldn't be regarded as luxury items but as everyday necessities, they managed with a single campaign to revive falling sales all round the world. *Charlie* quickly became an all-time best selling perfume and that original campaign is still discussed with awe in cosmetic journals. It was the gimmick that broke all rules and all the sales records and it introduced into the advertisements the concept of an emancipated, self-confident young woman. To make the point as direct as they could Revlon even put the model in their advertisement in trousers.

Today there are many other products sold along those same lines. There are products such as:

'*Florissa*. The fragrance of a new generation'
'*Fidji*. Woman is an island. *Fidji* is her perfume'

'*Cachet*. As individual as you are'
'*Rive Gauche*. N'est pas un parfum pour les femmes effacées'
'*Blasé*. For the girl who doesn't have to prove a thing'

Even Chanel have come in on the act with an advertisement which shows a beautiful woman in a check suit and tie sitting in a men's club. The headline is 'The unexpected *Chanel*'.

Not that these new strategies have replaced older ones. They've merely been added to the repertoire, and many companies make products that satisfy the old-fashioned woman and the new-fashioned feminist.

Avon, for example, make *Ariane* ('. . . its soft warm undertones gently unveil all the sensuousness that is essentially woman') *Avon Chic* ('it's a light, understated fragrance for the girl on the move who knows where she is going and what she wants – and how to get it too!') and *Emprise* ('She's elegant and assured and disconcertingly feminine – and she knows heads turn wherever she goes. *Emprise* makes sure of that. . .'). They do the same thing for men too and in their own words 'have a fragrance to match whatever image he chooses to present to the world'.

There is no doubt at all in my mind that whatever social changes may occur in the coming years and decades the cosmetic companies and their advertising agencies will be more than capable of blowing with the winds of change and coming up smelling of roses!

THE PHLOGISTON FACTOR – PSEUDOSCIENCE

Many cosmetic products are sold not just as superficial beauty aids but also scientifically tested and approved aids to good health and beautiful looks. Advertising copywriters very often produce laudatory comments intended to emphasize the quasi-medicinal qualities of the products they are promoting. The scientific arguments they use are often extremely convincing and the promises they make frequently irresistible.

In this part of the book I intend to look critically at some of the claims that have been made, not because I want to scoff or mock the manufacturers of such products but because I hope to show that in some cases the cosmetics have been 'oversold'. I have to confess that although I have over a number of years become accustomed to dealing with the hyperbole favoured by some manufacturers of medicinal products I was quite astonished to discover just what is promised by cosmetic manufacturers and the extent to which those worried about ageing, baldness, shapelessness, dry skin and so on are being misled by large international companies. The individual products which I describe are not the only ones on sale, of course, and I have no doubt that before the presses have finished printing this book there will be many hundreds of additional products in the shops. My hope is that after reading this section consumers will be better able to deal critically with the claims and promises that are made.

Before I begin to discuss some of the specific ways in which scientific information about cosmetic products is supplied I'll describe some of the general ways in which consumers are likely to be misled.

To begin with there are, of course, many ways in which technical jargon can be used to impress consumers and even to confuse and muddle a specific issue. Sometimes the terms used are simple ones which have, with repeated use, acquired meanings which they don't really deserve. The best simple example of a word in this category is probably the term 'moisturizer' which is often used to describe skin products. Manufacturers frequently use the word in such a way that customers might imagine that the product they are buying will actually 'moisturize' their skin. The scientific truth is that products sold as moisturizers do not actually put water into the skin but prevent it being lost by the skin. Some moisturizers, it is true, contain substances called humectants which can attract moisture from the air, but not even these products are able to push water or any other kind of moisture into the skin cells.

Another word that is often used to describe skin creams is 'nourishing'. There are many products which are said to fall into this category, and manufacturers say things like 'The skin should be able to absorb all the nourishment it needs in twenty minutes' and 'If a rich moisturizer is being used, then the best time to apply this is just before stepping into the bath, when the warm steamy atmosphere will help the absorption'. Again the truth is different to the interpretation. The fact is substances that *are* absorbed by the skin are usually quickly disseminated throughout the body. The skin itself cannot be nourished from outside.

However much copywriters love these simple terms, they love genuine scientific jargon far more. For example, many companies describe in magnificent detail the ways in which their products have a beneficial effect on the 'pH acid mantle' of the skin. Now it is certainly true that dermatologists have established that human skin is normally acidic when tested, but the importance of this isn't really understood. All we know for certain is that if the skin's acidity is altered in any way by any artificial factor then the skin will restore itself quite quickly without any outside interference.

Most companies are happy to use long words when short ones would do and this habit leads to considerable confusion. I wonder how many people buying *Vichy's Dermatological Cleansing Bar* found the name bewildering. Stop and think about it for a moment. And I wonder how many people were impressed by the prospect of owning an *Idrophysiotreating massage bath* with its antiphlogistic action? This latter device, sold through the Hairdresser's Tool Centre, will, according to its brochure, produce rising oxygen in water. The promoters say that 'oxygen assimilated through breathing and skin (bath permeated) improves the whole organism', but I wonder if they realize that if we could absorb oxygen through our skin we would all be able to breathe under water?

Clinique, who manufacture and sell an impressive range of skin products proudly tell customers that their skin type and needs will be assessed on the Clinique computer which has been 'programmed by a group of leading dermatologists'. The word computer suggests to many people a device capable of storing and analysing thousands of pieces of information but Clinique's computer isn't quite in that category. It consists of a device on which the customer can answer a total of eight questions in any of four ways. The questions include such searching inquiries as 'Colour of eyes?' and 'Surface facial lines?' To this second question the customer can reply 'Many', 'Several', 'Few' or 'Very Few'. When all eight questions have been answered and eight answers appear in the relevant windows the predominant shade of the answers will give your skin type. Clinique points out that 'in the case of a tie your Clinique staff assistant will ask you a tie-breaking question'. At the end of all this you'll know that your skin is Type 1, Type II, Type III or Type IV. Good scientific sounding stuff isn't it?

Many companies take advantage of the fact that vitamins are currently extremely fashionable and they stuff their skin products with these and other nutrients designed to turn wrinkled, leathery old skin into soft, pink peach-like skin. Let's examine some of the things they put into their products and look at their claims in detail.

Vitamin E and Vitamin F are among the most popular constituents of skin creams and this may or may not be due to the fact that we do not as yet know much about these particular vitamins. Whatever information there may be about them there certainly is nothing that I've been able to find to suggest that they have any useful effect on the skin when they are rubbed on to it. Nor have I been able to find any evidence to suggest that rubbing such delicacies as liquorice, hazelnut oil, oil of avocado, shark oil or milk and honey on to the skin is going to produce any miraculous change in skin condition. Rejuvenating creams often contain a number of these constituents, and my award to the company managing to cram the most substances into one product goes to the manufacturers of *Son d'or wash cream* which 'contains at least 19 vitamins, plant oils, proteins, trace elements, natural hormones and enzymes' while it is also 'rich in Vitamin E' and 'has a natural acid base like my skin'.

If you study the advertisements for beauty products you'll soon come across advertisements for products containing either feminine hormones or collagen or both. The advertisements for these products usually point out that the ingredients have a positive effect on ageing skin. I'll examine these two ingredients in turn.

Female hormones have been available in creams for many years but today there are limitations governing the amount of hormone which can be put into a cream. The main reason for this is an excellent one: the female hormone can cause serious skin problems if used in excessive quantities. But there are other disadvantages too. For example, the skin can become a hormone junkie needing its daily fix of special cream to stay healthy. In addition, there is no proof that I have been able to find to show that female hormones in skin creams relieve dryness, retain moisture or do anything useful to the skin.

Collagen is even more popular than the hormone oestrogen as a skin product ingredient and you can buy it, together with other ingredients, in such products as *Celaton Face Lift*, *Collagen IX*, *Galenco Deep Penetrating Skin Conditioner*, *Mary Quant Skin Programme* formulations and *Supplegen*.

It is perfectly true, as the advertisers say, that the tissues contain collagen and that this is an important constituent of healthy skin, but the vital question is whether or not collagen can be absorbed through the skin when applied as a cream. If it can, then it may well help prevent signs of ageing. If it can't, then applying it is probably a waste of time.

I made searching inquiries to investigate the value of collagen in skin creams and finally ended up with an Italian technical journal called *Relata Technica* in which I found details of a research programme organized to investigate the effectiveness of collagen in skin creams. It is undoubtedly this research which provides the scientific basis for the claims of some manufacturers.

The author of the paper begins by pointing out that the research was 'conducted to find out whether the Collagenon contained in a cosmetic preparation applied to the skin is absorbed by it and is included in dermal metabolic processes, exerting influences on formation of connective tissue and in particular on synthesis of collagen'. That is a good start.

The conclusion of the paper is that 'it thus exerts its action regulating the production of collagen fibres through an inhibition of protocollagen-proline hydroxylase which is manifested in an effect curbing the overproduction of interfribrillar bridges and therefore preventing occurrences of cutaneous sclerosis'. A good end.

However, if you then study the meat of the research and look at the work upon which that optimistic conclusion was based you find that the work consisted of an experiment done on ten male guinea-pigs. Each animal had 16 square centimetres of skin shaved and on that shaved area of skin was placed 100 mg of cream which was kept in contact with the skin by means of an occlusive dressing. The cream was kept in position for two hours.

There are, in my view, three enormous problems associated with this piece of research.

First, to transfer the results from guinea-pigs to humans we have to believe that human skin is similar to guinea-pig skin.

Second, to expect the same results with human beings the skin would have to be covered with an occlusive dressing after cream had been applied. It is well known that an occlusive dressing will hasten the rate at which a product penetrates the skin.

Third, since the cream was applied to the guinea-pigs at a rate of approximately 6 mg per square centimetre a human expecting a similar effect would presumably have to apply the cream in a similar quantity. I estimate that a woman of normal physique would have to apply nearly *one and a half kilogrammes* of cream to her face to obtain the same effect.

I have been unable to find any more evidence relating to the effectiveness of collagen in skin creams. Nor have I been able to find any evidence suggesting that there is any particular point in rubbing on to the skin products containing placenta, elastin, bananas or any other substance.

By now it should be clear that it is often difficult to actively disprove the claims made by advertising men. If a copywriter writes a piece of prose claiming that elderberry juice is a universal panacea he may be unable to produce any evidence proving his claim but critics will also be unable to produce evidence disproving the claim. By repeated publication the claim may eventually become a part of our growing scientific folklore and will then itself provide evidence for further claims. For example, a future copywriter may say 'We know that elderberry juice is a universal panacea but the Coleman Chemical and Cosmetic Company has now produced a type of elderberry juice which also acts as a sexual stimulant.' The folklore has suddenly become established fact.

This process is even more likely to continue if at some stage a small genuine scientific fact is thrown into the argument. If, for example, a mention of pH of the skin is made or a reference to the evidence about rats deprived of Vitamin E is tossed in, the whole argument can be given an even more stable appearance.

Undoubtedly many people want to believe what they read and are prepared to take what they read very seriously – whether the information they obtain is contained in an editorial or an advertisement. People who are sick or afraid or vulnerable in any way are easy game for those with quasi-medical solutions to sell.

Having so far dealt with scientific claims in general terms I'm now going to be rather more daring and deal with some specific companies and their advertised products. I chose these half-dozen products at random – simply because they were the first products I heard about. They are discussed in no particular order. They are all skin care products.

Crème B23 from Orlane

This product is advertised with the line 'B23 helps to combat dryness and dehydration (which can look so ageing) by actually working to hold moisture in the skin.' Orlane tell me that the product contains Colloid OR 38 and that this substance 'is spectacular in improving the respiration of the skin'.

I don't know what Colloid OR 38 is but I do know that according to all the sources I've consulted human skin doesn't respire. So how can this product improve a function that doesn't exist? If we breathed through our skin we'd drown every time we bathed wouldn't we?

On a more positive note I see that according to research that Orlane did, 96 per cent of women who tried *Crème B 23* found that it spread very easily. Isn't that nice?

Millenium from Elizabeth Arden

Millenium is described as a 'remarkable breakthrough in skincare technology' and as a 'cell renewal strategy. For skin that looks, feels and functions younger.'

According to the company brochure '*Millenium* works on and within the epidermis to accelerate the natural cell renewal process which is the normal revitalizing function common to every skin.' In simple language I suppose that means that *Millenium* will reverse the ageing process as it affects the skin. As we grow old our skin cells are replaced less frequently – this product is designed to reverse that trend. It is also, in the manufacturer's own words, supposed to produce 'cells of better quality'.

I asked Elizabeth Arden to let me see their background research material. I am not convinced from what I have seen that *Millenium* does anything more than an ordinary moisturizer. The research work they described to me consisted of a comparison between the effect of using *Millenium* and of using no product at all. The research shows that if *Millenium* is used the skin benefits.

But it is known that if an ordinary moisturizing cream is used the skin will benefit. If Elizabeth Arden's scientists can offer me better evidence I'll reconsider my verdict.

Crème de Jouvence from Jean d'Eveze

The brochure advertising this product claims that 'it is composed of cosmetically active substances of plant origin, and these give it a high power of penetration which effectively stimulates the renewal of the cells of the skin'. The brochure also claims that 'the cream helps to slow down and to reduce the signs of ageing in the skin by actively stimulating natural functions of the cells'. It is also claimed that the product regenerates the dead skin of scars.

I have been unable to find any independent scientific evidence supporting these dramatic claims and I fail to understand why a product which apparently has such miraculous effects has not been studied more widely by independent dermatologists. To me it seems as unlikely as the chance of independent motor engineers ignoring a combustion engine said to run on water.

Biogen Super from the Dr Babor Cosmetics Range

Described as 'the ace product' of the range *Biogen Super* contains such 'strongly regenerative substances' as royal jelly and ginseng and is said to produce 'increased permeability of the tissue, increased oxygen resorption and stimulation of the cell division'.

I confess that I do not really understand what Dr Babor means by oxygen resorption. I don't know of any evidence showing that royal jelly or ginseng are 'strongly regenerative substances', and it is my view that any product that can stimulate cell division could be dangerous.

Moisture Secret from Avon

They say that '. . . at Avon, just as much research goes into the creation of effective and reliable skin care products to meet your skin's individual needs and problems, as could go into any major technological development' but point out that 'despite the vast amount of scientific research and rigorous testing that goes into the creation of each Avon skin care product, they still couldn't be simpler or more pleasant to use' and ask 'Isn't it great to know about Avon?'

One of the latest lines to come from the Avon Laboratories is *Moisture Secret* and the former Vice-President of Product Research and Development at the Avon Laboratory in New York explains that the *Moisture Secret* products contain an 'unusual combination of humectants, which attract moisture, and emollients, which retain moisture'. I'm not sure that this preparation justifies the claim about Avon's research resources but the product is undoubtedly an effective moisturizer.

Evidence from Beecham

The advertisements for this product are very engaging. There are such headlines as 'With new *Evidence* your skin can lie about your age'. The product is described as a moisturizer, a long-term protector and a nourishing cream.

According to an article in *Manufacturing Chemist and Aerosol News* research and developmental work on the product started in 1975 when 'The marketing department was convinced that the product area of moisturizers was one of great commercial interest and the r & d department believed that as almost no proof of efficacy of moisturizers was being advanced by competitors, this would be a very interesting area in which to develop products with performance that could be scientifically substantiated.'

Early research showed that moisturizing lotions were much less effective than moisturizing creams and that the stickier, more effective moisturizing creams were less acceptable to consumers, so the aim became simply to produce two products, an efficient acceptable lotion and an efficient acceptable cream. It was decided that the efficiency of the products could be improved by the inclusion of a sunscreen ingredient.

So this new product seems to be little more than a moisturizer with an added sunscreen agent. I asked Beechams to let me see any evidence they had for the new product and received a letter in which they admitted that 'we shall no doubt produce papers for the scientific literature in due course, after we have accumulated sufficient experience of consumer use to reinforce our confident expectations that we have made a useful advance in skin care treatment'.

So with regret, occasioned by the fact that the Beecham research staff provided me with much general information and advice about the world of cosmetics, I have to confess that I do not believe that *Evidence* is any great improvement on any other moisturizing creams.

My general conclusion is that none of these products is distinctly superior to an ordinary moisturizing cream. Certainly I have not seen any evidence which supports claims that these products are likely to improve skin condition with any more success than are ordinary moisturizing creams.

One of the important general lessons which I think can be learnt from the claims made for many other skin products is that tests and trials offered in evidence are often poorly organized and scientifically inadequate – often because the product has been compared not to a competitor but to nothing. And that is rather like testing a new car and pretending that no other motor vehicles exist. The car on test is obviously going to be better than bicycles, roller skates and pogo sticks.

In an attempt to show just how apparently solid evidence can be manufactured and then misapplied and misinterpreted, I've prepared a short example of just what can happen.

Imagine, if you will, that a general practitioner wants to study the incidence of skin disease among his patients and he records in a diary information about the patients he sees in five consecutive surgery sessions. He finds, let us say, that out of 20 patients who come with skin problems 16 are female and 4 are male.

Consequently he concludes that according to the survey women have more skin problems than men. He then decides that since the main difference between the way that men treat their skin and the way the women treat their skin is the fact that women use make-up and cosmetics more often than men, that make-up and cosmetics cause skin disease.

Now is that conclusion reasonable? In truth, of course, it is entirely unreasonable, and to show you some of the ways in which so-called evidence can be ripped apart I've prepared a list of some of the more obvious holes in this particular argument.

1 There is no report about whether or not the skin disorders involve the face or hands or any other part of the body. If twelve of the women had skin disorders affecting the soles of their feet, it is unlikely that the problems were caused by make-up.
2 There is no account of the number of men and women seen in those surgeries. If, for example, a total of 135 women and 28 men were seen in those five consecutive surgeries then there

would be a higher percentage of men with skin problems than of women.

3 The occupations of the patients have not been recorded. These are important since if all the women patients worked in factories the skin disorders may well have been caused by industrial pollutants. Even if the women didn't go out to work at all the problems could have been caused by a widely used detergent or bleach.

4 The general practitioner has ignored sexual, genetic and hormonal differences. It is well known that hormonal differences can produce skin changes, and these may explain a higher incidence of skin disorders among women. (If indeed there is a higher incidence of skin disorder among women.)

5 The statistics do not record the ages of the patients. If the female patients were all children they are unlikely to have been using make-up.

6 There is no record of whether or not the problems are long term or short term. If the patients are all suffering from long-term problems, such as psoriasis, then it is unlikely that make-up will be responsible.

7 There is no account of the general state of health of the patients concerned. Nor is there any account of what drugs they are taking. Women take the contraceptive pill more often than men and there is an association between this product and skin reaction.

8 The report doesn't even tell us whether or not the women concerned actually use make-up. They may all be nuns.

9 The sample is so small that if a group of three or four men came in all suffering from an allergy rash caused by a product they'd been in contact with at work, the overall result would be changed completely.

10 The severity of the disorders has not yet been reported. Women are more likely to visit the surgery with their children than men and while in the surgery the women may mention problems not severe enough to merit making a special appointment. Some of the women may not have turned up if they hadn't taken their children to the doctor's surgery.

The point I hope that I've made is that trials and tests are difficult to plan and the results can easily be misinterpreted. The short research project I have described here is very simple and straight-forward but many scientific projects are a great deal more complicated and consequently the number of potential pitfalls for those interpreting the results are greater.

I'm afraid that many of the trials organized by cosmetic companies fail to provide convincing evidence because they are badly organized and poorly interpreted, and I suspect that bad organization and poor interpretation are often used to disguise the fact that a product has no solid evidence behind it.

BACK TO NATURE

This section of the book would be incomplete if I ignored the fact that many companies are today catering for the growing number of people who are anxious to 'get back to nature' when it comes to buying medicines and cosmetics. The trend is partly the result of a reaction against orthodox medicine in general and modern pharmaceutical processes in particular.

It isn't difficult to understand exactly why this reaction has set in; after all, it is widely known today that high-technology medicine can often cause, as well as treat, life-threatening ailments. Powerful remedies are always likely to produce severe side-effects and although those side-effects may be considered acceptable by prescribers, they are often regarded as unacceptable by those who are affected.

In the world of medicine the reaction has meant that those selling alternative remedies are enjoying a boom period that few of them could have anticipated, while in the world of cosmetics the reaction has led to a move away from scientifically prepared cosmetics and a move towards herbal, natural products. A number of companies, some small and some international, boast that their products are made without synthetic chemicals of any kind, and there are also companies and individuals whose sole purpose is to provide raw materials for those anxious to manufacture their own cosmetics and toiletries.

The number of plants used in the manufacture of 'herbal' cosmetics seems endless, and the claims made for individual products vary from the simply imaginative to the completely bizarre. I've seen remarkable claims made for avocado, grapefruit, tomato, wheat germ, soya, sage, wild chamomile, wild pansy, common mallow, juniper, arnica, St John's Wort, hazel, ribbed melilot, elder, alpine lady's mantle, borage, honey, rosemary, cucumber, marigold, nettles, and just about anything else you care to name.

The simple truth is that there is no unequivocal evidence that any one of these substances has any useful effect on the skin or that the inclusion of any one of them in a cosmetic of any kind will improve the value of that cosmetic or reduce the risk of an allergy reaction or chemical side-effect.

On the contrary, it seems to me to be likely that so-called natural products may actually be more prone to cause side-effects and allergy reactions. After all, a good many of these products and their additives have never been adequately tested. In addition there is the undoubted problem that the absence of preservatives in natural products makes infection more likely. For this reason 'natural' or 'herbal' products should always be freshly prepared and used within a short period of time.

In conclusion, my view is that 'natural' cosmetics should be judged in the same way that all other cosmetics are judged; with effectiveness and price being the two most important criteria.

CONTROLS AND LEGISLATION

VOLUNTARY AND STATUTORY

The manufacturer of cosmetics must ensure that his products do not contain ingredients known to be dangerous and he must avoid selling his wares in such a way as to openly invite accusations that he has blatantly misled potential customers. On the whole, however, the cosmetics manufacturer has a fairly easy time of it as far as statutory legislation is concerned. As is so often the case, the balance sheet is the most important restriction on the manufacturer since no producer of cosmetics is going to deliberately market a product that is likely to be dangerous. He knows that once customers are upset, they may be lost for ever, and that such a route inevitably leads to ruin in an industry where customer satisfaction is such a vital but nebulous quality.

Nevertheless, the evidence suggests that the balance sheet doesn't always prevent the use of misleading advertising or the over-enthusiastic promotion of products with a quasi-medicinal purpose. Indeed, the evidence seems to suggest that, on the contrary, companies which 'oversell' rarely lose. Customers are likely to blame themselves or ill fortune rather than the product they have bought if the promised miracle doesn't take place. The 'mark' is always going to be unwilling to admit that he has been conned.

In the cosmetics world this is perhaps of little significance. One can argue that the woman buying a perfume which promises social success and sexual ecstasy is paying for a dream which she does not, in reality, expect to achieve. She has willingly 'bought' the con. On the other hand, in the no man's land between medicines and cosmetics the consumer is fired by anxiety or fear, and disappointments are likely to be more important. It is in this area that some form of control is needed.

THE FUTURE

Those who consider that the current state of the cosmetics industry needs controlling and that in the future the production of cosmetics and toiletries must be subject to some legislative control, usually begin by pointing out that whereas there are some controls on the production and sale of medicines, there are very few controls on those products which are marketed as having medicinal qualities but are classified officially as being cosmetics. The anomaly means that one company producing a skin cream described as suitable for the treatment of dry skin will have to list the ingredients in the cream on the side of the package, whereas another company which produces a cosmetic cream with almost identical qualities will be under no compulsion to release such information and may indeed do all in its power to resist the release of that information.

I believe that this problem could be simply solved by insisting that all products which have any alleged medicinal qualities be officially classified as medicines while only those products sold purely as cosmetics should be sold in such a secretive fashion.

This minor change in the way that cosmetics and medicines are defined would also mean that those products for which manufacturers have claimed medicinal qualities would be sold with clear directions about how best they should be used. Products sold purely as cosmetics could continue to be sold without any such information being supplied.

There are many critics of the cosmetics industry who would go further than this, and it has been suggested that details of all ingredients should be included on the package in which cosmetics are marketed. It is said that if this were done customers who are allergic to specific constituents would be able to avoid products to which they may develop allergies. I suspect that this is impracticable since many cosmetics, and in particular products such as perfumes, contain so many different ingredients that the printing containing these details would have to be unreadably small. Patch testing new products and then sticking with items which do not cause allergic reactions is probably the best way for the allergic individual to avoid trouble from cosmetics.

My feeling is that we do not need to change the legislation controlling the manufacture or sale of cosmetics but simply to change the way in which cosmetics are defined, so that those products currently in the area of no man's land are in future placed firmly in the world of medicines where legislation is slightly more burdensome and customers' expectations are easier to define and control.

I suspect that the result of this would simply be that a great many manufacturers of cosmetics would suddenly find that their products had purely aesthetic qualities after all. Consequently, the public would be spared the effort of dealing with an enormous quantity of misleading, pseudo-scientific advertising.

PART TWO
THE PROFESSIONALS

INTRODUCTION

If you want to have central heating installed these days you don't speak to an engineer, you consult with a specialist. If you have rats at the bottom of your garden you get in touch with the local rodent exterminator. And so it goes on. Everywhere you turn there are consultants and specialists and experts.

The proliferation of experts in general and the specific abuse of the words 'specialist' and 'consultant' has meant that more and more consumers are becoming cynical and sceptical and looking for ways to identify the real experts. It is, after all, now well known that it is possible to buy a doctorate for a few pounds and that many companies and private educational establishments issue diplomas and certificates at the drop of a fiver.

So how can one differentiate between the real expert who has spent several years acquiring knowledge, experience and skill and the pseudo-expert who has spent a few hours being indoctrinated by a single company with a single range of products to sell? How do you tell which expert to believe when you're searching for help with a specific problem?

That is exactly what this section of the book is intended to be all about, and so I'll explain just what a chiropodist does and how much difference there is between a hairdresser and a trichologist. I'll also describe the techniques and equipment that the experts use. The beauty world is full of pseudospecialists, and I hope that when you've read this section you'll have a better idea of how to tell whether or not the expert you're speaking to really is an expert – and just what you can expect him or her to know.

The best experts are those who are aware of the limits of their own knowledge; in other words those who know what they don't know. In my experience the more someone knows the more he becomes aware of his own ignorance. As a general rule, therefore, I recommend that you beware of the brash and over confident expert who *knows* that if you use such and such a product or undergo this and that treatment you'll look more beautiful. In beauty care, as in medicine, there can be no guarantee, and the real experts will only recommend and advise.

BEAUTICIANS AND OTHER EXPERTS

When I began to investigate the qualities and qualifications of beauticians I found, to my amazement, that there are quite a number of associations and institutes which exist to train and certify those anxious to work in this rambling speciality.

There is, for example, the British Association of Beauty Therapy and Cosmetology Ltd which defines a beautician as someone who specializes in skin care, facial treatments, make-up, manicuring, pedicuring and removing unwanted hair by wax depilation. They say that the beautician should also be able to apply eyelash extension, and tint eyelashes and eyebrows. A beauty therapist, they say, is someone who specializes in body treatments such as slimming and toning, and what they call 'losing weight and losing inches'. An aestheticienne they define as someone who combines both the work of a beautician and a beauty therapist. An electrologist (who practises a speciality sometimes known as electrolysis) is defined as a person specially trained to treat the removal of superfluous hair by the use of an electrical current applied with a very fine needle.

For entry to a training course run by the Confederation of Beauty Therapy and Cosmetology which is the Education Board of the British Association of Beauty Therapy and Cosmetology Ltd a student needs a minimum of three O levels or their equivalent. She will attend a course at a private school or college of further education for between six and twelve months. The Confederation does say that shorter courses in selected subjects are also available.

Most of the training period is apparently spent 'on practical work to help you develop poise, confidence and ability', and at the end of the training diplomas are awarded. The beautician course and the beauty therapist course both cover a minimum of 300 hours training and at the end of that time the successful candidate is entitled to a diploma and membership of the BABThC.

Some of the Confederation courses are run to the standards set by the Comité International d'Esthetique et de Cosmetologie (CI-DESCO) which is described by the Confederation as 'the only genuinely world-wide beauty organization'. Training must last for at least ten months before the standards of this organization will be met.

I don't know whether the International Therapy Examination Council would agree with the Confederation's opinion of CI-DESCO. The ITEC claims to have examined more candidates than all the other comparable examining bodies put together in at least one recent academic year.

Then there is the Shaw College of Beauty Therapy which describes itself as 'one of the world's most successful Beautician Training Establishments instructing students from all over the world', and which claims that Shaw College diplomas are 'internationally recognized as a passport to success in the Beauty Business'.

And there is the National Health and Beauty Council which is the consultative organization representing the Society of Health and Beauty Therapists, the Institute of Male Masseurs, the Finnish Sauna Society, the Association of Beauty Teachers and the Health and Beauty Employers Federation.

The International Health and Beauty Council looks after the examination systems for all the members of the National Health and Beauty Council and approves official qualifications for those who have passed the requisite examinations. If you have an International Beauty Therapists Diploma you are entitled to put FSBTh after your name, while a Beauty Specialists Diploma entitles you to the letters MSBTh and a Manicure Certificate is denoted by the letters ASBTh. The Institute of Male Masseurs issues a Diploma in Health and Beauty Therapy which entitles holders to the letters FIMM, and the Finnish Sauna Diploma gives its holders the right to the letters FSS. There are many more. For example, you can get a Beauty Therapists Certificate from the City and Guilds London Institute.

My reason for describing at some length the confusion which surrounds the qualifications held by beauticians, beauty therapists and others is not to belittle those with these qualifications but to hopefully point out the limitations which must necessarily affect those involved. The best way to judge a therapist is not by his or her diploma but by personal recommendations.

Beauticians and cosmeticians often seem keen to banish any idea that they do not belong to the healing professions. One advertisement even goes so far as to suggest that 'the happy medium between a dermatologist and a beautician is the Janet Sartin Skin Care Programme' while Janet Sartin herself is described as a 'world famous Scientific Cosmetologist'. However, in my view beauticians simply are not trained in the same way that members of the healing professions are trained. In a textbook entitled *Principles and Techniques for the Beauty Specialist* by Ann Gallant, published by Stanley Thornes (Publishers) Ltd, the author advises students that 'new products or treatments should be introduced to keep the clients aware of fashion trends and abreast of current developments in the beauty industry. If she is made to feel up to date and knowledgeable, it is more likely that she will avail herself of the new concepts available in the establishment rather than in more neutral or commercial surroundings where she is not known'. She also says that 'specialized treatment products should be advised where possible, so that items recommended can only be purchased at the salon, thus assuring repeat sales and avoiding the client seeking unknowledgeable cosmetic advice from chemist or store'.

Now that is perfectly sound commercial advice but it isn't the sort of information one would expect to find in a textbook intended for members of a learned profession. Not even doctors and lawyers are quite so brutally frank about their intentions!

Even more worrying, if one considers beauticians to be professionals in the health and beauty business, is the fact that that book's index does not even include the word 'cancer' although there are naturally many pages devoted to skin care and skin afflictions.

What to let a beauty therapist or beautician do

A skilled and experienced beauty therapist or beautician (I don't really think that the title is important or particularly relevant) should be able to:

advise on general skin care
advise on the use of make-up
provide specific treatment for hirsutism
recommend specific cosmetic products

help you relax by providing a face pack or massage
provide a manicure or pedicure

Don't expect more from your beautician and you won't be disappointed.

What NOT to let a beauty therapist do
Don't let her:

interfere with warts or moles
bleach patches of dark skin
interfere with red veins, skin infections, eczema, skin ulcers and other medical conditions
do skin peeling, either with a machine or a chemical (see p. 65)

CHIROPODISTS
The only course in chiropody training recognized by the Society of Chiropodists and by the Chiropodists Board of the Council for Professions Supplementary to Medicine for the purpose of official, state registration lasts three years and involves full-time study. The qualification of state registration is necessary if a chiropodist intends to work within the National Health Service, and I suggest that if a private chiropodist's attention is needed you should make sure that the practitioner you intend to patronize has this qualification. Treated badly or ineffectively, foot problems can get worse.

DENTISTS
Qualified dentists register with the General Dental Council whether they practise solely privately, solely within the health service or do a little of both, and whether they practise as specialists or as general dental surgeons.

Dental hygienists and dental nurses do not necessarily have any official training and are only qualified to work directly under the supervision of a qualified dentist.

ELECTROLYSISTS

The British Association of Electrolysists has approximately 400 members, all of whom must have had at least 200 hours' experience of practical epilation over a period of not less than six months. After passing the initial examination members may use the letters ABAE after their names and after two years' continuous experience members may use the letters MBAE. After seven years' continuous experience members automatically become fellows. These qualifications are not listed in *Whitaker's Almanac* or in any of my dictionaries. The syllabus for students of electrolysis includes anatomy, physiology and clinical pathology.

HAIRDRESSERS AND TRICHOLOGISTS

Apprentice hairdressers have to spend three years learning their art and studying all aspects of hair cutting, styling and colouring. There is more to it than that, of course, and young hairdressers are expected to study the anatomy of human hair so that they can more effectively use and understand the chemicals used in salons and the effects that they are likely to have on both the hair and the scalp.

The *Shorter Oxford Dictionary* defines trichology as the 'study of the structure, function and diseases of the hair', and those who describe themselves as trichologists have their own institute which was founded in 1902 'to promote the scientific study, research and honourable practice in all that pertains to the treatment and care of the human hair and scalp in health and disease and to supply comprehensive instruction and training in trichology'. Those who have satisfied the entrance requirements and joined the institute as full members put the letters MIT after their names although this abbreviation is not included in Whitaker's Almanac where the usual professional qualifications are listed at length.

Personally, I do not feel that trichologists can offer a great deal more than good hairdressers. I feel that if you have a serious hair or scalp problem then you should see your own doctor who will, if necessary, arrange an appointment with a dermatologist under the health service. Hair transplantation operations and other similar operations should only be done by or under the supervision of a qualified surgeon.

OPTICIANS

There are two types of opticians in Britain: ophthalmic opticians who test sight and usually also supply and fit what the General Optical Council rather quaintly calls optical appliances; and dispensing opticians who do not test sight but only supply and fit optical appliances. Ophthalmic surgeons are qualified doctors who have specialized in the study of eye disorders and who are entitled to treat disorders of the eyes with spectacles, medicines or surgery, as they see fit.

BEAUTY EDITORS

'Now, hold your horses, Rufe,' I said indulgently. 'You don't really believe this works, do you?'

'Why not?' he snapped. 'Says so in the paper, don't it?'

'Sure, sure,' I said, 'but you've got to understand about the cosmetics industry.' I made a short, incisive talk, not one word of which he heard, explaining how the journalistic peony thrives in the rich humus of publicity and advertising. . . .'

The Most of S. J. Perelman
Eyre Methuen 1978

Beauty editors are the eunuchs of the cosmetics industry. A remarkably high number of them seem happy enough to copy out chunks of material from the publicity hand-outs produced by the major cosmetic companies and strangely reluctant to question any of the information they are offered. Secrets are easy to keep when no one wants to know them. It's difficult to imagine motoring correspondents writing such laudatory and uncritical comments, and if book critics would only follow their example many authors would suffer far less.

What I find particularly depressing is the sad fact that many beauty editors and writers seem to have very little understanding of basic human anatomy or physiology. Some do not even understand such fundamentals as the way in which a moisturizing cream works. The ignorance of beauty writers leads inevitably to the perpetuation of a number of bizarre myths and their uncritical approach makes things far too easy for the confidence tricksters who abound in this particular industry. I read one piece in which a beauty writer sniffed that 'orthodox doctors tend to be very cynical about anything that can't be proved in a series of controlled scientific experiments'. Personally, I wish that one or two beauty writers would replace some of their sycophancy with a touch of scepticism.

Finally, I must condemn the beauty writers who so enthusiastically use technical words which may or may not be used correctly. Professional jargon is often the refuge of the insecure, uncertain and uneducated who need to hide their lack of solid factual information or basic background knowledge behind a protective hedge of untrimmed verbiage. The beauty people even outdo the sociologists when it comes to jargon. My advice is simply this: if you don't understand what you read in a magazine or newspaper – ignore it. The chances are high that the writer didn't understand it either.

BEAUTY PARLOURS AND WHAT THEY OFFER

Before visiting a beauty parlour of any kind it is essential that you have some idea of what you expect to gain from your visit. Some parlours offer a wide variety of therapies while others specialize in electrolysis, hydrotherapy or massage.

To help you differentiate between the various procedures offered by different parlours I have prepared a series of pen portraits of the techniques and services most commonly offered.

AROMATHERAPY

Rubbing sweet, pleasant smelling oils into the body is a long established form of treatment. The Egyptians, Greeks and Romans all used oils as essential aids during massage, but it was not until 1928 that the term 'aromatherapy' was first coined by a French chemist called René-Maurice Gattefossé who claimed that some oils had healing powers. An Austrian beauty therapist, Madame Marguerite Maury, helped to make aromatherapy popular in London when she introduced treatments to relax, to stimulate, to treat dry skins, to help develop the bust and to improve poor circulation. Today the Aromatic Oil Company claims that aromatherapy is 'the practical application of the essential oils of plants to maintain or help restore natural harmony in the human organism'. The brochure advertising the company's products concludes: 'The aroma of a natural essence can have subtle effects on mood and emotion, and different essences may be used to soothe or excite, to uplift or refresh, and generally to enhance one's own aura, bringing about a state of harmonious well being.' One well established London practitioner claims that aromatherapy is a method of rejuvenation. My feeling is that aromatherapy is probably a good way to relax.

BALNEOTHERAPY
Literally, balneotherapy means treating with the aid of baths. There are many variations on this theme ranging from simply lolling in a warm bath, to dropping in bath salts and to adding such exotic things as mud, seaweed and oatmeal. There is no reason why you shouldn't add anything you fancy to your own bath, and one of the easiest ways to do this is to hang a bag of herbs under the hot tap before you turn it on. Do remember, however, that too much soaking in the bath can make the skin dry.

BODY WRAP
Clinics which offer treatments designed to reduce weight or inches sometimes offer a remedy called 'body wrap'. The client is smeared with a special gel and then wrapped in bandages. I've discussed this type of treatment at greater length on p. 218. Unless you have a mummy fixation I can see no reason why you should pay to be wrapped in bandages.

CATHIODERMIE
Said to have been the brainchild of French cosmetic chemist René Guinot cathiodermie involves the use on the skin of the extracts of sea plants, herbs, flowers and fruit together with electrical currents. According to an advertisement in *Hair and Beauty* this technique is said to be useful for the treatment of difficult skin conditions such as acne and in the oxygenation of the skin and cell regeneration. *Cosmopolitan's Health and Beauty Guide* suggests that the combination of galvanic current, gel and special cream releases oxygen which activates the cell regeneration process. I do not understand how releasing oxygen on the surface of the skin can in any way improve the condition of dead cells.

CHIROPODY
Properly qualified chiropodists (see p. 50) are capable of dealing safely and effectively with any foot problem. A chiropodist's training includes an analysis of those disorders which can sometimes present as foot problems. I do not recommend that you allow anyone not properly qualified as a chiropodist to deal with your feet.

CYTO-LOGISTIC THERAPY

This is the name for the technique favoured by Peter Stephan who maintains that with it he can arrest the ageing process. A great many claims have been made in recent years for treatments said to have a regenerative action. As far as I know there is no undisputed scientific evidence to support any of the claims which are made.

DEPILATION

Beauty specialists use several techniques for removing excess, unwanted hair. They will, according to the client's taste and purse depth, offer to cut, shave or pluck hair. They may also offer to use special hair-removing creams, bleaches, hair-removing waxes and electrical treatments such as epilation and electrolysis.

DEPILATORY WAXES

Wax can be used to help remove excess, unwanted hair. The wax is simply applied to the skin and then peeled off – the hairs should come with it. The advantages are that large numbers of hairs can be removed in one session and that the skin is left very smooth immediately after removal. The disadvantages are that the hairs grow again and cannot be removed with wax until they have grown to a noticeable length. Some people find the procedure painful and occasionally skin reactions occur.

DERMABRASION

Dermabrasion involves the use of a rotating wire brush which is designed to remove the superficial layer of skin cells. When an ordinary rough face cloth is used the skin is being thinned to a small extent; thinning with a wire brush is simply an extension of the same philosophy. Unfortunately, there are many potential problems, and the exposure of a layer of raw, untanned skin can result in temporary or even permanent damage. Dermabrasion is sometimes offered by beauticians who do not have medical training, but should, in my opinion, only be attempted by dermatologists or plastic surgeons and even then only in most exceptional circumstances. There may be, and probably are, beauticians who know how to do this operation safely, but I know of no way to help readers differentiate between the capable and the incapable. A medical qualification seems, therefore, to be an essential pre-requisite to be on the safe side.

DIRECT HIGH FREQUENCY TREATMENT
High frequency currents alternate so rapidly that they do not stimulate the muscles. When applied directly to the skin these currents are said to have a germicidal effect which is produced by the formation of ozone on the skin's surface. Whatever the truth of this may be, the fact is that it is impossible to do more than temporarily remove all the bacteria living on the skin's surface, and I can see no possible reason for using this treatment.

EAR PIERCING
The overlap between the responsibilities of doctors and beauticians is usually extended by beauticians rather than medical practitioners, but there is one exception to this general rule: ear piercing. Many family doctors will now pierce ears as well as syringe them, and in view of the number of girls I have seen with infected ear lobes it might be wise to take advantage of this strange development. Alternatively it is best to patronize a salon where piercing is done with a gun and sterilized stud. Afterwards the ear lobe should be carefully cleaned each day with a little liquid antiseptic.

EFFLEURAGE
Soothing massage movements are usually described as effleurage. The flat of the hand is used to help stroke the muscles and the aim is to improve the circulation and prepare the muscles for more aggressive forms of massage.

ELECTROLYSIS
The operator needs to be skilled since tiny needles have to be put into each hair follicle one at a time. The needle then destroys the hair root by using electricity to produce a chemical reaction. The main disadvantages of electrolysis are that the process is slow, expensive, sometimes painful and occasionally produces a skin re-

action. The major advantage is that if the operation is done properly the hairs do not return.

EPILATION
Short wave diathermy or electrically produced heat is used to destroy permanently the hair root and hair follicle. It is an excellent way to remove unwanted hair. (See p. 125.)

ETHEIROLOGY
According to those who follow the philosophy of René Furterer etheirology is the care of the scalp and hair. Those who practise this speciality provide their clients with special scalp treatments and use massage and brushing techniques to improve the health of the scalp and hair. Personally, I don't think there is much difference between an etheirologist, a trichologist and a good hairdresser.

FACE PACKS AND FACE MASKS
The Egyptians used a complex recipe when preparing face masks but the technique they employed was similar to the one used today. The mixture was applied directly to the skin and allowed to dry, and as moisture evaporated from the mask the skin was first cooled, then drawn and constricted. The aim was to clear dead cells from the skin's surface, to draw out toxic wastes from within the skin, to remove wrinkles and even to improve the circulation.

Today there are so many different types of face mask available that to attempt to provide a comprehensive list would be impossible. Whatever the type of mask the rules about its application are very similar: the mask must be applied on clean skin, it must be rinsed off thoroughly, and afterwards the skin must be covered with moisturizing cream. Face packs and face masks may well produce some temporary improvement in the skin of the face but the improvement is unlikely to last more than an hour or two. However, it may be sufficient to give extra confidence for an evening out.

One company, French of London, makes a pair of special pink masks. One mask, made of pink PVC and shaped rather like the masks that highwaymen and the Lone Ranger made famous, is used in conjunction with a product called *Collagen Protein Skin Control Cream* which is described as 'a specially formulated skin regenerating cream which renews the skin's elasticity, tones and moisturizes the skin and leaves it smooth, firm and youthful looking'. The cream is first patted on to the skin, and then the mask, which has been gently heated in a saucepan of hot water, is tied on and left in place for ten or fifteen minutes. The alternative mask known as *Pink Ice* is filled with a gel and should be chilled in the refrigerator before being tied on. It is said to 'bring relief from tension, ease migraine headaches and even hangovers' and also to 'soothe away eye irritation and puffiness caused by polluted atmosphere or overwork'.

FACIAL SAUNA
You can in fact have a facial sauna at home simply by filling a bowl with boiling water and holding your face over the rising steam. (Obviously you should not use water so hot that it causes pain or burns.) The theory is that the steam, by causing the production of sweat, will open and cleanse the pores. If herbs such as chamomile, rosemary, comfrey or lavender are added to the water the sauna will smell good.

Facial sauna can be most refreshing but it is important to remember to cleanse the face thoroughly with fresh water afterwards.

FACIAL VACUUM TREATMENT
The lymph vessels are sometimes drained by manual means (cf. lymphatic draining massage) but they can also be emptied by mechanical means. The operator applies a small vacuum device to the skin and uses the suction to control the flow of lymph. This is just as silly as manual massage done for the same purpose. In fact it seems to me to be a modern cosmetic equivalent of the old medical practice of bleeding patients with the aid of leeches.

FARADISM
Faradism refers to a type of electrical current which, when controlled by a physiotherapist, can be used to treat damaged muscles.

The current induces muscular contraction and thereby provides a type of passive exercise.

Beauty therapists use faradism to stimulate muscles such as those of the face. The movement of these muscles helps to temporarily improve the local circulation. A similar effect can, of course, be obtained by simply exercising the facial muscles yourself.

FRICTION MASSAGE
Friction massage involves rubbing the skin with the fingers!

GALVANIC SKIN TREATMENT
This is one of a number of different electrical treatments favoured by beauty therapists. Galvanic treatment can be used to remove surface oils (a procedure known as desincrustation) or to introduce water soluble substances through the skin (a procedure given the grand sounding name of iontophoresis). I know of no research which substantiates these claims or which proves the procedure to be entirely safe. I do not believe that any improvement which could be obtained with the aid of this type of treatment could be anything more than temporary.

HYDROTHERAPY
Hydrotherapy simply means treatment with water. You can drink it, splash it on to your body, wash in it, sit in it, bathe in it, swim in it, and exercise in it. If you're recovering from an illness, that is a good way to exercise.

Some people enjoy being massaged by jets of water under pressure. This is known as hydro-massage and you can either buy an expensive 'jacuzzi' type of bath or a special tub such as an *Agua Caliente Hot Tub*, or you can mess around with the shower attachment next time you have a bath.

KINESIOLOGY
The strict definition of kinesiology is the 'science of motion' and kinesiologists usually spend their time studying the actions and

relationships of bones and muscles during movements of all kinds. The term does not really have anything to do with beauty treatments but some keep fit ladies with delusions of grandeur sometimes describe themselves as kinesiologists.

LASER BEAM THERAPY

The removal of unwanted tattoos is a tricky business. Several methods have been tried and found to be unsatisfactory, and such techniques as plastic surgery and dermabrasion have been discarded by a number of experts as unsuitable.

The latest technique involves the use of laser beams and although there seems to have been some success I strongly advise anyone contemplating such treatment to consult his or her own family doctor first.

LYMPHATIC DRAINING MASSAGE

Special facial massage techniques are used by some beauty therapists to empty the lymph ducts of the face. I cannot see any possible reason for paying for this service. If you massaged the visible veins on your forearm you could temporarily increase the flow of blood in that region but I don't know what good it would do. (See also p. 60.)

MANICURE

The professional manicure doesn't just involve cleaning, filing and painting the finger-nails. The hands are also given attention. Everything that can be done by a beauty specialist can also be done at home, but a number of people certainly enjoy the pleasure of being pampered and having their hands and nails attended to by a professional, and of course some people find it difficult to deal with their dominant hand.

MASSAGE

Small advertisements in shop windows have given massage and masseurs rather a bad name. However, not all the masseurs and masseuses and not all the massage parlours now open offer pleasures to the exclusion of all other forms of treatment. When it is well done by experienced hands massage can help relieve pain and ease tension all over the body. Massage should not be done on inflamed or damaged skin and should not be attempted without the use of oils to make the skin more malleable. (See also effleurage, friction massage, petrissage, tapotement and vibration massage.)

ORTHODONTICS
The objective of orthodontics is the prevention and correction of malocclusion of the teeth. An orthodontist is, in popular terms, a dentist who straightens crooked teeth, and since children's teeth are more likely to respond to treatment than those of adults, orthodontists usually deal with children.

OZONE STEAMING
According to one textbook of beauty therapy ozone steaming is a 'natural means of activating the circulation of the subcutaneous vessels and providing them with oxygen'.

At first sight you might think that this means that the ozone filters through the skin. I suspect that what really happens is that the steam (whether or not it contains ozone) increases the temperature of the skin and that the local circulation increases in an attempt to reduce the skin temperature. The increase in the rate at which blood circulates through the skin means that the tissues are provided with extra oxygen.

Ozone steaming may be pleasant but it is unlikely to produce anything more than a very temporary effect on your skin.

PARAFFIN WAX TREATMENT
Paraffin wax treatments are recommended for use on those with stiff joints. They are also recommended for those who are worried about their general skin texture and condition. Relief is likely to be temporary. Joint pain and stiffness may well be relieved by the use of a hot wax treatment.

PEDICURE
If your feet don't look as pretty as you think they could do and you have difficulty in attending to them yourself then you might enjoy having a pedicure. It is, however, important to realize that if there is anything wrong with the feet (any infections, callus or nail disorder) then a chiropodist must be seen.

PERIODONTICS
This is the prevention, diagnosis and treatment of conditions which affect the jaw bones and gums.

PETRISSAGE
This is a type of massage which involves pinching, kneading and rolling the skin. Larger muscles are relaxed and the general skin condition is said to be improved.

PHYSIATRY
Physiatry should not be confused with psychiatry or physiotherapy. It is, according to a report in a British daily newspaper, a special technique which can, among other things, shift fat from a woman's stomach to her breasts. I don't believe in flying saucers either.

PRESSURE SPRAY TONING
Instead of dabbing facial tonics on to the skin from a bottle some beauticians spray the tonics on. Indeed you can buy vaporizers so that you can enjoy this facility at home. You can even buy mineral waters in sprays. I suppose that some people really will buy anything but I find it difficult to understand why anyone should pay money to have anything sprayed on to his or her face.

PROSTHODONTICS
Prosthodontics is the science of maintaining and restoring oral function, comfort, appearance and good health by the provision of prostheses. For most people the word 'dentures' or 'false teeth' can be used instead of prostheses. Any dentist will provide this service.

SAUNA

The experts claim that a sauna will help relax a tired human and by increasing the rate at which sweat oozes out will clean the pores and the skin. Certainly few saunas are equipped with telephones and that simple fact alone will ensure that most patrons enjoy rest and relaxation. A Turkish bath is rather less extreme than a sauna with the temperature being slightly lower, while in a steam cabinet the body only is immersed in a steam-filled box.

A recent correspondence in the *Journal of the American Medical Association* discussed the question of whether or not there are any physiological explanations for the fact that steam baths often relax those who favour them. The conclusion seems to have been that there is no known reason why steam baths help to relax people, but they do. Those who suffer from heart disease or any other ailment needing medical attention are advised not to take a steam bath without first obtaining their doctor's permission.

SHORT WAVE DIATHERMY

Short wave diathermy is used by some beauticians for the removal of unwanted hair. (See p. 125.)

SKIN PEELING

Skin peeling is an effective way to remove dead skin cells and to help unblock sebaceous glands. Peeling can be done chemically, mechanically (see p. 57) or it can be done with simple abrasives such as a rough face cloth (see p. 153). Since skin peeling done with chemicals or by dermabrasion can be dangerous I do not recommend that it be done by a beauty therapist.

SLIMMING TREATMENTS

Slimming treatments such as *Kwik Slim* and *Quickslim* are discussed on p. 128.

SWEDISH MASSAGE

The phrase 'Swedish massage' always seems to attract giggles and guffaws but I don't really know why. There isn't really any difference between 'Swedish massage' and 'Polish massage' or 'Australian massage', but I suppose that since the Swedes seem to have a reputation for sexual skill and strength, massage in the Swedish style might be expected to have a saucier flavour.

TAPOTEMENT
Tapotement is the stimulating form of massage that involves beating, whipping, slapping and tapping the skin. This type of massage is done to stimulate and tighten the skin.

TATTOOS
I very much doubt if anyone contemplating the addition of a tattoo or two to any part of his or her body will read this book but I mention the procedure simply to remind readers that individuals having tattoos done may risk acquiring hepatitis. The use of unsterilized needles by tattoo artists may cause this infection.

TRICHOGRAMS
If you think your hair is falling out you can visit a trichologist and have a trichogram done. Hairs are taken from the scalp and examined under a microscope. A study of the number of hairs which are growing and the number which are resting will give the expert an idea of the health of the hair at that particular time. Unfortunately, if your hair is falling out there isn't much that a trichologist can do about it.

ULTRAVIOLET TREATMENT
Sun lamps and other artificial sources of sunshine produce ultraviolet light. These lamps are therefore used to help induce artificial tans. Some beauty experts claim that the lamps help improve oily skin. The problems of such lamps are described at greater length on p. 235.

VACUUM SUCTION
This is the name given to the type of treatment sometimes used to help improve the flow of lymph and sometimes used as a slimming aid. It involves the use of a suction pump and a number of cups. I don't recommend it since I do not see how it can possibly have anything more than a temporary effect.

VIBRATION MASSAGE
Vibration massage involves a delicate tapping and circling of the skin with the fingertips in an attempt to stimulate the circulation. Electric vibrators are also sometimes used. The only risk is that the subcutaneous tissues may be damaged if the massage is not done carefully, This type of massage is often used to relieve tension. Some clinics offer a special type of vibratory massage which, among other things, is said to stimulate the flow of digestive juices. I do not recommend this unusual remedy.

VIENNESE FACIALS
Facial massage is a favourite in the beauty parlours. Clients can often choose from French, Japanese and Viennese massage, but although the style of massage may be different there won't be much difference in the end result. Facial massage can produce some temporary improvement in the tone and appearance of the face but the improvement will not last. Viennese massage seems to involve the indirect use of a high frequency electrical current.

DOCTORS – PLASTIC SURGEONS AND DERMATOLOGISTS

There are times when the search for cosmetic improvement leads not to a beautician or the cosmetic counter of a pharmacy or store but to the doctor's surgery. Those who feel that they have physical deformities of some kind which are responsible for social embarrassments as well as mental anguish may look for surgical help, while those with disorders of the skin, nails or hair may need the skilled and specialist attention of a dermatologist.

When a dermatologist's advice is needed there are few problems about how or where to find a suitable specialist. The patient's general practitioner will simply arrange for the appropriate referral and write an introductory letter. Whether the patient chooses to see a specialist working within the National Health Service or a specialist who is in private practice, the procedure will be the same. Most people with skin problems will find that they have a choice between public and private care, although there may be a small number of people needing purely cosmetic care who will have to pay for the appointment. I do not know of any dermatologists who are prepared to see patients not referred by their general practitioner.

The world of plastic surgery is rather different.

Plastic surgery is, of course, a relatively new speciality and although there is evidence that many cosmetic operations were performed in Egypt some thousands of years ago, it was only after the First World War, when surgical techniques had been changed by the introduction of antiseptics and anaesthesia, that the speciality began to flouish. The horrifying burns suffered by airmen in the Second World War intensified the development of this speciality and the improvement of appearance became as important as the restoration of function. Today the world of plastic surgery is different from almost any other branch of medical care and there are a great many private clinics and hospitals advertising widely in magazines and newspapers and offering a full range of services to those dissatisfied with the shape or size of their noses, buttocks or breasts. The man or woman wanting plastic surgery can, therefore, select a specialist with or without the help and advice of his or her general practitioner.

This ready availability of facilities for plastic surgery may seem at first sight to offer those in search of physical improvement many advantages. A number of people have, after all, reported that general practitioners are not always as helpful as they might be when confronted by patients wanting plastic surgery and the health service facilities are in appalling short supply with the inevitable but deplorable consequence that waiting lists are long and growing longer.

There are, however, problems associated with some of the private clinics and the number of confidence tricksters operating in this rather unique area of medical care seems disturbingly large. One factor that undoubtedly makes the availability of private facilities for plastic surgery operations particularly dangerous is that many clinics use attractive and persuasive sales staff to convince those inquiring about surgery that it will indeed satisfy their need. These so-called experts have little or no training, and because so many seem to be paid on commission they are obviously more likely to emphasize the potential advantages of surgery than to discuss the dangers and shortcomings. Few of those selling breast surgery operations, for example, will inform potential clients that as many as 50 per cent of these operations have been reported to be unsatisfactory, with women complaining of rock hard and uncomfortable breasts which cause more social and sexual problems than were present beforehand. Another undoubted problem is the fact that those actually performing plastic surgery do not have to be medically qualified. The law in Britain simply says that no one who is not fully qualified and registered with the General Medical Council may claim to be qualified, or use dangerous drugs. There are no laws which prevent unqualified people from performing delicate and potentially dangerous operations.

Yet another problem associated with private clinics, which do not require the consent of a potential client's general practitioner, is simply that there is a potentially hazardous lack of medical continuity. The individual seeking plastic surgery may not be aware of specific contraindications such as, for example, sensitivities to particular drugs or anaesthetics. The lack of contact with the client's own family doctor may also mean that vital information about past medical problems is likely to be overlooked.

Finally, there is the problem of what happens if anything goes wrong. Plastic surgery operations are like any other in that there are always risks of disaster, infection, disfigurement and even death. The risks are slight when the medical attention is good but they are nevertheless there, and when the qualifications of the surgeon are in doubt and communications with the family doctor poor or non-existent the consequences can be tragic.

The individual who has had surgery and returned home will naturally need help if anything goes wrong. But at three o'clock in the morning when a wound reopens or starts to bleed the staff of the private clinic which may be a hundred miles away are unlikely to be of much help. The clinic's customer will inevitably have to call her own doctor for help, and he will know nothing of the operation and have no details of the care and services provided already. The consequences of such a total lack of communication can be fatal.

Less vital, but nevertheless important, is the fact that when things do go wrong the individual who has paid for surgery at a private clinic may have difficulty in obtaining any sort of financial compensation. Qualified and fully registered practitioners of all sorts are usually members of defence societies which, for an annual premium, provide both doctors and patients with insurance against accident and negligence. Private clinics will sometimes insist that before surgery patients sign away all their rights and even when this isn't done, the possibility of obtaining any financial compensation may be slight without this insurance cover.

The simple, important truth, which is often overlooked, is that plastic surgery is a branch of medicine not cosmetic science and it must be carried out by experts if the risks are to be minimized. The surgeon who performs a cosmetic operation needs to be not only qualified as a medical practitioner but also an accepted specialist in the field of plastic surgery. He will usually be a Fellow of the Royal College of Surgeons. Operations to change the shape of a nose or to improve the shape of the bust require experience and a delicate touch. A lack of either can lead to disaster.

I'm afraid, therefore, that I strongly recommend that anyone contemplating plastic surgery should first of all consult their own general practitioner. Whether a private appointment or a health service appointment is to be made the general practitioner will first write a letter of referral, introducing the patient to the surgeon. Most reputable surgeons in Britain will not see any patient without such a letter.

Anyone who has a half-way decent relationship with his or her general practitioner should be able to discuss the need for plastic surgery without too much difficulty, and even the most stubborn family doctor will, I hope, be prepared to write that essential letter of referral if he is convinced of the sincerity of his patient. If the patient explains that she does not want to visit any private clinic that would mean the exclusion of the family doctor from the plans for the operation most doctors will be flattered into cooperation.

At the first appointment good plastic surgeons will want to convince themselves that the operation is necessary and that the patient actually wants to have it done. Good surgeons will explain the limitations and risks and will discuss with the patient the possible opportunities. It just isn't possible to always provide the patient with a button nose or an eye-popping chest.

The surgeon will also want to be sure that the patient is not likely to develop an unpleasant keloid scar after the operation. It is a simple fact that some people have a tendency to produce exaggerated scars after any type of surgical intervention. These scars are called keloid and obviously when they occur after plastic surgery they can make the whole operation pointless. Attempts to remove the keloid scars simply make things worse. Dark-skinned individuals are more likely to get keloid than others, but the problem can occur with any patient, and if there is a family history of keloid then plastic surgery should be avoided.

BEFORE CONTEMPLATING PLASTIC SURGERY

1 Decide exactly what it is that you want changed. If the condition is the result of an injury, a disease, a surgical operation or a major congenital defect you will almost certainly be entitled to treatment under the National Health Service. If the problem does not fall into one of these categories you are unlikely to be able to arrange for surgery under the health service unless you can convince your family doctor that your problem causes you real physical or mental pain.

2 Talk to anyone you can find who has had a surgical operation for a cosmetic problem. You can often learn much more from those who have had real experience of plastic surgery than from those whose experience is only second hand.

3 Talk to members of your family and find out whether any of them have ever suffered from 'keloid'. If they have then you should abandon the idea of undergoing plastic surgery of any kind.

4 Decide exactly what you expect to gain from the operation. You should not expect any major improvements in your social or economic status as a result of the operation. Nor is it wise to undergo surgery in order to rescue a failing relationship. A plastic surgeon can help his patients explore their natural potential but he cannot change their personality.

5 Recognize that plastic surgeons can only adapt what features are already present. However skilled a surgeon may be, he cannot turn 'Whistler's Mother' into the 'Mona Lisa'.

6 If you are paying for an operation, don't borrow money or spend more than you would normally be prepared to squander on a holiday or some similar extravagance. If you go into debt to pay for a plastic surgery operation you're unlikely to be satisfied by the simple correction of a cosmetic flaw.

THE JARGON OF PLASTIC SURGERY
Apronectomy: removal of abdominal fat
Blepharoplasty: eyelid surgery
Mammaplasty: breast operation (can either be a reduction or an augmentation)
Otoplasty: ear-lobe surgery
Rhinoplasty: a nose job
Rhytidectomy: a face-lift

HEALTH FARMS

Health farms are the twentieth-century equivalent of the spa town hotels that were so popular a few generations ago. But many do not confine themselves to offering cures and treatments for medical conditions – they offer beauty therapy and treatments of many kinds.

A number of the therapies they offer are the same as the treatments which can be obtained in beauty parlours, but in view of their size, country location and price, health farms do offer what sound like unique forms of treatment. The one service that is offered by many so-called farms is hydrotherapy – a posh medical sounding word which simply means treatment with the aid of water. The snag is that most forms of hydrotherapy require long-term treatments. Swimming exercises, for example, need to be kept up for several months if full benefit is to be obtained. The term balneotherapy sounds even more impressive than hydrotherapy but this simply means treatment by the use of a bath, and those who run these farms seem to have really stretched their imaginations in the search for new and exciting things with which to fill the bath tubs. You can, if you feel up to it, bathe in brine, peat, pine, seaweed or oatmeal, and although I don't know of any reason why any of these substances should make you look or feel exceptionally healthy or beautiful it is I suppose perfectly possible that you'll feel stimulated by them. However, if you want to try bathing in any of these substances you can do it at home by buying the ingredients at a local pharmacy for a few pence. And if you want a Scotch Douche or a Sitz Bath you can have one of those at home too: the first involves an alternating hot and cold spray, while the second means sitting in alternating hot and cold water.

But all of this is superficial trimming of course. What health farms really offer is peace and quiet. And that is why so many people patronize them. The truth is that if you can get away from it all for a few days and relax then when you return to the fray you probably will look more attractive and feel healthier.

My advice to anyone thinking of spending money on a visit to a health farm is to spend it instead on a trip to a hotel for a few days. If you pick a quiet, country hotel you'll get just as much peace and quiet, and it will cost you only a fraction of the price of a health farm. The other services, such as a swimming pool and a hairdresser, can be found in most small towns.

And if a hotel is out of the question, the next best thing is to disconnect the telephone, the doorbell and the television aerial and to spend the weekend doing absolutely nothing.

PART THREE
CLASSIFIED SECTION

GENERAL ADVICE ABOUT BUYING COSMETICS AND TOILETRIES

There are two important questions which have to be answered by the potential purchaser of any cosmetic product. Those two questions are: what to buy? and where to buy it? I'll deal with them one by one.

WHAT TO BUY

It is difficult to provide specific advice about 'best buys' for three reasons. First, the introduction of new products is a continuous process which means that every week the customer's choice widens or at least changes. Second, each individual's requirements are inevitably peculiar to her or himself. A product which suits one purchaser may prove to be entirely unsuitable for another. Third, a great many companies manufacturing cosmetics and toiletries are extremely reluctant to share details of their products with the public. This means that it is sometimes difficult to produce an accurate scientific assessment of all the items which fall within a specific category.

With these three difficulties in mind I decided that it would be helpful to produce some general advice which can be used to supplement the specific advice available in the latter part of the book. Here then are my ten tips for consumers:

1 It is always wise to test any cosmetic product before buying to make sure that you aren't likely to find yourself allergic to an expensive purchase.

2 When you are buying a toiletry such as soap or shampoo, buy the product that has the fewest number of additives and which costs the least. Often the cheapest products are also the simplest – they're usually the best. Learn to use the same criteria that you use when buying groceries and judge cost

and quantity rather than advertising material and packaging.

3 Don't buy a cosmetic or toiletry because the manufacturer says that it will have medicinal qualities. Cosmetics are not medicines, and if you buy a product expecting it to serve two needs you'll be disappointed.

4 Don't buy in excessive quantities. It isn't economical to buy products that are going to be left in the bathroom or which will go off before you use them. There is also the risk that you might become allergic to a product and find yourself with an economy-sized bottle of it. Trial or sample offers are often a good buy.

5 If you suffer from allergy reactions to cosmetics then buy from one of the companies specializing in the production of hypoallergenic cosmetics. There are no non-allergenic products, and any company claiming to make products which *never* cause allergies should not be patronized.

6 If you have problems with a product you have bought, do write to the manufacturer and complain. Manufacturers rely heavily on feedback from their customers.

7 Don't buy cosmetics that have been made in out of the way places by unheard of companies. Some imported cosmetics contain dangerous ingredients such as lead.

8 Well known companies tend to be careful about what they sell under their own brand name. If faced with a choice between two almost identical products, costing more or less the same amount, then you are probably wise to choose the product made by the better known manufacturer.

9 Don't let companies con you. Learn to read between the lies and study my account of the tricks used by advertising copywriters (see p. 18).

10 When using a colourant or perm or any other potentially dangerous product do read the manufacturer's instructions carefully and then make sure that you follow them.

WHERE TO BUY

It may seem strange to devote a separate section to explaining the advantages and disadvantages of buying cosmetics in different places, but there are good reasons for doing this. I hope you'll understand what I mean when you've read a little more.

There are three types of shops which sell cosmetics and toiletries and of these three types the chemist's shop or pharmacy is probably the most traditional. In many ways it is also the best place to buy a cosmetic. Although pharmacies are unlikely to be able to compete with price-cutting stores and supermarkets they do often have a wider range of products, and since they are unlikely to be linked closely with any particular manufacturer sales assistants will often be able to offer less biased advice than 'consultants' in stores. It is also worth remembering that only in a pharmacy will it be possible to obtain proper advice about treatment for minor medical conditions. Some manufacturers, such as Vichy, believe strongly in the advantages of the chemist's shop and sell their products in this way alone.

The big stores are another obvious and traditional site for the sale of all kinds of cosmetics. Like chemists' shops they usually have sample bottles and 'testers' on display so that customers can try out products they think they might buy, but unlike most chemists' shops they often also have staff working directly for individual manufacturers. These single manufacturer consultants usually work in kiosks or on clearly labelled counters so there is no question of the customer being duped, but it is important to remember that a consultant working for one company is unlikely to offer unbiased advice.

More recently many supermarkets and chain stores have started to sell cosmetics. These shops can often sell at lower prices but they usually sell shrink-wrapped cosmetics and rarely have 'testers' on display. The other disadvantage is that there are unlikely to be knowledgeable salesladies on the premises and so the customer is left very much to herself. Some modern 'drugstores' fall into this category.

It is my feeling that if you are buying a toiletry (such as soap, shampoo or toothpaste) or a cosmetic product that you have already used and found suitable then it is probably cheaper to buy that product in a supermarket. The disadvantage with this philosophy is, of course, that eventually pharmacies and stores will stop selling cosmetics if they don't have any customers, and then there will be nowhere to test products or obtain advice.

Cosmetics can also be bought at home. Many products can be bought by mail order, either through newspaper or magazine advertisements or through catalogues. Many magazines now offer their readers guarantees that they will not lose money if an advertiser doesn't deliver goods that have been paid for. The magazine itself promises to pay out what has been lost. Readers are usually advised that they must report their loss within a fixed time period. At least two companies, Beauty Vision Ltd and the Universal Beauty Club, offer to sell world famous cosmetics at low prices through the post, and if you want to try out a variety of products it might be worth replying to their advertisements. Both these companies offer to refund money to unsatisfied customers.

Guarantees are also offered by companies such as Avon which sell through local representatives. Avon's brochure includes a guarantee which promises that 'if for any reason whatsoever an Avon product is not found satisfactory, it will be cheerfully exchanged or the full purchase price will be immediately refunded upon its return to us or to your representative'. Oriflame, a company which has beauty consultants who deliver orders personally, also has a guarantee which states that 'if any product or product packaging proves to be unsatisfactory in use the product may be returned to us and your money will be repaid in full'.

Finally, I should mention the fact that many companies now sell raw materials with which customers are encouraged to manufacture their own cosmetics. This is a splendid idea, but it is important to remember that home-made cosmetics can cause allergies and that if they do not contain preservatives they may become infected. This risk can be minimized by making small quantities of each cosmetic.

GLOSSARY OF TERMS

Every science has its own private language which is often used by professional practitioners to confuse others. There follows a short glossary of some of the terms most commonly used by those who sell, promote and write about cosmetics of all kinds. I must point out that these definitions are specifically designed for this book and that some of the words mean other things in other contexts.

abrasive something that rubs or wears away unwanted skin or accumulated tartar on the teeth, for example.

aerosol solid or liquid particles suspended in a fine spray or mist.

aftershave a preparation which usually consists of a mixture of alcohols, astringents and perfumes.

alopecia loss of hair.

anhidrosis an inability to sweat.

anti-perspirant a product designed to stop sweating. Anti-perspirants usually consist of aluminium derivatives designed to clog the pores.

antiseptic substance which destroys small organisms which may harm living tissues.

application any substance which is applied to the body. For example, a cream or ointment.

aromatherapy strictly speaking there is no such medical speciality but I assume that those who practise this science would describe it as healing by smell.

astringent something which makes tissues contract and draw together.

axilla armpit.

balm an aromatic ointment that is traditionally used to help heal a wound or soothe pain. Balms are commonly used in the treatment of rheumatism.

balsam an aromatic, oily preparation which usually has some medicinal qualities.

barrier cream a cream which prevents the skin coming in contact with substances which might otherwise prove harmful.

beautician anyone who specializes in helping people (usually women) make themselves look as beautiful as possible. Those who describe themselves as beauticians may be well trained or they may not be trained at all.

bleach a substance used to lighten the colour of some part of the body – usually the hair.

blusher see **rouge**. Although a blusher is theoretically the same as rouge, the former term seems to be preferred today when subtle colouring of the cheeks is implied.

brilliantine an oily hair dressing that is nearly all oil.

bubble bath a detergent in solution. Bubble baths often have a similar composition to shampoos.

cleansing milk an oil and water emulsion which is used instead of soap. It is usually light on oil and heavy on water and it works because some impurities are soluble in water while others are soluble in oil.

cold cream a thick cleansing cream which contains a relatively high proportion of oil in an oil and water emulsion.

cologne water a perfume that really was first made in the German city of Cologne.

conditioner a product designed to improve the state of a part of the body, e.g. a hair conditioner is supposed to improve the health and appearance of the hair.

cosmetic a preparation designed to improve the appearance of the user.

cream a substance with the consistency of the oily part of milk. Creams spread more easily than ointments which tend to leave the skin sticky.

dental caries tooth decay.

dental hygienist a dentist's assistant who teaches patients how to keep their mouths clean.

dentifrice a preparation used for cleaning the teeth. An abrasive is often the active constituent.

deodorant a product designed to remove (or prevent) unwanted body smells. A deodorant may contain a disinfectant intended to destroy organisms which might otherwise break down human sweat and in the process produce a nasty smell, and/or perfumes designed simply to disguise unpleasant smells.

depilatory something that removes hair.

detergent any substance used for cleaning purposes.

disinfectant a substance which destroys small organisms which may produce infection and harm living tissues. The word 'disinfectant' is usually kept for products which are used on inanimate objects which need to be kept clean (dirty sheets may be washed in disinfectant), whereas the word 'antiseptic' is usually kept for products used on the human body (mouthwashes, lotions, creams and so on). This distinction is, however, not always followed, and the two words are often used by some medicine manufacturers as though they were interchangeable. Just to make matters even more confused, there are manufacturers who claim that their products contain antiseptics and disinfectants. For practical purposes the words antiseptic and disinfectant are interchangeable.

dusting powder fine powder which is shaken on to the body like talcum powder.

eau de Cologne (see **cologne water**)

electrolysis in cosmetic terms this usually refers to the destruction and removal of hairs by electrical means.

emollient an application rubbed on to the body to help soften and relax it.

emulsion a mixture of two immiscible liquids, one dispersed throughout the other in small droplets.

essential oil an oil which has the characteristic smell of the plant from which it came.

eye-liner make-up to help define the edges of the eyelids.

eye-shadow make-up for the eyelids.

face powder usually consists of a powder such as talc mixed with pigments to give the necessary colour.

fixative usually something which is used to 'fix' or 'set' colours.

fixed dental prostheses false teeth fixed into position.

fixed oil an oil that isn't easily turned into a vapour or gas. Fixed oils do not, therefore, have much in the way of smell.

foundation cream an oil in water emulsion used before make-up is applied.

fragrance a sweet or pleasing perfume. Some fragrances are immediate but short-lived; others are subtle but more persistent.

gargle solution for rinsing mouth and throat.

gominas cheap, thick, gum-like hair dressing used most commonly in South America.

hair lacquer a sticky spray which is virtually a varnish to keep the hair in place in high winds.

hair straightener substance designed to straighten curly or crinkly hair.

hirsutism excess body hair.

hydrogen peroxide a mixture of hydrogen and oxygen which is used to bleach the hair.

hyperhidrosis a tendency to sweat too much, often when sweating is physiologically inappropriate.

liniment an oil liquid preparation to be rubbed on to the skin.

lip salve a preparation designed to protect the lips by providing them with a fatty coating. Lip salves are usually colourless.

lip-sticks consist of fatty bases with stains or pigments included.

lotion a liquid preparation for bathing a part of the body.

manicure the treatment or application of treatment to the hands or nails.

mascara make-up for the eyelashes.

moisturizing cream an oil in water emulsion which contains a high proportion of water and a small amount of oil.

oil a substance that is usually liquid, lighter than water (so that it will float on the surface if mixed with water) and rather sticky.

ointment a semi-solid preparation for external application to the body which may contain a medicinal substance. Ointments are stickier, greasier and messier than creams but can be useful on very dry, crusty skin.

orthodontics the prevention and correction of malocclusion of the teeth. An orthodontist is a dentist who specializes in straightening crooked teeth.

paint an application which is put on with a brush – like any other paint.

paste a semi-solid preparation, usually applied to the skin. Pastes are firmer than ointments.

perfume a single substance or a mixture of substances which has a pleasant smell. There may be over 100 ingredients of plant, chemical and animal origin in a single perfume.

periodontics the prevention, diagnosis and treatment of the gums and jaw bones.

perm literally permanent waving, this is the use of heat or chemicals to produce a change in hair shape or style.

peroxide a substance which contains an element combined with as large a quantity as possible of oxygen (see **hydrogen peroxide**).

plaque teeth which are not cleaned regularly acquire a layer of plaque. This is a hard substance rich in bacteria which causes infection and destruction of the tissues.

pomade a perfumed ointment usually used on the head.

powder a lot of tiny particles obtained by grinding a solid mass. Chemists used to use a mortar and pestle to make powders (the mortar is the bowl).

prosthodontics the restoration and maintenance of oral function and appearance by the use of fixed or removable dental prostheses. A prosthodontist is someone (probably your dentist) who fits false teeth.

protective cream consists of an emulsion of water in oil which is suitable for all types of skin (oily, normal or dry) and which covers the skin with a protective barrier of oil while keeping the skin itself moist.

removable dental prosthesis dentures or false teeth.

rub a substance suitable for rubbing on to the body.

scent see **perfume**.

shake lotion a convenient way of applying powder to the skin. The water in which the powder is suspended evaporates, cooling and soothing the skin, and leaves the powder behind. Obviously needs to be shaken before use. Calamine lotion is a good example.

shampoo a preparation sold for the cleansing of the hair which contains a particularly soluble detergent which will remove grease without making the hair sticky.

shaving cream, foam and soap a preparation designed to hold water in contact with the area to be shaved.

soap a substance manufactured by combining oils and fats which is used for washing and cleaning.

solution an evenly distributed solid available in liquid form.

spirit a volatile or distilled liquid.

spray a liquid which is available as a mist – a host of tiny droplets.

sunscreen a substance which helps to filter out some of the sun's rays and to therefore protect the body.

talc is the name used for a variety of minerals but it is usually used to refer to magnesium silicate which may or may not be mixed with aluminium silicate.

talcum powder powdered talc or French chalk which may or may not be perfumed.

toiletries a general term used to describe a whole range of products sold for the maintenance and preservation of personal cleanliness.

toilet water a mixture of alcohol, water and perfume designed to give the user a fresh feeling; it usually has a short-lived effect.

unguent see **ointment**.

vanishing cream a cream which can be rubbed into the skin without leaving any trace. These creams usually consist of a small amount of oil and a large amount of water.

volatile oil see **essential oil**.

EYES

Some pious drops the closing eye requires

'Elegy in a Country Churchyard' by Thomas Gray

ANATOMY

This isn't the place for a full account of the anatomy of the human eye. A proper explanation of the functions of the retina, cornea and lens would require a disproportionate amount of space and would be of relatively little value.

There are nevertheless some points which are worth making and some facts which may strongly influence the use and understanding of cosmetics.

To begin with it is important to understand that because it is such a delicate organ the human eye is surrounded by protective mechanisms. We do not always appreciate the effectiveness or the importance of these devices.

The eyeball is, of course, protected behind, above, below and on each side by bony walls and a thick layer of cushioning fat. At the front, where such fundamental forms of protection are obviously impractical, the eye is guarded by the eyelids which when closed protect the surface of the eye from injury and which when blinking continually keep a fresh supply of fluid spread across the cornea, pumping excess tears away as quickly as possible. These tears help wash away small irritants which land in the eye. In addition a row of special glands secrete a substance which helps to keep the lid margins slightly greasy. Normally the tears which have been produced by the lacrimal gland and spread across the eye by the eyelids drain through a small duct into the nose, but when the amount of secretion becomes excessive, either through cold, irritation or excessive emotion, there may be an overproduction of fluid with the result that tears escape from the eye and run down the cheeks. The eyelashes, a delicate extension of the eyelids, help provide additional protection.

The inside of the eyelids is lined by the conjunctival membrane which also covers the surface of the eyes, stretching across the sclera which is the opaque white area and the cornea, which is the central transparent sheet covering the front of the eyeball. The iris, which is the coloured part of the eye, can be seen through the cornea and it is the iris which, by responding to the amount of light falling on the eye, governs the size of the aperture through which light will reach first the lens and then the retina. The aperture in the centre of the iris is known as the pupil, and from the retina light images are transmitted to the visual cortex of the brain.

LOOKING AFTER YOUR EYES
In an introductory essay to a symposium on opthalmology published in *The Practitioner* in June 1980 a leading eye specialist wrote that he wished that doctors could persuade the public that most disorders get better by themselves by the following morning, that most medicines are therapeutically irrelevant, that the less we put in our eyes the better, that in general we should wear dark glasses only if we have an inflammation, are albinos or admit ourselves to be psychopaths, and spectacles only if they make us see sufficiently better to justify their nuisance value!

I've quoted him because I think there is much truth in what he says. Perhaps including it here will ensure that it reaches a small part of the audience for which it was intended.

The British eye care market was more or less created by and is now dominated by Optrex, a company which proudly announced recently that its promotional activity within one twelve-month period pushed sales up by a quarter.

Personally I firmly believe that if all the eye drops made and sold without prescription in Britain were poured down the drains the effect on the health of the nation would not be noticeable.

Phenylephrine hydrochloride is one of the commonest constituents of eye remedies. It is a substance which helps to dilate the pupil and to constrict the dilated blood vessels in a red eye and it is present in products such as *Degest, Eyeclear Eye Drops, Eyesoothe Eye Lotion, Optabs* and *Steri-fresh*. Although probably safe in the short term, these products can be dangerous when used regularly or when continually reapplied to the eyes. The manufacturer's warnings and instructions should be carefully followed.

The Optrex products, *Optrex Eye Lotion* and *Optrex Eye Ointment* both contain antiseptics. *Optrex Eye Lotion* contains witch-hazel, boric acid, salicylic acid, chlorbutol and zinc sulphate while *Optrex Eye Ointment* contains gramicidin and aminacrine hydrochloride. Another product from this company, *Optone Eye Drops*, contains witch-hazel, borax and chlorbutol. I cannot think of a single condition for which I would recommend any of these products and the same thing goes for other concoctions such as *Boots Eye Drops*, *Lanes Eye Lotion*, *Pennine Eye Drops* and *Visimax Eye Lotion*.

I do not recommend these products because I believe that if a condition needs treatment then it needs a doctor. No one is more in favour of home treatment than me, but I have yet to work out a foolproof way of explaining to readers which conditions can be safely treated without expert advice and which need to be seen by a specialist. I'll go further than that and admit that when patients come to me with eye problems I frequently have to ask an opthalmic surgeon to decide whether the condition needs his attention or not. Eyes are tricky areas, and differentiating between the benign and the potentially troublesome can be difficult.

Nor do I recommend any of the creams and lotions sold to help the skin around the eyes. Elizabeth Arden, for example, make a product called *Visible Difference* which is said to 'build up a moisture bank'. The advertisements for this product claim that only Elizabeth Arden can call an eye treatment *Visible Difference*, and if the company has registered the name I suppose that is true. But so what? Clarins make a range of products called *Around the Eyes* which don't seem to me to have any advantage over any other kind of moisturizer.

I suggest that to protect your skin round your eyes you use the moisturizer that you use on the rest of your face, and seek medical advice if you develop eye symptoms which you think need treatment out of a bottle or tube. There are, of course, many minor problems which can be dealt with at home. Eyes which are tired and sore can be soothed simply by putting a fresh, damp flannel on to the closed lids, or, if you're feeling extravagant or fruity, by using expensive pads or even cucumber slices. Cotton wool pads dipped into cold water are as good as anything if your face-flannel is grubby (which it shouldn't be).

You can help avoid sore eyes by keeping out of smoky rooms and you can avoid headaches usually associated with 'eye strain' by working in a good light rather than by struggling to read by the light of the television set. You won't go blind by reading in a poor light any more than you'll go blind by masturbating, but the first of these two habits is likely to cause headaches.

When you use a hairspray and any other aerosol be careful to make sure that you don't direct it towards your or anyone else's eyes. Aerosols send out small particles at high speed and these can damage the eyes. Be careful with soaps, shampoos and rinses, all of which can irritate the eyes.

If you get an eyelash or small piece of dust or grit stuck in an eye and you can't flick it out with a twist of paper tissue, dissolve a tiny amount of salt in water in an eggcup and splash your eye a few times in the water. That should free the foreign object but if it doesn't the local pharmacist may be able to help.

Finally, remember that eyelashes and eyebrow hairs fall out as often as hairs anywhere else on your body.

Sunglasses

There are thousands of different types of sunglasses on the market and it would be pointless to try and differentiate between all the various different makes since there are few major differences between the available products.

Best known perhaps are the Polaroid ones which cut out unwanted reflections and which, according to some advertisements, enable the wearer to study bathing belles with less difficulty. The problem with Polaroid spectacles is that they seem to make pretty patterns on some car windscreens, and so they can make driving rather an adventure.

Recently, the photochromic lenses have become very fashionable. These get darker as the light gets brighter and then lighter as the sun goes in. In Britain photochromic lenses have to work very hard.

The most exotic sunglasses are probably those with mirror lenses which enable the wearer to hide completely between twin reflections of those in front of him. There is something rather sinister about mirror lenses, and I've never really worked out who is seeing what when two people wearing these wretched things come face to face.

Whichever type of sunglasses you choose you should naturally buy a pair that fit well and comfortably. You can usually bend the arms a bit if you are careful, should the pair you choose be too tight or too loose. It is important to make sure that the lenses are clear and that there are no scratches or defects, and if you plan on wearing your sunglasses while doing anything hectic then plastic lenses are probably safer. People who wear spectacles normally can have special lenses made, buy clip-on shades or simply wear two pairs of glasses.

Two important warnings are essential. First, don't wear sunglasses while driving at night. You may think you can cut down the glare of oncoming headlights by doing that, but it is dangerous because your vision will be badly impeded. Second, don't ever try looking at the sun while wearing sunglasses. You'll damage your eyesight permanently if you do.

PURELY COSMETIC

Even the most attractive eyes can be made more alluring with the aid of cosmetics. For several thousand years the eyes have been the features women have usually chosen to emphasize. With the aid of the correct make-up, both the shape and set of the eyes can be changed, with small eyes made to look larger and wide-set eyes made to look closer together. Fashions change as far as colours and styles are concerned, and I don't intend even to touch upon the distinctions between 'midnight violet' and 'spirit of aubergine'. Here I am concerned only with the types of product offered and their advantages and disadvantages. Price and style I'll leave to you with the single warning that all else being equal, it is rarely worthwhile buying expensive make-up since the extra money you pay usually goes on packaging rather than contents.

An enormous variety of useful products are available, but most can be categorized quite simply. Eye-shadow adds shade and colour to the eyelids, while eyebrow pencils are designed to lengthen, darken or adapt the shape of the eyebrows. Eye-liner is used to pick out the edges of the eyelids, and mascara is used to emphasize and sometimes lengthen the eyelashes. You can buy specific products for each of these specific tasks or you can use one product to do several jobs. Mascara, for example, which can be bought in a liquid form, ready mixed on what is known as a mascara baton, as a cake which needs wetting, or in a soap-based block, can be used in place of eye-liner as can eyebrow pencil. How many different products you buy is really a matter of convenience, taste and purse depth. Most experts seem to agree that buying make-up in large sizes is a false economy because the make-up will probably become lumpy and unusable or else you'll get tired of the colour.

The ideal cake mascara will contain soap, so that when the wet brush is rubbed on the cake an emulsion will be formed, making it easy to transfer the colour to the eyelashes; it will also contain wax and fats which help to make the mascara waterproof. The more difficult it is to turn the mascara cake into an emulsion, the more the mascara will resist water when it is on the eyelashes. Any waterproof mascara can be removed with an ordinary moisturizing cream.

In a cream mascara the water has already been incorporated into the mixture. The manufacturer can usually put more pigment into a cream than a cake, but obviously the risk of smudging is likely to be greater.

Eye-shadows usually consist of a base, which may be made of melted beeswax, mineral oil, lanolin and petrolatum, and colouring, together with a substance such as titanium dioxide added to add opacity. Eye-shadows that have a metallic look are made by adding very finely ground silver, gold or aluminium powders. Frosted shades contain pearlescent materials such as mica and bismuth oxychloride.

The hardwear you need for using eye make-up is very limited. If you want to buy brushes with which to apply make-up then the best ones to buy are probably goat or sable hair artists' brushes. An ordinary toothbrush is said to be the best way to deal with eyebrows, and if you're buying eyebrow tweezers choose ones with slanting ends; and do make sure that the ends come together. An ordinary pencil sharpener is perfectly adequate for sharpening an eyebrow pencil as long as you keep it for just that purpose.

Having introduced the types of product used, the next important point to make is that because the skin around the eyes is extremely delicate and sensitive it is vital to ensure that products used do not contain any potentially harmful or irritating ingredients. All the major cosmetic companies are extremely aware of this problem and do take care to ensure that their eye make-up contains only safe constituents. To further reduce the risk of developing any signs of irritation in or around the eyes, it is important to resist the temptation to borrow or lend any eye cosmetics. Infections are easily spread from person to person in this way. To prevent packaged cosmetics becoming infected most major cosmetic companies do two things. First, they include a small amount of preservative in the product and second, they put their product into a tube or bottle which is usually kept sealed before use and closed between uses afterwards. The advantage of bottles and tubes with self applicators is that there is very little chance of contamination taking place. Now that many smaller companies are making cosmetics and are indeed encouraging women to make their own cosmetics at home, it is well worth making the point that these home-made products do not usually contain preservatives and that consequently they do not keep for very long. They need to be used up fairly quickly and not left lying around for months at a time.

Three other safety points which need to be made now are: first, you should always visit a doctor if any apparent infection or allergy persists more than a day or two; second, you should never apply eye make-up in or on any moving vehicle – it is very easy to damage the eye with an eyebrow pencil or mascara brush when a sudden, unexpected lurch occurs; third, do not buy cosmetic products from companies you don't know. It is quite simple for anyone to set up a company selling cosmetics without any knowledge of the potential hazards which can be associated with cosmetic products.

If you are careful about what you buy for the skin around your eyes and yet you still find that you suffer from allergy reactions, do remember that other products can affect the eyes too. For example, most of us touch our eyes with our fingers many times a day, so it may well be your nail varnish that is causing that allergy reaction.

While on the subject of allergies I must mention eyelash dyes which I have seen advertised. According to an advertisement from Louis Marcel Ltd, their *Eyelash Dye* lasts for up to six weeks. I have no evidence suggesting that this product is dangerous but I am very worried by any product which is said to have such lasting power. If the product causes any allergy reaction (as many dyes do), then its long-lasting quality could be a disadvantage. You simply would not be able to remove the dye. The makers of another product called *Dylash* make a similar claim for the longevity of their product, but again I would not recommend using such a product. The other point about these dyes is that although they are said to last for several weeks, new lashes will undoubtedly grow within that period.

While discussing eyelashes it is, I think, essential to give a word of warning about eyelash extenders to those who wear contact lenses. Lash extenders usually contain tiny synthetic fibres which stick to the lashes and make them look longer and thicker. If you get one of these tiny fibres behind your lens you will be most uncomfortable. So beware.

So far I've dealt only with cosmetic products designed for use in or around the eyes. There are, of course, products which are designed to be used on the eye itself.

Eye dew, which is advertised with the riveting slogan, 'make the most of a quick flash', is made by Optrex and so are *Optone Crystal Clear* drops. Since both these products are advertised as cosmetics rather than as medicinal drops I must assume that the manufacturer expects some, at least, of its customers to use the drops regularly.

I do not recommend using any drops of this kind regularly. If they contain anything which has a positive action on the eyes then they are potentially dangerous and if they do not contain anything which has a positive action on the eyes there is no point in using them.

EYE PROBLEMS

Introduction

To the doctor equipped with the necessary equipment the eye is a window through which evidence of many different types of general disorder can be identified and studied. All the reader needs to know is that medical attention should be sought whenever there is a persistent or severe pain in or around the eye or when there is any loss of vision, whether that loss of vision is permanent or temporary, partial or complete.

Those are the main warning signs of potential trouble and they need to be taken seriously. There are, of course, many less dramatic symptoms which indicate that less threatening disorders may affect one or both eyes and may need attention.

Not unnaturally, since it is the superficial covering of the eye, the conjunctiva is perhaps most commonly affected by infection. The symptoms usually include a gritty feeling, a redness of the membrane and a stickiness which may cause the eyelids to be stuck down first thing in the morning. Allergic reactions are commonly confused with eye infections, but the symptoms are usually rather different. The stickiness and grittiness are absent but there is redness, swelling and itching. Usually the reaction can be related to the use of a new eye make-up, but if the eye symptoms are accompanied by sneezing fits or occur regularly in the early summer months then the diagnosis of hay fever cannot be dismissed.

When a small piece of grit or dust gets into an eye then the symptoms will usually include pain, grittiness, redness and profuse watering. On most occasions the patient will be aware that there may be a foreign body irritating the conjunctiva. As a first-aid measure it helps to fill a clean eggcup with water in which a little salt has been dissolved and to then hold the eggcup against the eye and blink so that the eyelid splashes in the water. If this fails to remove the offending matter then a doctor should be seen without delay.

There are, of course, many other symptoms and signs affecting the eyes. Squints, double vision, drooping eyelids and styes are but four of the other problems. Whatever the symptom, however, I don't believe in home remedies for eye disorders. A doctor's advice may not always be essential, but it is rarely possible to decide that medical advice is not necessary without seeing a doctor.

Allergies

Since many women consider themselves improperly dressed without eye make-up the development of an allergy can be a temporary disaster. It is important to realize that the problem is invariably short lived and usually easy to avoid in future.

The usual symptoms include redness, itching and swelling of the eyelids and tissues around the eye itself. The sight and eyeball itself are usually unaffected and this fact alone makes a differentiation between an allergy reaction and an eye infection easier to make.

When an allergy reaction develops the most important thing to do is to remove any make-up that is on the skin and to ensure that the skin is left free of all cosmetics for a day or two. Any product that has been used on or around the eyelids and lashes may be considered suspect, and it is probably safest to throw away any product which may have been responsible for the reaction if you can't eliminate it immediately. It is naturally also sensible to avoid buying any similar eye make-up product in the future.

If you choose to use a natural, herbal or home-made product because you've been allergic to eye make-up, remember that the possible absence of a protective antiseptic may make the product likely to become infected if kept for more than a week or two. Such products should be bought and used fresh. They are not suitable for storing.

Infections

Conjunctivitis is, as already mentioned, the commonest type of eye infection. The symptoms usually include redness, a stickiness and a feeling of grittiness, and the eyelids may be stuck together first thing in the morning. When these symptoms develop it is important that other members of the family do not share towels or face-cloths since conjunctivitis is very easily spread. Eye infections can easily be spread in any one of a number of different ways and for this reason it is important to remember never to share eye make-up.

Conjunctivitis can usually be cleared up without too much trouble by the prescription of eye drops or ointment, and anyone with the symptoms described should visit a doctor without delay, although some relief may be obtained by bathing in a weak salt solution and wearing dark glasses to protect the eyes from sunlight.

There are other types of eye infection, of course, and the symptoms of many of these are usually similar to those of conjunctivitis. Whatever the precise diagnosis may be I do not recommend the use of any home remedies for eye infections. If the right diagnosis is made the treatment will usually prove effective in a day or two. If the wrong diagnosis is made the consequences may be serious and long lasting. When symptoms of an infection develop, and during the period that treatment is being applied, it is wise to avoid the use of eye make-up. Make-up that has been used just prior to the development of an obvious infection should be thrown away since the causative organisms may be harboured and reapplied to the eyes with the make-up.

Sight problems

If you wear spectacles you presumably do so because your eyes need some help. So however important the frames may be, the lenses are always more important. That common sense fact is mentioned simply because many individuals seem prepared to buy new frames at regular intervals while they forget to have their eyes checked and new lenses prepared when required. If you wear spectacles then you should have your eyes tested if you cannot see properly. By the way, do make sure that the frames you choose do not impede your vision. Some very fashionable frames have remarkably wide arms which cut down vision to a dangerous extent.

Those who wear contact lenses should remember to put their lenses in before applying any eye make-up. Make-up around the eyes should be applied sparingly, and flaky, powdery make-up should be avoided altogether since small specks of powder can slip behind the lens and cause irritation. Waterproof mascara is the wisest choice. Contact lens wearers should also avoid lash extenders since the fibres can, if they slip into the eye, cause a similar problem. Finally, remember that when putting contact lenses into place the hands should be quite free of cream or oil and that if any cream or make-up gets on to a lens, a special lens cleanser should be used.

There are a great many commercial products available for the cleaning, storing, and wetting of hard or soft contact lenses, but readers should accept the advice of their optician or opthalmologist when choosing a product.

Squint

The movement of each eye is controlled by a number of tiny muscles attached at one end to the eyeball and at the other to the socket in which the eye is suspended. When those muscles aren't tuned to perfection the two eyes will not move together. The result will be a squint which may be present all the time or which may only become apparent when the eyes are moved in one particular direction. The precise nature of the squint will, of course, depend upon the position and duties of the affected muscle.

Squints can occur at any age but they most commonly become apparent during childhood. Some experts believe that somewhere between 5 and 8 per cent of British children have squints.

It is the child's appearance that takes most parents along to the doctor's surgery, and help is often sought for cosmetic reasons rather than anything else. It is important to realize, however, that when a child has a squint one eye may become lazy if early treatment is not provided. The medical term for a lazy eye is amblyopia and this condition is said to affect between 2 and 5 per cent of the population in the United Kingdom. That means that there are about a million people in the country who are more or less one-eyed and who go through life with a social and cosmetic disadvantage.

If seen by a specialist as soon as possible squints can very often be corrected by using spectacles, patches or surgery. Many thousands of half-blind people could have full vision if they had been seen early enough. And the visual improvement would inevitably have been accompanied by a cosmetic improvement.

Wrinkles round the eyes

Changes affecting the upper and lower eyelids occur relatively early on in the ageing process. The skin there is thin and easily wrinkles. In an attempt to reverse this process women and men between them spend many millions of pounds every year. They buy creams and oils, vitamins and electrical vibrators. They spend many thousands of hours between them practising special exercises in front of the bathroom mirror and trying to massage away those first telltale wrinkles.

Most of the time and money spent is wasted because the ageing process is irreversible. There are only two things you can do to hide or disguise the fact that you have wrinkles around your eyes.

First, you can buy creams which cover up and hide the wrinkles. The thicker the wrinkles are, the thicker the cream you'll need. And when the cream is removed the wrinkles will still be there underneath. I suggest that you experiment, starting perhaps with your favourite moisturizing cream and then moving on to a thicker cold cream if that doesn't work. I don't see why any of the creams sold specially for this purpose should be better than cheaper, multi-purpose products, but if your wrinkles are particularly noticeable then a masking cream may be more suitable. Masking creams are discussed in the section headed 'Birthmarks' on p. 185.

Second, you can have plastic surgery done to remove the wrinkles. Like all plastic surgery operations the eyelift needs to be done by a professional who is both trained and properly qualified. The only way to find such a surgeon is, in Britain at least, through a general practitioner. There is no other way, and any surgeon prepared to operate without a letter of introduction from a family doctor is not worth seeing.

The eyelids do have genuine functions to perform; by spreading tears across the corneas they prevent them from drying, and with the aid of the involuntary muscles which control the blink reflex they help to protect the delicate eyes. Performing a surgical operation on the eyelids obviously requires considerable skill.

Most patients stay in hospital for two days and go back to work a day or two later. Sutures are removed a few days after the operation, and although eye cosmetics have to be avoided for a fortnight and the sunshine for a few months the long-term results of the operation are usually good. The effects usually last for ten or fifteen years, and the scars are often completely invisible. The black eyes that usually last for a few days after the operation can be hidden with dark glasses.

The eyelift operation is today one of the most successful and popular operations done by plastic surgeons. Many operators report that the number of men having an eyelift done is growing. It seems that men are becoming more conscious of their appearance and more aware of the need to compete with young-looking executives. It may also be that men are aware of the fact that they look old alongside their surgery-aided, wrinkle-free wives.

Finally, three tips to help you prevent wrinkling of the skin around your eyes:

1 Wear sunglasses when the light is bright. Screwing up your eyes may cause wrinkles.
2 If you smoke, use a cigarette-holder to keep the smoke out of your eyes.
3 When you moisturize your face don't forget the skin around the eyes. Be very gentle and apply cream in a thin layer, but do remember that the skin there needs protection as much as the skin anywhere else.

HAIR

One that is ever kind said yesterday:
Your well-belovèd's hair has threads of grey,

'The Folly of Being Comforted' by W. B. Yeats

ANATOMY

Most animals have hair on their bodies to keep them warm. Few human beings, however, have enough hair to provide any useful insulation. The hairs of the eyelashes and eyebrows do provide some slight protection for the eyes, and the hairs in noses and ears which stand guard over the entrances to their respective organs are of some use, but on the whole human hair is decorative rather than functional. When hair is damaged or missing, therefore, the problem is usually cosmetic rather than medical.

There are various different types of hair on the human body, but most people have the greatest number of hairs on their heads. A good head of hair will consist of about 150,000 individual hairs, each one of which will have been produced by its own manufacturing plant or follicle.

The follicles which produce head hair have a long active phase which means that individual hairs can grow to enormous lengths. Eventually the follicle goes into a resting phase, and the hair stops growing. Then a new hair is formed, and as it starts to grow so the old hair will be shed. An average scalp hair grows for three years, rests for three months and then gets replaced. This process is continuous and it explains why there are always a few odd hairs in the comb and at the bottom of the wash basin. The whole cycle can be interrupted by a large number of factors. A high temperature, a loss of blood, a major operation or a severe emotional upset can all push some or all of the scalp hair follicles into the resting phase at the same time with the result that individual hairs stop growing and are displaced *en masse* about three months later by new growing hairs. This causes temporary baldness which may be partial or total. Since hair grows about a third of a millimetre a day it obviously takes some time for the replacement hairs to grow to the same length as their predecessors.

Except for the follicles in the male beard region the follicles which produce body hair have a shorter active phase. This means that body hairs grow to a limited length, stop growing and are then replaced by new hairs. If our body hair grew at the same rate as our facial and head hair then we would all either look like monkeys or spend most of our time shaving each other. The life expectancy of single body hairs varies from individual to individual, and so the effectiveness of temporary methods of hair removal also varies.

The growth and distribution patterns of some body hairs are influenced by sex hormones, which is why hair grows in the pubic region and underneath the armpits from puberty onwards. It also explains why facial hair starts to grow at that time. This hair doesn't have any practical purpose, but some people find it sexually attractive, and the hair around the genitalia presumably exists to highlight the importance of these regions. The active phase of hair in the pubic region is obviously rather longer than the active phase of hair on other parts of the body.

The colour of human hair depends upon the amount of melanin pigment (see 'Skin anatomy' p. 145) present as well as on variations in the surface structure of individual hairs which are believed to affect the way that light is reflected. Straight hairs look round when cut and examined in cross section under a microscope, whereas wavy hairs are alternately oval and round. Very curly hair is shaped like a twisted ribbon.

The individual hair follicles are arranged within the skin in such a way that hairs emerge from the surface at an angle – rather like shot coming from the mouth of old-fashioned cannon. Thin muscle fibres which are attached to the follicles can, by contracting, make the follicle and its hair stand up straight. When this happens the skin is puckered and develops what are usually known as goose pimples. When this happens to animals it makes them look bigger and provides them with better protection against such varied enemies as predators and the cold. When it happens in humans as an automatic response to fear or low temperatures it has no useful function because the body hairs are too small.

Human hairs are also equipped with nerves which make them very sensitive to slight pressure. If you touch the tiny hairs on your arm very lightly you will be able to feel a slight sensation in that area. This mechanism is similar to the one which makes the cat's whiskers so useful.

The sebaceous glands which exist to lubricate the skin and which are sometimes closely associated with hair follicles in purely anatomical terms are described in the section on skin anatomy (p. 148).

LOOKING AFTER YOUR HAIR

Beautiful hair is an asset worth taking care of. There is a great deal that you can do to protect your hair from damage, but let us begin with a discussion of the various types of shampoos and conditioners that are available. These are, after all, the products most widely associated with hair care. I'll discuss the two types of product separately since in my view it is totally illogical to expect one product to both cleanse and condition the hair. It is as unscientific to expect to find a hair care product capable of serving both functions as it is to look for a skin care product which can act as a cleanser and moisturizer.

Shampoos fall into four main categories: those intended for normal, dry and greasy hair and those for dandruff sufferers. Dandruff shampoos are considered on p. 122 since here we are only concerned with the care of healthy scalps and hair. Dry and greasy hair are discussed at length on p. 124 and p. 132 respectively.

The hundreds of different types of shampoo available give the consumer many problems since the claims made are often conflicting. According to the trade journal *Manufacturing Chemist and Aerosol News* it has been said that: 'the poor consumer has only a one in a hundred chance of selecting the correct shampoo for his or her hair type'. So with these odds in mind let's take a look at the constituents of the available shampoos and try to decide what advantages specific products can offer.

The basic ingredient of most shampoos is a detergent which is included to loosen oil and dirt from the hair. The amount of detergent in each shampoo varies according to the whim of the particular manufacturer. The inclusion of a detergent is important because it is by using such a substance that the sebum and hair oils which actually bind dirt to the hair and scalp can be removed. Unlike soaps, detergents do not usually result in the production of a great deal of scum.

Many shampoos also contain an element included to modify the properties of the cleansing agent. The modifying ingredients are included to improve the amount of foam produced, to reduce the irritancy sometimes associated with cleansers and to add a conditioning component to the finished product. Conditioning agents such as lanolin, minerals oils, herbs and balsam are included in greater quantities in shampoos sold for the treatment of dry hair although, as I have already pointed out, this seems to me to be rather an illogical approach.

In addition to these ingredients most shampoos also contain other substances designed to add colour, perfume or body to the finished product. In the *Manufacturing Chemist and Aerosol News* it was reported that 'opaque, pearlescent products suggest mildness to the dry-haired consumer and formulations for shampoos frequently include agents to achieve this'. There are other criteria, and obviously the final consistency of a shampoo must be designed according to the packaging in which it will be sold. A product which will be sold in a sachet, tube or jar must be more viscous than a product to be sold in a bottle. Knowing that many customers are more satisfied that their shampoo is working well if it produces a great many bubbles, a number of manufacturers include special ingredients to increase the amount of lather produced. Bubble production and viscosity are in fact quite irrelevant and are not related to the efficacy of a shampoo.

Looking through the advertisements for shampoos it is difficult to remember that most of the products on sale contain nothing more important than a simple detergent. The other added ingredients about which so many manufacturers get so ecstatic are of very little real value in the cleaning of hair.

There are, for example, shampoos which contain beer. The *Linco-Beer Shampoo* is one of these. The advertisements for this product claim that there is no need to use a conditioner afterwards and to a certain extent this claim is justified. After all, beer can act as a conditioner. However, as already mentioned, I do not recommend products designed to cleanse and condition at the same time. Many shampoos are said to contain herbal constituents designed to give the hair a more natural, healthier look. Klorane make shampoos which contain such ingredients as white nettle, quinine and nasturtium, while Laboratoires Leryss make products which include carline thistle, tower mustard, golden maidenhair, safflower, water mint, great figwort, wild angelica, quaker bonnet, bitterherb and mugwort. Some *Weleda* shampoos contain rosemary and chamomile, and *Country Born* shampoos contain such ingredients as sunflower and meadowherb. There are also a number of companies making shampoos which contain lemon. If you shampoo with soap, then lemon juice, which is acidic, might help rinse out the scum that can form, but since detergents don't leave any scum and most shampoos are detergent based the inclusion of lemon is of doubtful value. I know of absolutely no evidence which suggests that a shampoo will do its job more effectively because it contains a herbal constituent of any kind. Nor do I know of any reason to buy a shampoo according to its pH content.

A number of companies make dry shampoos which are designed to be used when ordinary shampoos are impractical. These products consist of absorbent powders which are supposed to absorb grease from the hair before being brushed out again. These really are emergency-only shampoos since they can leave the hair feeling gritty as well as dirty. If you want to try a dry shampoo there are products such as *Aero Dry Shampoo*, which is sold in a 'puffer pack', and *Batiste Aerosol Dry Shampoo*, which is made by a company called Schwarzkopf. It is most invigorating that a company making beauty products should be called by the German translation of 'blackhead'.

Some shampoos are said to have almost mystical qualities. The *Jojoba Super Shampoo*, for example, is said to have been developed by a Dr Gomez of the Republic of Mexico, and a brochure for the product claims that 'a big improvement in the appearance and condition of the hair is noticeable within a week to ten days. Hair loss decreases to normal within a few days and the scalp condition continues to improve. Each replacement hair becomes progressively stronger and longer. The thin hair area gradually grows smaller, as the old fuzz and weak hair along the edge slowly develop into longer, healthier hair'.

If that claim can be justified by the manufacturers of the *Jojoba*

Super Shampoo, then I'll recommend it. Until I see evidence proving those claims, however, I don't recommend it.

I cannot recommend any specific brand of shampoo for several reasons. First, and most important, different shampoos suit different people. Second, shampoo brands vary and disappear quite regularly. My advice therefore is to ignore the advertisements appearing for shampoos and to remember that shampoo sales exceed £50 million each year. In any area of big business there are bound to be exaggerations and disputable claims.

The purpose of a shampoo is to help you clean your hair. Obviously, therefore, the qualities you should look for are effectiveness as a cleanser and ease of removal. When using a shampoo it is important that hair should be wet thoroughly before the cleanser is applied, both to help remove surface dirt and to prepare the hair for cleansing, and that it is rinsed thoroughly after shampooing. It is easier to wash hair under running water because then the shampoo can be removed more efficiently. If the hair is only washed once a week then two applications of shampoo may be needed. If the hair is washed more often than that one application of shampoo at each washing should be sufficient. It is important to remember that the purpose of shampooing is to clean dirty hair and that consequently if the atmosphere in which you live or work is dirty more hair washing will be needed. Hair absorbs environmental pollutants such as cigarette smoke, and city dwellers usually need to wash their hair more often than country folk.

The best shampoo for you is probably the cheapest that doesn't cause an allergy rash, that doesn't contain unwanted perfume and that doesn't contain any other unnecessary ingredients but which simply enables you to wash your hair easily and effectively.

There are as many conflicting claims for conditioners as there are for shampoos, but the most sensible advice is probably that from the Institute of Trichologists who claim that 'if the hair is particularly dull and brittle, difficult to comb because of tangling, or lacking in "body", a conditioner may be helpful'.

A conditioner usually works by attaching itself to the surface of the individual hairs, thereby giving those hairs more body and making both the individual hair and the hair in general look thicker and more luxurious. Conditioners usually contain protein, and by sticking to the outside of the hairs they can also provide some protection against potentially damaging chemicals. It is important to remember, however, that if too much conditioner is used the hair can become matted and impossible to comb or control. People with greasy hair don't really need a conditioner.

Many conditioners are described as containing special ingredients designed to provide the hair with something special. *Ultra Care High Performance Conditioner* is said to help hair grow up strong and healthy. 'By penetrating the shaft of the hair itself,' says the advertisement of this product, 'it builds up protection from the inside and leaves your hair supple and shining.' *Sunsilk Deep Action Conditioner* 'is rich and thick with a special formula that penetrates deep down and revives damaged hair'. *Agree Conditioners* are made 'from a unique blend of non-oily conditioners' which are 'designed to bind to the shaft, to smooth down the roughened surfaces and penetrate deep into the hair to condition it thoroughly'.

You can also buy conditioners which contain mink oil or which have added vitamins to help the hair regain its strength and good health.

I don't think that any one claim for any specific conditioner is particularly convincing. Some products contain less oil than others, some are pH balanced and some contain other ingredients, but the basic task of a conditioner is, as I have already explained, to help give hair more body and to help make it more controllable.

When you choose a conditioner I think that you can afford to be influenced by price more than content. Once you have found a conditioner you like, then stick to it. Don't be tempted to use more conditioner than the manufacturer suggests and don't leave the conditioner on the hair for more than a minute or so. After a conditioner has been applied the hair should be rinsed so that excess conditioner is washed away. There are, by the way, conditioners that are obtainable in aerosol cans and these may be worth trying. A conditioner needs to be applied to the hair and not the scalp, and the ends of the hair naturally need more conditioning than the hair near to the scalp (the sebum has a lot further to travel, and the hair at the end is much older than the hair nearer to the scalp).

Shampoos and conditioners are in my view the only two types of general hair care product worth buying. There are however a great many other products on the market. *Silvikrin* is an organic hair tonic which contains seventeen amino acids, aqueous alcohol and sodium lactate while *Saul Hair Care Therapy* is said to improve the condition of the existing hair, to improve the blood circulation of the scalp, to tone up the scalp's skin tissue, to reactivate a return to actual growth of hair roots lying dormant in suspended telogen, and to moderate excessive greasiness or, in the case of a dry condition, to improve sebaceous gland activity. To obtain this wonderful treatment you can simply phone or write to Karen in London telling her your health, age, sex, hair condition and shampooing habits. A trichologist will then prescribe your *Supercare* medication which will be posted to you immediately 'under plain wrapper'.

Jochen's Hormone Preparaat will, according to the brochure advertising it, 'in practically every case stimulate dormant hair roots into healthy activity again', while *Head High Capsules* which 'go into your mouth, not on your head' will 'help you keep your healthy good looks from your toes right up to the hair on your head'.

Hair care hardware is another important part of the beauty industry and there are many companies making combs, brushes and other pieces of equipment. The *Lady Jayne* catalogue, for example, contains photographs of twenty-nine different types of hair brush and twenty different types of hair comb. Other companies have similarly large ranges of products.

The Institute of Trichologists claims that combs made of hard materials such as bone, ivory or tortoiseshell are best but that a vulcanized rubber comb will do just as well and will be less expensive. They also claim that natural bristle brushes are safer than nylon or plastic brushes. Personally, I don't think it matters what a brush or comb is made of as long as the bristles are not sharp at the ends and not too close together. Rounded bristles don't damage the hair as much as rough ones, and wide-toothed combs mean less pulling at the hair. It isn't wise to brush or comb the hair too often since these procedures can be damaging. It is important to remember to keep brushes and combs clean and free of hair, and to clean them all such implements should be immersed in warm soapy water.

Hair dryers are dangerous and bad for the hair if they get too hot, so if you can dry your hair without an electric dryer then do so. Gently dabbing with a soft towel is safer than using electrical heat, but allowing the hair to dry naturally is the best method. If you buy an electric hair dryer do see that it has an automatic shut-off which is intended to operate if the equipment overheats.

And do remember not to use any electrical equipment in the bathroom or to cover up the air intake.

Hair rollers can damage the hair if they are pulled too tight, and hair grips that aren't rubber tipped can also break and damage hairs.

For many people choosing a hairdresser is an important step in their hair care. On p. 51 some of the aspects of professional hair care are described but here it should be pointed out that although good hairdressers are usually expensive, expensive hairdressers are not necessarily good ones. It's sometimes said that the best way to choose a hairdresser is to find the one who can't fit you in for a week, and I suppose there might be some sense in that rather cynical comment. More important, your stylist should discuss his plans with you before starting work and you should listen to him and ask for his advice. Do remember that complex styles that need lots of setting lotions, sprays and gels will be difficult, if not impossible, to manage by yourself. One final myth that must be exploded: it used to be said that singeing was good for split ends. I remember when I was a boy seeing barbers touching a lighted taper to the hair of their customers. The idea of that was to stop the goodness oozing out of the cut or split hairs. In fact it just made the hair more brittle and more likely to split again. The truth is that if your hair has split ends it has grown too long. If a conditioner doesn't help then the solution is simply to cut an inch or so off the length of the hair.

Hair care

1 Remember that sun, heat, salt water and chlorinated water can all damage the hair. Wear a floppy, broad-brimmed hat when sunbathing, don't use rollers that are too hot, rinse your hair thoroughly after bathing and if possible wear a bathing hat.
2 Don't brush or comb your hair too much, and don't use too hard a brush or comb. The bristles shouldn't be sharp or too close together. When wet, your hair is particularly likely to be damaged by fierce brushing.
3 Shampoo your hair gently in hand hot water, putting shampoo on to your hands first to ensure an even spread on the hair. Rinse the hair thoroughly after washing.

4 When drying your hair, do it naturally whenever possible. Wrap a towel round your hair turban style to absorb the moisture.

5 If you use a conditioner, do rinse your hair thoroughly afterwards. Choose your conditioner the same way that you choose a shampoo – by price and effectiveness on your hair. Use a conditioner after a shampoo. Using a conditioner before washing your hair is as sensible as putting your make-up on before you wash your face.

6 Hair is easily damaged by bleaching, tinting, stripping, straightening or perming. None of these operations should be done too often and as a general rule no two should be done within the same seven-day period.

PURELY COSMETIC

At some time or other most women feel an urge to change or improve the appearance of their hair. It is hardly surprising therefore that in the last few years the profits made by the major hair care product manufacturers have risen fairly consistently. Today the business of selling hair dyes, colourants, straighteners and waving lotions is worth many millions of pounds each year. The companies know that a new style or a new colour can make a woman feel she has a new persona.

We'll begin this section with the group of products which now contribute most to those healthy profits – the hair colourants. These compounds fall into three fairly distinct categories: permanent colourants, temporary or semi-permanent colourants and blonding agents or bleaches. Whether they are marketed for men or for women and whether they are aimed at those anxious to disguise a change in their natural hair colour or at those who simply fancy something different, these products all need to be treated with considerable respect. Like all cosmetic hair products they are unsuitable for use on diseased or infected hair or scalps.

The simplest hair colourants are naturally those which can easily be washed on to the hair and then washed off again at any time. These products, sometimes called temporary rinses, work by coating the shaft of the hair with a colour and do not penetrate the hair shaft or change it in any way. Because they can easily be washed away they are extremely safe to use. The big snag with temporary rinses is that if you wear one and go out into the rain you may be in for some considerable embarrassment. The hair colourant that will wash out in the bath will also wash out in a shower of rain! Hair rinses of this kind are most useful for those who think that they might like to have their hair dyed but who would like to try out their chosen colour first.

Before going on to semi-permanent colourants and permanent colourants I should perhaps mention that hair conditioners can sometimes be used to give more shine and apparent colour to hair that is lifeless and looks 'flat'.

Semi-permanent hair colourants coat the hair shafts but also slightly penetrate them, and so these products aren't normally washed away by a single shampoo. They usually disappear slowly over a period of some six weeks or so, although if you get tired of the colour you can of course wash it out with a really thorough shampoo and rinsing. Semi-permanent colourants, like temporary colour rinses, are best used to darken the colour of the hair. These colourants are probably the strongest and most powerful products which are suitable for home use, and even these need to be treated with considerable respect.

When using a semi-permanent colourant it is important to test a patch before colouring the whole head. Many different types of dye are used in hair colourants, whether they are permanent or semi-permanent, but all of the dyes can cause allergy reactions. The results of a reaction affect the scalp, not the hair, and the usual symptoms involve itching, redness, swelling and even oozing of the skin. It is vital to remember that you can develop an allergy to a product you have been using for years, and so patch testing should be done before any use of a hair colourant. The manufacturer's instructions should be followed, but most companies suggest trying out the product behind an ear. If, after twenty-four hours, there has been no reaction then it is safe enough to continue.

While mentioning the problems associated with hair dyes I should perhaps mention the fact that hair dyes have been linked by some reports with the development of cancer. Back in 1977 a report in the *British Medical Journal* by four research workers from the Cancer Epidemiology and Clinical Trials Unit in Oxford commented on the fact that many permanent and semi-permanent hair dyes are strongly mutagenic according to a laboratory test. They also pointed out that some female hairdressers had a higher incidence of breast cancer than other women. The hazards associated with hair dyes were discussed in the *Lancet* in 1978. One correspondent, N. J. Van Abbé writing from the British Industrial and Biological Research Association in Surrey, argued that 'a lady who has her hair tinted ninety times with a permanent hair dye and ten times with a semi-permanent one is unlikely to suffer greater chromosomal damage than if perhaps she undergoes routine dental X-rays or occasionally catches a cold'. Mr Van Abbé's argument did not, however, seem to carry much weight with correspondents from the Department of Cytogenetics at the Royal Marsden Hospital and the Institute of Cancer Research at the Royal Cancer Hospital who wrote pointing out that 'the experimental evidence that many hair dye constituents are mutagenic and that some are carcinogenic is irrefutable'. Incidentally, an article published by Mr Van Abbé in the journal *Cosmetics and Toiletries* a month earlier had described him as representing Beecham Products.

The controversy over hair dyes has still not died down. A recent short paper in the *American Heart Journal* by a scientist from the Department of Cytogenetics and Immunogenetics at the Institute of Cancer Research concluded that the available results suggested that 'hair dyes were penetrating the scalp and causing untoward genotoxic effects in the lymphocytes'.

More dramatically a paper entitled 'Use of permanent hair dyes and cancer among registered nurses' published in the *Lancet* showed, as a result of a survey of 120,557 nurses in America, that there was a statistically significant association between the use of permanent hair dye and the development of cancer of the cervix, vagina and vulva. The paper's authors concluded that 'women who had used permanent hair dyes for twenty-one years or more before the onset of cancer had a significant increase in risk for all sites combined compared with "never users". This increase was primarily due to an excess number of observed to expected cases of breast cancer.' What this means is that women who use hair dyes seem to have a greater chance of developing cancer somewhere in their bodies later in life.

The *1979 Year Book of Dermatology* supports this conclusion, and a writer points out that many constituents of hair dyes are known to have caused chromosomal damage and that research on people who tint or dye for a living has shown that they may be particularly at risk.

If you do use hair colourant, certain precautions should be taken: rubber gloves should be worn to protect the hands and a barrier cream such as *Vaseline* should be smeared around the hair-line to ensure that the forehead doesn't get dyed. Once the hair has been dyed it is important to realize that even a semi-permanent colourant will weaken the structure of the hair and that it is not wise to subject the hair to any other type of cosmetic operation for at least a week.

In permanent hair colourants the dye is mixed with a substance called hydrogen peroxide, and when dye and peroxide are left on the hair the new colour (which can be lighter or darker than the natural colour) will slowly develop. Heat speeds up this process, but after a fixed interval, which will usually be decreed by the manufacturer of the colourant, the dye must be washed out. It is important not to leave the dye on the hair for too long since if this happens the hair can be badly damaged.

Permanent colourants are not permanent, of course, since the hair is always growing and new hair of the original hue will gradually appear. A permanent hair colourant doesn't permanently change the colour of the hair any more than spilling paint on the lawn changes the colour of the grass. In addition to the slow regrowth of hair, the dyed hair will also fade as a result of sunlight, shampooing and brushing. To disguise the gradual fading and the emergence of hair of the original colour the hair is usually retinted and touched up. Retinting is usually done with a semi-permanent colourant while the touching-up of the roots can be done with either a permanent or a semi-permanent colourant.

Because they are more powerful than semi-permanent colourants and have a greater effect on the structure of the hair, permanent colourants need to be used with very great care. Patch testing is vital, and the hands and skin have to be protected too. Many experts believe that if you want a permanent colourant applied you should visit a hairdresser.

When the aim is to lighten the colour of the hair and turn it blonde, the principal traditional ingredient used is hydrogen peroxide which strips away the colour of the hair and which can, if done carelessly, damage the hair very badly. It is important to read the manufacturer's instructions very carefully if you are contemplating bleaching your hair and it is important not to try and use any type of domestic bleach for this extremely delicate and potentially dangerous operation. The whole business of turning blonde is so fraught with danger that I really do not recommend that you attempt such an operation by yourself.

The problems of hair growing out a different colour when a permanent dye or bleach is used can be avoided by highlighting, streaking or tortoiseshelling the hair. In these procedures streaks of colour are put into or taken out of the hair by dying or bleaching isolated strands. This is more time-consuming, of course, but it is less damaging and in the long run it causes fewer problems. After a permanent dye or bleach has been used on the hair, conditioning is important, and it is vital not to have any other operation performed on the hair for at least a week. If you subject your hair to a permanent wave and a permanent colourant at the same time then you really ought to have a wig ready in the wardrobe because these twin traumas can produce hair loss.

One other point about dyes and bleaches is that they both can be dangerous if they're used on any other part of the body. I don't recommend that you try dyeing your eyelashes or eyebrows, and if you try dyeing pubic hair then do so with great care if you want to avoid soreness that will be painful and embarrassing.

Before leaving the subject of hair colourants altogether I should mention the problem of grey hair, which isn't necessarily a problem since it can look very attractive. Grey hair isn't really grey at all, but white. The fact that there will be a small number of white or unpigmented hairs growing among a large number of coloured hairs means that the overall appearance suggests greyness. It is not true that people can turn grey (or white) overnight, and although the precise reasons why hair begins to grow out without any natural colour aren't understood, the fact is that this development is usually associated with age and genetic susceptibility. The answer is to use a colour rinse or semi-permanent colourant, although when Henry IV of France went grey his courtiers all powdered their hair white to keep him company. So if you have royal blood, that alternative may be a real possibility.

Just as the ways in which you can change your hair colour vary according to the strength and permanence of the rinse or dye used, so the products available for changing the shape of your hair vary according to the strength of their constituent chemicals.

The most powerful products are those which give the hair a new style or shape, and whether they are used to add or to remove curls the process used is the same. The hair has to be structurally damaged and then reshaped.

Until the 1940s permanent waving involved the use of heat and such instruments as curling tongs. The heat disrupted the chemical bonds within each hair and made it possible for the hair to be curled or straightened according to taste. Unfortunately, using heat in this way damages the hair very badly and I don't recommend that you try it. The classic foolishness usually involves young girls who traditionally lay out their long hair on the ironing table and then frizzle it.

If you want to straighten hair with heat it is safer to put some oil on to your head and then spread it over the hair with a hot comb. The oil is used to transfer heat gently to the hair from the comb, and some of the hair bonds will be broken in this fairly temporary and safe procedure. Men, of course, simply use oil to do this job when they use brilliantines or pomades to plaster their hair down straight.

Today most permanent waving is done chemically with the substance involved usually being the thioglycollates. The waving lotion is first applied to the hair and this disrupts the chemical bonds which hold each hair in its shape. Flexible in its new form, the hair will retain new shapes when wound around hair curlers. After ten or twenty minutes the hair is rinsed and then neutralized, either with a separate solution containing an oxidizing agent such as hydrogen peroxide or by being allowed to oxidize slowly in the atmosphere. If the permanent waving lotion is allowed to stay on the hair too long or is not properly neutralized it can damage the hair badly and produce brittleness and split ends. Allergy reactions are also possible and so patch testing is vital. Hair that has been dyed or bleached and hair that is particularly fine or coarse is not likely to take a permanent wave well without suffering damage.

When using a permanent waving lotion at home it is vital to read the instructions carefully and to make sure that you understand exactly what to do. It isn't possible to do anything else while perming your hair, and I think it is probably wise to take the telephone off the hook and, if possible, to disconnect the front door bell. A useful trick when doing a home perm is to try the solution on a test sample of hair first. If the curl is too limp, then the time the solution is allowed to remain on the hair needs to be increased. If the curl is too tight, then the amount of time that the solution is left on the hair needs to be decreased.

If you are uncertain about how well you'll manage a home perm then you're probably better off letting a hairdresser do it for you. An advantage of a salon perm is that since the professionals usually use stronger solutions their perms may be more effective and even last longer.

However, those who are frightened of traditional perms may be interested to know that two companies, Gillette and Chesebrough-Ponds have recently introduced special home perms which they say are safer than traditional home perms. Gillette was the first company on to the market with a product called *Lightwaves* which does not contain any ammonium thioglycollate. *Lightwaves* is said by Gillette to be very gentle, to have no smell and to be suitable for use on bleached or dyed hair. It is also said to be suitable for gentler styling than traditional perms. *Rave*, a product from Chesebrough-Ponds, is also said to be very gentle and to be safe for use on bleached or tinted hair. These less dangerous home perms may be products for the future.

I'll discuss hair straighteners together with permanent waving lotions since the thioglycollate straighteners used in perms are sometimes used in straightening solutions. For straightening the bonds within, the hairs are broken with the thioglycollate but no curls are put into the hairs. Alkaline creams and bisulphites are also sometimes used as straighteners or curl relaxers. Like thioglycollate straighteners these produce reversible changes in the chemical bonding within individual hairs. Straighteners of this kind are fairly safe but they shouldn't be used on damaged, brittle or bleached hair. It is also important to remember that long hair is old hair and therefore particularly likely to break or split.

More temporary shaping of the hair can be arranged with the aid of setting lotions, gels, liquids and aerosols. These products are often used to hold or fix the hair in a particular style although they are sometimes intended to add extra gloss. Aerosol sprays range from those which offer a light hold to those which virtually varnish the hair. Sprays often also contain perfumes and may include plasticizers which make the products more workable. Boots claim to make the only hairspray that is unperfumed. Gums, gominas, brilliantines and other similar oily hair dressings are traditionally used by men to fix their hair into some sort of shape. When using an aerosol spray on the hair it is important to be careful not to spray the eyes or any nearby cigarettes or candle flames. People have been badly burned by hair sprays which have caught fire. Hair sprays can usually be brushed out without too much difficulty.

There is a great deal of hardware available for those who wish to shape or style their own hair. Electric hair rollers, curling tongs, curling brushes, curling wands and styling brushes are made by a number of different companies. All of these products can effectively help in the styling of hair but it is vitally important to remember that heat can damage the hair. These tools should only be used on hair in good condition and even then the manufacturer's instructions should be obeyed to the letter.

HAIR PROBLEMS

Introduction
There are two serious problems associated with hair. The first, which usually causes most concern when it affects the hair of the scalp, is alopecia or the loss of hair. The second, which is invariably only a problem when it concerns the body hair, is hirsutism or an excess of hair. These are problems only because they are often in direct opposition to what is regarded as normal, ideal and therefore attractive.

At any one time something like 90 per cent of the hairs on a human head will be growing normally while about 10 per cent will be resting, before being replaced by new hairs. This steady turnover means that under normal circumstances anything up to 100 hairs are lost each day without there being any noticeable thinning of the scalp hair. Indeed there has to be a considerably greater loss of hair before there is any appreciable baldness.

There are a number of different causes of hair loss but statistically the most important is inherited male baldness. This and other causes, which include such varied problems as infection, stress and the use of prescribed drugs, are dealt with in the section on baldness on p. 118.

For the simple reason that both conditions are common among men hirsutism, like alopecia, is really only a major worry when it affects women.

Again there are a number of possible causes ranging from gener-
alized hormonal problems to the simple fact that some families tend
to be hairier than others. Generally speaking the development of
body hair in women follows the same pattern as the growth of
body hair in men. In other words, it usually affects the beard area,
the chest, the legs and a line from the pubic area to the umbilicus.
The causes of hirsutism are discussed in the section on p. 125 and
the various treatments are outlined on pp. 126–31.

Although alopecia and hirsutism may be the most important
conditions to affect the hair, dandruff is probably the commonest
problem. It has been estimated that nine out of ten people suffer
from dandruff which must make it a close contender, along with
dental decay and the common cold, for the title of the commonest
disease. Dandruff is discussed on p. 122.

The sebaceous glands control the greasiness of the scalp. When
they are too effective the hair becomes greasy and lank, when they
are not effective enough the problem is dry hair. These problems
are discussed on p. 132 and p. 124 respectively.

Baldness

The causes of baldness can be divided into four main groups.

In the first group are those systemic, general disorders which
result in the loss of hair from the scalp but which are usually also
responsible for other symptoms not necessarily affecting the condition of the scalp or the growth of hair at all. Specific disorders
which come into this category include a variety of hormonal problems ranging from thyroid disorders to the menopause although
general illnesses of any sort, physical or mental, can cause baldness.
Pregnancy and the taking of the contraceptive pill can cause hair
loss because of their effects on the quantity and quality of circulating female hormones, and drugs, particularly those used in the
treatment of cancer, are also likely to produce hair loss. I think
that it is unlikely, generally speaking, that in any of these cases hair
loss will be the symptom initiating a medical consultation. That is
not true, however, of a condition known as alopecia areata which
is included in this section because, although its precise cause is not
known, most doctors believe that the sudden and sometimes total
hair loss that results is caused by anxiety and stress. Alopecia areata
most commonly affects young people in their teens and their twen-

ties and it affects women as often as it affects men. It causes hair to fall out in handfuls, leaving genuinely bald patches all over the scalp, and the best way I can describe it is as a hair root strike. Usually the condition resolves itself with the hair growing again more or less completely after a few months. Alopecia areata is the only type of baldness that really can cause baldness within days.

The second group includes localized diseases which can produce baldness and in this category I include problems such as dandruff, eczema and so on. Some of these conditions produce baldness because when the itchy scalp is scratched hairs are broken.

The third type of hair loss is the commonest and it usually only affects men. I'm referring, of course, to what the hair experts call 'male pattern baldness'. This is a type of baldness which depends upon two things: male sex hormones and a genetic tendency to baldness. (The only two sure ways to avoid male pattern baldness are either to choose your parents carefully, ensuring that your male ancestors have good heads of hair late in life, or to have a castration operation done to stop the circulation of male hormones.) Baldness is a dominant gene among men and this means that if a man inherits the tendency to baldness from just one parent he will go bald. When the gene is there and the tendency to baldness present male hormones shorten the growing phase of head hair so that the hair becomes shorter and thinner, eventually being nothing more than a short fuzzy growth. It is said that one in ten twenty-five-year-old men will be partly or completely bald, while a mere ten years later a third will be showing signs of baldness. By the age of about fifty years some 50 per cent of all men are bald or balding.

The fourth type of hair loss involves factors which affect women more than men. This is the group which includes all the cosmetic causes. Baldness can, for example, be caused by tight hair styles which literally pull the hair out by its roots. This type of baldness known as traction alopecia is commonest at the front of the head and is often caused by styles such as pony tails, pigtails, braids and buns. Using a comb with fine, rough teeth or a brush with stiff nylon bristles can also cause baldness by damaging and even breaking the hair as can the careless use of all sorts of chemicals. These types of baldness are usually temporary but they are none the less worrying. Bleaches, dyes, hair straighteners and perms can all make hair dry, lifeless and fragile. Too much heat can have the same result and the careless use of curling irons or dryers can produce baldness. Hairdressers are responsible for this type of error almost as much as women themselves. Finally it seems that too much scalp massage can cause hair loss too, as can the use of rollers that are too tight.

If you want to check whether you are going bald, one suggested way is to comb your hair over a white towel every day for a fortnight using the same brush or comb and the same number of strokes. Count the number of hairs lost each day to see if the number is increasing or is greater than the usual average of about one hundred hairs.

Whether or not you can do anything about your baldness depends, of course, upon the cause.

Baldness due to a general disorder or a localized scalp disease will usually disappear when the illness is treated, and hair loss caused by cosmetic carelessness is rarely permanent. It is the baldness that affects men which is most commonly permanent and most often the target of those with remedies to offer.

There is nothing new about trying to treat baldness, of course. In ancient Egypt they did it with ointment made from the fat of the lion, the hippopotamus, the crocodile, the tiger, the snake and the goat, and in North America a traditional recipe involved the use of bear grease. Today's remedies tend to be rather more sophisticated but no more effective.

Before I go any further I must point out that sadly there is no cure of any kind for permanent baldness. Those individuals and companies which can produce photographs of bald men who have been given full heads of hair have probably been dealing not with male pattern baldness but with cases of alopecia areata – which would have got better with or without the magic treatment. The only way you can help your hair is by looking after your scalp properly, by keeping it clean, washing it carefully and rinsing thoroughly. There are no magic solutions. Those who promise that with the aid of magic diets, special mixtures or tonics or electrical treatments that they can cure all types of baldness are lying.

Having said that, let me go on to some of the ways of disguising baldness. To begin with the remaining hair can be combed over the bald patches or a conditioner can be used to make what hair there is seem thicker. These solutions are only of use in the early stages of baldness where there is still some hair left.

A solution many people favour is to buy a wig or a toupee. The

Egyptians, Persians and Assyrians all used wigs, and Louis XIV and his courtiers would probably have felt quite naked without their wigs. The King and his pals had fairly complicated wigs, but one of the King's mistresses, the Duchess de Fontagne, designed an extraordinarily complex false hair piece for herself which involved the use of wire, flowers and ribbons. That was called a *fontagne* in her honour and was popular with all the other women who either were or who wanted to be the King's mistresses. People have often made fun of those who wear wigs and the Roman wit Martial once wrote:

The golden hair that Galla wears
Is hers: who would have thought it?
She swears 'tis hers, and true she swears,
For I know where she bought it.

Still, for all the fun making, wigs are still pretty popular both with men and women, and there are dozens of different companies making and selling wigs today. In the *Hairdressers Journal* recently, several experts voiced the opinion that wigs are going to be more fashionable than ever before in the 1980s, although they were undoubtedly talking more about high fashion wigs than about wigs bought to cover up baldness.

Good synthetic wigs are probably as good as real hair wigs and they are certainly likely to be cheaper. They're usually tougher, too, but it's important to make sure when buying a wig that it looks natural. The drawers of Britain's bedrooms are probably bulging with wigs that have never been worn.

A good wig should have a loose mesh base so that it doesn't get too hot and although it needs to fit well, a wig should not be tight enough to give the wearer a headache. Wigs can usually be washed and they should be stored carefully. Incidentally, if you wear a wig it is a good idea to take it off whenever you can because even in cool weather wigs can cause sweating and produce scalp problems. It is also important for bald people to remember to wash their scalps and whatever hair is present.

There are a good many more permanent ways of dealing with baldness. Despite the fact that baldness is a visible sign that there are male hormones circulating in the blood, many bald men feel embarrassed by their hair loss and want to disguise it. Perhaps it's something to do with the fact that they don't like looking older.

Hair transplantation is a very fashionable solution, but it is important to be aware that problems can arise. One of the reasons for the difficulties which occur is that few leading surgeons or dermatologists are prepared to do hair transplantations, either because they don't think the operation a good risk or because they feel it's rather beneath them.

A hair transplantation doesn't increase the number of hairs on the scalp but merely rearranges them. Hair is moved from the side or back of the scalp to the front where it continues to grow quite happily. The hairs are moved in batches of about a dozen, being taken along with small cylinders of skin which are placed in holes made in the scalp. They are temporarily kept in place with a special non-stick dressing. It takes about a fortnight for each transplant to take and at least ten sessions are needed before there are any real signs of improvement.

If things go wrong with a transplantation the hair may fail to grow or the area may become keloidal.

More exotic treatments include such remedies as hair weaving, in which artificial hairs are knotted or fixed in some way to the existing hair, and the implantation of entirely artificial hair or the hair from someone else's head. Anyone contemplating hair implantation might be well advised to read an article in the *Journal of the American Medical Association* for 22 June 1979. In that article horrifying stories of a number of men who had had implants were told. The report stated that 'the majority of implantees have local or systemic infections, either of which may be life threatening' and the typical patient was described as appearing with a scalp that resembles 'a piece of stinking red meat with pus pouring out'. I don't apologize for quoting such a horrible statement. In my view implantation should not be considered. If you must try some permanent remedy for baldness transplantation of hair from the back of the scalp to the front is the only method even worth considering. I do not recommend techniques which involve tying arteries or massaging the scalp to help the circulation.

Dandruff
Human skin is always being replaced. The steady turnover of cells means that small scratches and stains that affect only the superficial layer of the skin are quickly forgotten. Occasionally the skin pro-

duces new cells too quickly and the older, discarded cells seem to fall off or be pushed off the skin like snowflakes. When this happens on skin around the body the disorder is usually known as psoriasis (see p. 222); when it affects the scalp then it is dandruff. Whatever complex names trichologists may give it dandruff is simply the result of a superficial cell turnover that is two or three times the normal rate.

Exactly what causes this change in the rate at which cells are made and discarded has been the subject of many scientific investigations. I could fill pages with accounts of the work that has been done to try and define the precise pathways which lead to the development of dandruff, but such information would not help a great deal in the treatment of the condition. There just are not enough proven facts.

Still, the important thing is that we do know that there are several useful products for its treatment, some of which are sold as drugs and some of which are sold as cosmetics. Incidentally, this differentiation has led to some extraordinary situations in the USA where the manufacturers of drugs have to list only the active ingredients on the labels of their products whereas the manufacturers of cosmetics have to list all the ingredients. This means that the rules governing more or less identical products are quite different.

One of the most popular ingredients in products sold for the treatment of dandruff is zinc pyrithione. Evidence published in the journal *Toxicology and Applied Pharmacology* and information presented at the Hamburg Hair Congress in 1979 suggest that this product is both safe and fairly effective as a dandruff treatment. It is included in such commercial products as *Head and Shoulders* and *Revlon ZP11 Formula Medicated Shampoo*.

Another effective ingredient is selenium sulphide. Unlike zinc pyrithione this product can be dangerous if taken by mouth and is also potentially dangerous if used on inflamed areas of skin. Selenium sulphide is available in products as *Lenium, Selenium Sulphide Scalp Application BPC* and *Selsun*.

When using any of these products (or indeed any anti-dandruff shampoo) it is important to allow the shampoo time to work. It should usually be left on the scalp for a few minutes before being rinsed off, although the manufacturer's instructions should be followed carefully whether they agree with this advice or not.

There are a great many other anti-dandruff preparations available. Many of those on sale contain disinfectants or antiseptics which may or may not have a useful effect on dandruff, and I suggest that if you want to try an anti-dandruff shampoo you try one containing either zinc pyrithione or selenium sulphide. Just read the packet before you buy and see whether either of these constituents is listed among the contents. Both will usually be included as 1 or 2 per cent of the constituents.

Dry hair

Dry hair is dull, brittle and coarse and often difficult to set or comb. It may break easily and often splits at the ends. In purely medical terms dry hair can be more of a problem than greasy hair.

There are many factors which can make dry hair drier and normal hair dry, and if you suffer from dry hair it is important that you understand these factors thoroughly.

Sunshine is probably one of the worst offenders where dry hair is concerned and, indeed, any form of heat can cause problems. Electric dryers, sunlamps and curling tongs can make dry hair really difficult to handle and anyone who has dry hair should, whenever possible, allow the hair to dry naturally after washing.

Ironically, although the problem with dry hair is that there isn't enough oil, washing the hair frequently (which people with greasy hair always want to do, but are usually advised will cause rebound oil production) simply isn't the answer. The fact is that if you have dry hair the glands which produce sebum just don't work very well, and if you wash your hair a lot you don't encourage extra production of oil as quickly as you wash existing oils away.

However, some of the habits that those with greasy hair are told to avoid, such as frequent brushing and combing, are a good idea since if the glands are irritated they may well be encouraged to produce a little more sebum.

Conditioners are heaven sent for those with dry hair since these can give the hair more bounce and make it far easier to manage. The conditioner should be used directly after the shampoo and should never be applied with the shampoo or even before it. The shampoo is used to clean the hair and nothing else. The choice of shampoo and conditioner really doesn't matter and the simplest, cheapest products are usually the best. There is more about shampoos and conditioners on p. 103.

Since dry hair is exceptionally brittle and easily damaged it is vital to be careful when changing the shape or colour of the hair. These are potentially damaging processes at the best of times and when the hair is dry they are particularly likely to cause problems.

There are those, incidentally, who recommend eating an oil rich diet for dry hair. This is, in my view, a naive and nonsensical solution which shows an ignorance of human anatomy and physiology. It used to be said that greasy skin and acne were made worse by oily, fatty foods but I think that particular theory has long since lost credence. I'm saddened to see such an out-of-date theory revived by those who write about treatments for human hair.

If you want to improve dry hair with oil the only way is to rub the oil directly on to the scalp and the hair. Either oil itself can be used or a product such as *VO5 Alberto Hot Oil* can be tried.

Excess hair

Body hair is physiologically and socially associated with the presence of circulating male hormones and consequently excess hair only really becomes a problem when it affects women. For that reason the remedies available for the removal of excess hair are aimed almost exclusively at women. Hirsutism in men, however exaggerated, is rarely considered to be a cosmetic problem, but for women hirsutism is a cause of anxiety and embarrassment.

There are a large number of reasons for the growth of hair on women and although there are a number of fairly rare syndromes, most of which involve hormone abnormalities, which are associated with hirsutism, the majority of women who have too much body hair have inherited the tendency either through familial genes or racial propensities. It is a simple and established fact that the female members of some family groups are hairier than others, while it is well known that women from Southern Mediterranean countries and parts of Asia often have more limb and facial hair than their sisters from Northern Europe.

Whatever the cause of their excess body hair may be, the fact remains that many women find such hair unattractive and embarrassing and are prepared to pay almost any price to have it removed or remove it themselves. This is no new fashion for women have always been remarkably adept at removing body hair, particularly the hair from their armpits and pubic area which, although it may be linked with the presence of female hormones rather than male hormones, has been considered unhygienic by many. Roman women removed all body hair by shaving, singeing, plucking or the use of chemicals and most Roman statues are devoid of body hair. The Greeks had strong feelings about pubic hair too and even Aristophanes wrote about the tendency for Greek women to shave their pubic hair in an attempt to attract men.

Today, whether you are interested in shaping your pubic hair or merely concerned with removing excess hair there are five ways of getting rid of hair you don't want. These methods vary in cost, effectiveness and risk.

The first method I'll discuss involves the use of hormones and I mention it first simply to dismiss it from the reckoning before we go any further. Body hair distribution is governed by the presence of sex hormones. In men the male hormone makes the presence of body hair quite normal and the pattern of hair distribution follows a strictly defined pattern. Male pubic hair, for example, usually continues upwards from the pubic area with a thin vertical line of hair connecting the pubic area to the umbilicus. Female pubic hair does not usually grow across the abdomen but finishes with a clearly marked horizontal line. A woman with male pattern hair distribution, resulting from a higher than normal level of circulating male hormones, will, in addition to having hair on the face, abdomen and legs, have a deep voice, small breasts, no periods, small buttocks and an enlarged clitoris. Hormone therapy can reverse the abnormal distribution of hair, but unless the other abnormalities I've mentioned are involved it shouldn't be considered to be a real alternative. Nor do I recommend the use of hormone creams of any kind. The effectiveness of hormone creams in the treatment of any cosmetic condition is as doubtful as their safety.

The second method of hair removal is probably the simplest. It consists simply of cutting off the excess hair with scissors, knife or razor of some kind.

Wet shaving with a blade razor is the oldest established and probably the best way to get a smooth, close shave. It is important to remember that a wet shave really should be exactly that. Wet hair is softer and easier to cut than dry hair. The best method is to wash with warm or hot water and to then apply a shaving cream or soap which will help the hair to retain moisture. All shaving soaps, apart from the brushless creams, are basically soap preparations which simply need to be brushed on to the area to be shaved. The brushless shaving creams are modifications of the traditional vanishing cream and they usually contain a humectant to help retain moisture. These are good travelling aids but like ordinary shaving soaps they need to be used after the skin has been thoroughly soaked with water.

Whether you choose a shaving soap or a brushless shaving cream is largely a matter of taste, but those with dry skin are probably wiser to choose a brushless cream. Incidentally if you have dry skin it is important not to use an aftershave lotion which will probably contain an astringent.

It's important that the razor you use is sharp and clean, and rinsing the razor after each stroke is an effective way to make sure that it doesn't get clogged with hairs. Long, careful strokes against the grain are better than short, stabbing strokes, and it is always important to watch out for bony promontories and obvious varicose veins, particularly when shaving the legs. Styptic pencils or toilet tissue are traditional remedies for small cuts and scratches but if you have too many small cuts you'll look worse than if you hadn't shaved at all.

If you use a shaving soap which needs to be brushed on to the skin you may be interested to know that one company, Vulfix, makes over 200 varieties of shaving brush but will, in addition, make up brushes to your own specification. As for which type of razor is the best buy it is really a matter of personal choice. You can buy an ordinary safety razor, a cartridge razor or a throw-away razor. A *Which?* survey suggested that cartridge razors are likely to give the best shaves but that they are probably slightly more expensive than throw-away or safety razors. The prices of razors and blades do seem to vary a great deal, and the major companies often seem to have special offers available. There is no reason for a woman to buy a wet shave razor that is in any way different from a man's wet shave razor.

One of the main disadvantages with shaving is said to be that the resultant stubble feels bristly and that when the hair grows again it will be stiffer and stronger than it was before. Shaved hair may indeed feel bristly because it is simply cut off at skin level, rather than being removed or dissolved as it can be with other techniques. But it won't grow up any more bristly than hair cut or removed in any other way. The fact is that growing hair, being shorter, always feels stiffer than hair that has reached its full length. Hair that has been cut doesn't grow any quicker either.

Men who wet shave are often encouraged to buy special after-shave preparations which consist of alcohol, water and scent. These products are similar to the 'refreshers', 'skin bracers' and 'splash-it-all-over' products that are becoming so popular and they are basically scents, although the alcohol they contain may produce a temporary feeling of freshness.

These days electric razors are used by a growing number of women and by an enormous number of men. The principles involved are the same whether the razor is used by a man to shave his face or a woman to shave her legs and so I'll discuss both together.

Before shaving with an electric razor the skin has to be thoroughly cleaned and dried. There are, naturally enough I suppose (since the sale of a single electric razor would otherwise preclude further profits for several years), a number of pre-shave lotions and powders designed to prepare the face for dry shaving. And inevitably, there are also a great many aftershave lotions, creams, powders and astringents which are advertised according to the markets for which they are intended, the shaving products intended for men are often advertised by sportsmen to ensure that the right image is obtained for the product. I don't think that any of these products are necessary although the manufacturers will explain that their pre-shave products will help stiffen and raise the hairs ready for cutting, dry the skin with the aid of evaporating alcohol and even coat the skin so that the razor slides easily along without any drag. You can prepare your skin for electric shaving just as well by washing and then rubbing briskly dry with a dry towel.

The electric razors which are sold can be divided into two main groups: those which are operated by mains electricity and those powered by batteries. The former are cheaper to run but the latter are most useful if you spend time travelling by overnight train or camping, or if you need to keep a razor with you to deal with the emergency shadows when you find you can't get home.

Shavers can also be subdivided into groups according to the type of cutting blades they have. Foil shavers have a multi-bladed cutter vibrating underneath a flexible foil of thin metal, while rotating cutter shavers have two or three circular heads. Bar shavers have a flat cutter vibrating underneath a rigid metal cover. The three types of shaver can also be obtained with or without such extras as trimmers for keeping moustaches and beards in shape. The noises made by different shavers vary but I can't imagine that many people choose a razor according to the noise it makes.

Most of the major manufacturers make razors which are designed for men and razors which are designed for women. The differences between the two types involve the cases and names rather than the mechanisms.

The third method of hair removal is by using chemicals, usually obtainable as special creams. The first and most important point to make about cream depilators is that they can affect the skin and they should always be tested out first on a small patch of skin. Because of this risk they are not suitable for use on the face. Many of the creams available for this purpose contain a substance called calcium thioglycollate which reacts with human hair just as a waving lotion does. The difference is that the cream is allowed to continue its work for longer and to make the hair so weak that it can easily be removed.

If you're testing a depilatory cream leave it on a small area for the length of time recommended by the manufacturers (this will usually be ten or twenty minutes). Rinse the cream off thoroughly and then wait twenty-four hours to see if the small patch of skin shows any signs of an allergic reaction developing. If there is going to be any problem, the area of skin will be red, perhaps swollen and possibly itchy.

The effectiveness of these creams is obviously less when the hairs are thick.

One product, *HaarEXstop Gelée with CA plus Moisture Factor*, which is sold in Britain as *Lady's Epil Stop*, is said to lead to 'a complete cessation of aftergrowth'. This is obviously an important claim since most methods of hair removal produce only a temporary improvement. I was fortunate enough to see a clinical test report on the effects of *Lady's Epil Stop* performed by a Dr Friderich of Stuttgart. Dr Friderich reported that 'in a further series of tests which has so far lasted more than nine months we have examined the effects of *Lady's Epil Stop* on the hair-covered skin area of the lower arms of 7 men and 8 women. The object of these tests has been to establish whether continuous and regular application of the preparation on the same area is capable of influencing the re-growth of hair after previous depilation carried out according to different methods.' Dr Friderich then concludes that 'the regrowth interval on the treated areas in the case of 7 of these people was initially prolonged by 5 days' though he goes on to say that over a period of five months the hair-free interval was increased threefold.

Dr Friderich also studied the structure of the re-growing hair and concluded that 'the clinical picture now obtained after application over a 9-month period, in 4 of the 7 cases examined, corresponds, in my opinion, to the normal type of pilosity'.

I am afraid that I have not been convinced by the evidence I've seen.

A fourth method of hair removal involves the use of hot or cold wax which is put on to the skin and allowed to set. The theory is quite simple: when the wax sets the hairs will be stuck within it and will then be pulled away quite easily when the wax strip is removed.

Again, as with creams, I think it is important to do a patch test when using a wax removal technique. Using the wax technique can provide hair-free limbs, or whatever, for between three and four weeks and the wax can be used repeatedly but there are snags. Obviously the system can hurt, particularly if you don't pull the wax off sharply. Another problem is that you need to leave the hair to grow to a decent length (at least a quarter of an inch) before it can be pulled out with the wax. Obviously if the hair is too short it isn't pulled away. The wax techniques are most suitable for parts of the body where there are decent flat stretches of skin and obviously you can't easily use wax treatments on your face. If you want to try one of these products it might be best to visit a beauty parlour first and see how they do it. The main advantage of the wax treatment for hair removal is that because the whole hair is pulled out the skin does feel smoother.

Electrolysis is the fifth method of hair removal and this is the only method that will provide a permanent solution. You should only have electrolysis done by a skilled operator and it is important that the operator really is skilled. It can obviously be a fairly expensive procedure and it can be tedious since, if there are a great many hairs, the whole thing can take an awful long time.

The operator needs to reach the root of the hair with a needle through which a small electric current passes and if she misses the root the hair will grow again. Obviously, therefore, you don't really know how effective your treatment has been until a few weeks later when the hairs either have grown or they haven't.

The risks with electrolysis are that scarring may occur, infection can follow and regrowth rates, depending upon the skill of the operator, can be as high as 50 per cent. The risks are probably worth taking if you have very obvious hairs on your face which you want permanently removed. I've discussed electrolysis as a beauty parlour service on p. 58.

Those are the five main methods of dealing with unwanted hairs. There are other methods. A very old established method is to use an abrasive such as pumice stone to rub away the hairs. This may sound crude but it can be very effective. It is also a useful way to get rid of rough dry skin although I do suggest you use a moisturizing cream afrerwards.

Tweezing or plucking is another obvious way to get rid of unwanted hairs and this is probably the best way to deal with isolated hairs such as those which sometimes grow around the nipples. While mentioning isolated hairs, do remember that hairs which are on or near to moles shouldn't be touched until a doctor's advice has been sought. Moles that have hairs can be potentially dangerous (although most are not). If you are plucking individual hairs then it helps to press a warm flannel or face-cloth against the hair to prepare it for plucking. This method is one of the best ways to deal with eyebrows which need shaping, although if you are certain of the shape that you'll want your eyebrows to be in twenty years' time you can get the extra hairs removed by electrolysis. Do remember to pull in the direction of the growth of the hair and to clean the tweezers with alcohol before and after the operation.

You don't actually need to remove hairs to hide them of course. You can bleach hairs that you want to disguise, but bleaches can cause skin rashes and so you should perform a patch test first. Hairs that have been bleached repeatedly may eventually fall out. Excess hair does tend to darken and thicken with age, and so bleaches may be particularly suitable for hairs that used to be more or less invisible. Incidentally, this natural darkening of hairs is often wrongly blamed on the use of depilatories of one sort or another.

From the fact that bleaches are so popular and effective you can safely assume that if the body hair you're worried about is fair and downy then you can safely leave it alone.

Greasy hair

I really do wish that I could make some specific recommendations about how to deal effectively, quickly and permanently with greasy hair. But the fact is, I'm afraid, that there is no one shampoo that can be relied upon to turn lank, oily hair that simply won't hold any style or setting into easily manageable hair. Nor is there any one routine that can be relied upon to permanently change a greasy scalp into what the hairdressers sometimes call a 'normal' scalp.

Indeed if you read as many books and articles about the treatment of greasy hair as I have in the last few months you will begin to wonder if the experts can agree on anything about greasy hair. There are those who believe that greasy hair should be washed at least once every day, while at the other end of the spectrum there are dermatologists and trichologists who argue that greasy hair should be washed no more than once a week. Just about the only point they agree on is that greasy hair can be a real nightmare for the unfortunate sufferer.

Before dealing with shampoos and hair-washing routines I would like to discuss some of the factors which can make hair greasy. After all there isn't much point in hunting around for the perfect shampoo if you can stop your hair becoming oily simply by changing a habit.

It is the sebum produced by the glands on the scalp which make hair greasy and obviously, therefore, if those glands are irritated in any way they will increase their production of oil. So if you have a tendency to oily hair don't wear your hair in a style that needs too much attention, don't comb or brush hair too often, don't wear a hat if you don't really have to, don't use really hot water on your scalp, keep out of the sun as much as possible and be very careful about what you put on to your scalp.

Since longer hair usually needs more attention, gets dirty easily and looks worse when greasy it is obviously wise to choose a hair-style that keeps the length of your hair as short as possible.

Now to get back to when and how you should wash your hair and what sort of shampoo you should buy. The experts who argue that people with greasy hair should only wash their hair once a week claim that each time the hair is washed more sebum is produced. This, they say, means that the hair gets greasier and greasier until eventually the point will be reached where even daily washing doesn't control the amount of oil.

To a certain extent these experts are right. It is true that washing the hair causes what is known as reactive seborrhoea. But on the other hand it is very difficult for a girl with greasy hair to resist the temptation to wash her hair fairly regularly. She knows that unless she does wash her hair she looks a dreadful sight.

So in purely practical terms a compromise is necessary, and washing every two or three days (in warm not hot water) is probably the best solution. There is one important way that the production of sebum can be limited if this regime is followed and that is by washing the hair and not the scalp.

When they wash their hair many people scrub and rub at their scalps since they have been taught, quite rightly, that the scalp needs cleaning too. Unfortunately this scrubbing of the scalp is just what stimulates the production of oil. So the individual with greasy hair should perhaps be as gentle as possible and resist the temptation to try and rub all the oil away. A good rinsing should ensure that the scalp is kept clean.

The next question, of course, concerns the type of shampoo that should be used.

If you call into any shop selling shampoos these days you'll see row after row of specially made shampoos which are recommended for particular types of hair. There will be shampoos for dry hair, extra dry hair, normal hair and greasy hair as well as shampoos for combination hair, mildly greasy hair and so on. It would all be confusing enough even if you could rely on every manufacturer's claims but I'm afraid that you cannot. The truth is that some shampoos sold as suitable for greasy hair are better used on dry hair and vice versa.

I think that the only really important criterion that you should follow when looking for a shampoo for greasy hair is that the shampoo should not contain any additives. Conditioners will make greasy hair worse as may other 'special' shampoos. The sole purpose of the shampoo is to help you clean your hair, and for the purpose the cheapest, mildest and simplest product is best.

Once you have found a cheap shampoo that you like, stick with it. Use it two or three times a week if you like but wash your hair once not twice and make sure that it is rinsed thoroughly afterwards with plenty of clean water.

If you have split ends or any other problem that you think needs a conditioner then try and limit the use of the conditioner to the hair ends and keep it away from the body of the hair and the scalp.

Finally, do resist the temptation to use any other product on your hair, and ignore the next piece of dogmatic advice that you read about the treatment of greasy hair. There is no simple, magic solution and there are no miracle remedies. The advice I've given you won't stop your hair being greasy but it may make it easier for you to live with that fact. And remember that greasy hair, although it can be a nuisance, is stronger and less easily damaged than dry hair. There are some advantages!

NAILS

We recognize a doomed people by the way they sneeze or pare their nails.

Tiger at the Gates by Jean Giraudoux

ANATOMY

All creatures, great and small, that have toes or fingers have protective horny structures on the ends of them. Horses have hooves, cats have claws and we have nails. Our rather delicate and comparatively inoffensive nails may not have the same obvious duties as hooves or claws, but try picking a coin off a smooth table top or unknotting a piece of string without using your finger-nails and you'll soon see just how much you would miss them if they weren't there.

Finger- and toe-nails all consist of the same sort of cells as can be found on the superficial surface of the skin, but the cells that make up the nails are packed together far more tightly than the cells that make up the surface of the skin and it is, in part, this increased density which makes the nails so hard.

Nails are themselves colourless, but since they are translucent the pink colour of the skin underneath shows through. At the end of the nail nearest to the knuckle, however, where the nail is more opaque and the skin underneath is busy producing new nail cells there is a small white patch visible, rising like a pale moon.

It is called the lunula. Immediately underneath that semilunar opacity is a line of dead skin called the eponychium by anatomists and the cuticle by beauticians. This marks the point where the nail originally broke through the skin. The nail root extends back underneath the cuticle and the nail itself is firmly attached to the nail bed which lies directly underneath it.

It takes about six months for a finger-nail to grow to its full length, although growth rates slow down in cold weather and speed up in warmer times. Toe-nails grow at less than half the rate of finger-nails. Injury, disease and an inadequate diet can all interfere with the production of nail cells, and lines, ridges and black or white marks which appear, grow out slowly over the subsequent months. Ridges across the nails can be a telltale memory of illness from which an individual has long since recovered.

LOOKING AFTER YOUR NAILS

You do not have to spend a lot of money to look after your nails and you don't even have to actually *do* anything very much. The most important part of nail care is knowing what sort of things can be damaging and knowing just what not to do if the nails are not to be damaged.

The single most important cause of nail trouble among women is the fact that the hands, and therefore the nails, are for ever being immersed in water. Washing clothes, dishes and small children means that the average woman's nails are probably soaked more than a dozen times a day, and, perhaps even more important, are dried properly no more than once or twice. The kitchen towel is probably ancient and bald and missing whenever the doorbell or the telephone rings.

The detergents and soaps that are so much a part of daily household duties damage and irritate the hands and the nails and, together with too frequent wetting and infrequent drying, are responsible for many of the important disorders which afflict the hands and nails. The hands show their suffering by developing dry patches and ugly rashes (see p. 205) and the nails show that they have been damaged by becoming brittle, by splitting, by developing hangnails and so on.

It is obviously impossible for a woman with all these responsibilities to avoid these frequent soakings but it should be possible for her to limit the damage they do. There is no reason why any woman (or man for that matter) should sacrifice any part of her (or his) good looks to dirty dishes.

Wearing rubber gloves is the most obvious way to avoid damage. It is important to ensure that the gloves are large enough and that they are not worn for more than fifteen or twenty minutes at a time, since if worn for too long they can themselves cause skin problems. Wearing thin cotton gloves underneath the rubber gloves increases the level of protection provided. Some people argue that rubber gloves are clumsy and unmanageable but most can adapt to them quite easily with a little practice.

Where gloves can't be worn for one reason or another a long-handled dish mop is a good idea since it means that the hands can at least be kept out of the water for some of the time. It may seem strange to be writing about long-handled dish mops in a book on beauty treatments, but the fact remains that if doctors prescribed such simple implements they would probably do far more good than they do by prescribing powerful and only temporarily effective steroid creams for detergent-damaged hands.

When gloves and mop aren't practicable the only important weapons are a good soft towel and the ubiquitous moisturizing cream. The hands should be dried thoroughly every time they've been wet, even if the telephone caller has to wait another few seconds, and the moisturizing cream should be applied to the hands and the skin around the nails after each wetting.

Other chores can inevitably damage the nails and the nature of the chore determines the type of solution. If you use the telephone a great deal, for example, using a pencil to operate the dial will save your nails, while if you do a lot of heavy mechanical work or dirty gardening, gloves can provide invaluable protection. If you find that gardening gloves wear out frequently don't complain too much about that fact but just think how much damage you'd have done to your fingers if you hadn't been wearing gloves.

So far I've been very negative, detailing only the things that you shouldn't do if you want to protect your nails. There are positive things that you can do to keep your nails healthy too.

A weekly manicure is probably the best way to produce good healthy nails without too much effort. There is no strict ritual that needs to be followed as though it were some religious requirement, but there are some basic rules to follow.

First, it is important when cutting and shaping the nails to be careful not to take too much off the sides of the nails. If you do, you'll weaken them and they will be more liable to break. Smooth, even strokes with the rough, coarse side of an emery board or with a steel nail file are the best way to shape a nail, and if you file the nail in one direction you'll be less likely to develop rough edges.

The finer side of the file or board can be used to finish off the nail.

Second, when cleaning the nails don't be frightened to give them a fairly good scrub with a nail brush. You aren't likely to damage healthy nails or skin that way. A chamois buffer is a harmless way to polish the nails.

Third, do not forget to look after the cuticles. The cuticles can be pushed back with a towel or cotton bud if they are edging forwards, but don't be too rough on them. Do resist the temptation to attack the cuticles with anything sharp like a nail file, scissors, or the nails of the other hand. If you do, you're likely to develop paronychia (see p. 141). Use a little moisturizing cream to keep the cuticles soft and healthy.

And don't forget that unless you are pretty exceptional you'll have nails on your feet too.

There are products available which are sold as nail conditioners. *Super NuNale* and *NuNale Cream* (why, I wonder, do so many companies feel it necessary to mis-spell words when naming products?) both contain Keratol as their principal ingredient. The promotional literature for this product claims that 'this oily but non-greasy material penetrates to the nail matrix and encourages the growth of new, healthy, trouble-free, non-brittle nails'. Keratin is the name applied to the proteins which form the main constituents of horns and hooves but I don't know what Keratol is. The same company also makes a product called *NuKleen* which is a nail varnish remover which contains nail conditioning ingredients. I don't know of any irrefutable scientific evidence which supports the claims made for these products.

Finally Pifco now make a *Nailcare Kit* which consists of an electrically operated device for cleaning, shaping and polishing the nails. I can't help feeling that you really would have to have everything to feel a burning need to go out and buy this piece of equipment.

PURELY COSMETIC

Neat, well kept nails may be a good starting point but not many women are prepared to stop there.

Nail care products which come under the heading 'purely cosmetic' fall into two main groups.

First, there are the nail varnishes or enamels designed purely and simply for painting the nails a pretty colour. A basic nail enamel will contain four different types of component. The solvent is the vehicle in which the other substances are dissolved and it is chosen to ensure that none of the ingredients are left high and dry before any of the others. The solvent is usually a mixture of substances in which all the other ingredients of the enamel are soluble. It will usually contain one substance designed to speed up the first drying period, so that the enamel quickly reaches a point where it is hard enough to stand up to accidental knocks, and other substances designed to keep the whole solution stable during the final drying period. If the solvent isn't carefully prepared the enamel will dry in lumps and blotches. Too fast an evaporating solvent will produce fast-drying nail varnish, but can result in a messy finish.

The 'film former' traditionally favoured is nitrocellulose and the snag with this essential ingredient is that when left as a film on the nail it is quite brittle and doesn't stick very well. To overcome this problem a plasticizer is added to increase the flexibility of the finish and to make it stick firmly. Camphor was an early plasticizer but that was replaced by dioctyl phthalate, diethyl phthalate and castor oil, among others. Resins finally add lustre and pigments add colour.

Modern nail varnishes and polishes do not always adhere to this classical recipe. Synthetic resins and new plasticizers are being introduced all the time. To the consumer, however, the precise formulation is probably of little importance since the majority of products within this general category are produced to similar standards. The two major criteria for the consumer to look for are price and colour.

To satisfy the purely aesthetic demands of their customers all the major manufacturers make a huge range of colours. The *Maxi* range from Max Factor runs to '19 dazzling fashion colours'. Cutex make thirty different colours of varnish and Rimmel make over fifty varying shades with such descriptive names as *Grape Sorbet* and *Mulberry Wine*. Can't you just imagine a room full of elegant men in pinstripe suits sitting around a huge oval table struggling to think up a name for a new shade of nail varnish. Suddenly one of the men stands up and shouts: 'I've got it! Why don't we call it *Grape Sorbet*?' And all the others stand up and shout with delight. '*Grape Sorbet*! Why didn't I think of that!'

Outdoor Girl Super Cover Nail Polish, made in 'a riot of colours' is said to dry in a minute, while another product *Ten Set* consists of a spray that dries nail varnish 'instantly'. This product is also said to be enriched with cuticle oil so that 'as fast as it dries your varnish it softens your cuticles with a rapidly absorbed conditioner'. I can't imagine anything much more difficult than trying to spray finger-nails without spraying hands, clothes and anything else near by.

Nail varnish removers usually consist of acetone or ethyl acetate although both constituents may be mixed in the same bottle. The nails can be damaged if a remover is used too often or too liberally, so it's wise to touch up chips rather than remove the varnish and start again from scratch.

It is important to wipe the top of the bottle and fasten the lid properly after use since varnish can harden in the bottle as easily as it can on your nails, although some manufacturers do put a ball bearing into their bottles to help you keep the varnish fluid. The quicker setting varnishes may be more of a problem in this respect than ordinary varnishes.

Then, there are the products sold to women whose nails are either too short or broken. The products which fall into this group can again be subdivided into several categories.

If a nail breaks completely you can replace it with a completely artificial, pre-formed nail which is glued into position and which can then be filed into the precise shape required. Products in this category include *Fancy Fingers* and *Quik tips*. As with any cosmetic it is important to be aware of the fact that sensitivity reactions can occur, although with these products the glue is the only likely sensitizer. Alternatively you can buy artificial nails that are brushed or painted into position. A mould is placed underneath the shortened nail and the special substance from which the new nail is formed is then painted over the existing nail and the mould. When the mould is removed the nail can be filed and shaped. Products in this category include *Classic Nails* and *Lee Nails* and again the main danger is that an allergy reaction could develop. However, both these types of artificial nail are undoubtedly a great boon and the advantage of both is that the nail doesn't stop growing. It is important to realize that none of these products work well if you have misshapen nails.

NAIL PROBLEMS

Introduction

The number of separate medical specialities seems to rise each year in direct proportion to the rise in the number of diseases described in the medical journals and the number of new odd facts discovered by researchers all round the world. It just isn't possible for any one practitioner to be familiar with all the information that exists in modern medical libraries. Even specialists who might, twenty years ago, have known just about all there was to know about their subject can now only hope to have a passing acquaintance with a small part of it, which explains why the number of separate specialities is rising annually.

One of the next new specialities could well involve the study of those afflictions which concern human nails. There are now many general and specific problems which cause changes in the nails, and the science of unguistics cannot be far off.

Meanwhile, the important thing is perhaps to try and differentiate between those conditions which are self limiting, those which can be treated at home and those which need medical attention. Theoretically this could be difficult and important since many of the changes which affect the nails can betray signs of some general internal disorder. For example, iron-deficiency anaemia may cause the nails to be spoon shaped, in chronic arsenic poisoning the nails can develop transverse white lines and in a number of chest conditions the whole shape of the nails can be disturbed. In practice, however, these abnormalities are unlikely to precede by any significant interval the development of more noticeable symptoms. For example, by the time the patient with iron-deficiency anaemia has developed spoon-shaped nails, he or she will probably be appreciably breathless.

The commonest localized disorder of the nails is probably chronic paronychia, a condition which can be fairly easily diagnosed by the fact that the nail folds, the area where the nails meet the skin, are usually painful, red and swollen. This disorder can be caused by the careless use of a nail file or manicure scissors, by thumb-sucking or by too frequent immersion in water. It is a condition which is an occupational hazard of dishwashers, barmaids and kitchen hands, and since many people are exposed to similarly dangerous conditions at home they, too, frequently suffer from paronychia. Paronychia can usually be prevented and treated by keeping the hands as dry as possible (by using cotton-lined rubber gloves) or by making sure that when they have been wet the hands are dried carefully and thoroughly. Careful attention to the cuticles and cautious use of files, scissors and other implements is also essential.

Hangnails, slits along the side of the nails, are also commonly caused by too much washing and not enough drying and by injuries caused during manicure operations. By the way, it is important that if you have a sliver of skin sticking up by the side of a nail you don't pull it off and damage more skin but that you cut it off as neatly as you can.

Finally, there are two common but important conditions which usually affect toe- rather than finger-nails. An ingrown toe-nail can be painful and physically limiting and will need medical treatment if it persists, while onychogryposis, a condition in which the toe nails grow to a tremendous size will need the attention of a chiropodist.

Brittle nails

There are nearly as many explanations for this condition as there are experts, but the only scientifically justifiable theory I've come across (and the one which seems to be the one most favoured by dermatologists) is that split edges and brittle nails are caused by immersing the hands in powerful detergents or by using nail varnish solvents too frequently. This theory is substantiated by the fact that the condition seems to be confined to women who are guilty of doing these two things.

The best way to deal with the problem should be obvious. When washing up or doing anything which involves immersing your hands in anything other than plain water, wear rubber gloves. Modern chemicals are powerful enough to strip metals – they can certainly damage your skin and nails. And try not to change your nail varnish too often. If varnish gets scratched or chipped confine yourself to a touch-up job if you possibly can. Cleaning off the varnish (particularly with a remover containing acetone) and then reapplying from scratch only seems to weaken the nail structure.

Once brittle nails have developed there are several treatments you can try although I don't know of any undeniable evidence supporting their efficacy.

Applying a cream containing a mixture of equal parts of *Starch Glycerin BPC 1963* and *Salicylic Acid Ointment BP* every night is said to be helpful, and if you want to try this remedy ask your local pharmacist to make you up a quantity.

More widely advocated is the use of gelatin by mouth. It is said sometimes that dissolving one or two teaspoonfuls of gelatin in a drink and then swallowing the concoction will help give the nails added strength. Most experts are, however, in agreement that there is absolutely no evidence supporting this hypothesis.

There are a number of branded products available for the treatment of brittle nails. Some nail polishes, for example, contain nylon fibres designed to help give added strength to the nails, but it is obviously important that if you use one of these products you leave it in place for as long as possible. Removing the polish with a removing solvent will merely weaken the nail still further. Some of the other products sold to help strengthen the nails contain formaldehyde but it is now suspected that this ingredient can actually damage the nail and the cuticle.

On balance I think the best action to take is to protect the nails by wearing rubber gloves, to limit the number of times that nail varnish is removed and to keep brittle nails as short as possible to avoid embarrassing and uncomfortable breakages. I don't think that there is any point in spending money on chemical products sold to condition or harden the nails.

Nail biting
Nail biting is a psychological problem rather than a physical one. Nail biters are usually anxious, worried people who bite their nails for the same reasons and in the same half-conscious way that other worriers tap their feet, pull at their ear lobes and suck on pipes or thumbs.

The traditional remedy is to paint the nails with some nasty tasting substance to make each nibble so repulsive that the nails are eventually left alone. There are some branded products sold for the prevention of nail biting. *Stop 'n Grow* is a colourless liquid which is painted on to the nails like varnish and which is said to produce 'the most unpleasant taste known to man'. It is described by the manufacturers as 'willpower in a bottle', and they say that after you use it 'you'll have long, strong, beautiful nails in days'. Quite a few days I should think, since it takes a considerable time for nail to grow a noticeable length. Paints and liquids of this type sometimes work although the nail biter often then develops some other habit which may, according to fortune, be less or more annoying. The same thing goes for the trick of painting offenders' nails with shiny red polish. The polish may make the girl proud of her nails and therefore more conscious of them and more deter-mined to avoid nibbling, but the solution does not get to the root of the problem.

There are many different reasons why people worry and this really isn't the right book to include a comprehensive account of the stresses and strains that can cause such obvious manifestations of anxiety. If you can't think why nail biting continues I suggest that a visit to the family doctor may be the best solution. He ought to be able to analyse the possible causes. My book *Stress Control* is devoted to the management of stress-related disorders.

SKIN

Man is the hunter; woman is his game:
The sleek and shining creatures of the chase,
We hunt them for the beauty of their skins.

'The Princess' by Alfred, Lord Tennyson

ANATOMY

In many ways skin is the most magnificent part of the human body. It is forever adapting, permanently repairing itself, always responding to changes in body shape and requirements and at the same time responding to variations in the environment. It is a complex, multi-purpose organ which most of us treat with little thought and less respect. Good skin is such a tremendous asset that it is worthwhile spending a little time understanding how it is composed.

The skin consists of a number of different layers, and just as a piece of plywood is stronger than a single board of the same thickness so the skin is stronger and more resilient than it would be if it were composed of just one layer of cells.

There are two principal layers. The surface epidermis is thin but composed of four of five layers, while beneath that there is the thicker, bulkier and stronger dermis which is made up of two layers. Some idea of the inherent strength of the dermis can be obtained from the fact that leather is nothing more than tanned dermis.

The epidermis varies in thickness according to the needs of particular parts of the body. It is thickest on the palms and the soles where it gets most wear and thinnest over the eyelids and genitalia. At the very surface there is an upper layer of hard, protective, dead cells which are continually being replaced by the formation of new cells at the base of the epidermis. As new cells are formed they produce a substance called keratin (itself a complex mixture of substances) and a variety of lipids and waxes designed to give added plasticity and strength to the skin. The new cells take about a month to travel from the bottom of the epidermis to the surface but in conditions such as psoriasis this process is speeded up with new cells reaching the surface in a week or even less, pushing off old cells as they arrive.

Special cells which exist just below the bottom of the epidermis and which are called melanocytes produce a pigment called melanin. We all have a similar number of melanocytes but the amount of pigment these cells produce varies. Very active melanocytes give the skin a dark brown colour, while less active cells allow the skin to be coloured pink by the blood flowing through superficial vessels. A main function of the melanin is to protect the skin from ultraviolet rays, and so when a light-skinned individual is exposed to the sun the melanocytes become more active with the result that the skin acquires a brownish colour. When the melanocytes are not being stimulated by the sun the melanin production falls again, and the skin returns to its previous pale colour.

It is melanin which gives colour to the nipples, the labia minora and the penis and this is presumably to make us all more aware of each other's sexual qualities.

The normal elasticity of the skin is governed by racial and genetic factors and it is designed to accommodate size increases and changes and to allow for muscular movements. Just think of the changes which must occur in the skin to enable it to cover adequately and equally successfully a seven-pound baby who grows up to be a ten-stone woman. And remember that even when fully grown, the human body is rarely stable in size – pregnancy and dietary indiscretions are but two of the many causes of change in body shape.

If you study a stretch of skin carefully you will see that it consists of many tiny furrows; these lines tend to be more prominent over joints but they exist in all parts of the body and generally indicate the lines of tension within the skin. Because these patterns are particularly dramatic on the tips of the fingers where lines meet and form characteristic whorls and because the tips of the fingers are readily available for such purposes, forensic scientists use fingerprints to help in the identification of individuals.

As we age, the quality of our skin slowly changes as it becomes less elastic and more flaccid. Many obvious furrows or wrinkles appear as a result of repeated frowning or smiling and those areas of skin which have been exposed to the elements, usually the hands and the face, develop all the usual signs of wear and tear. Fortunately for the world's police forces, fingertips don't change with age.

Other changes in the skin occur fairly early in life. At adolescence body hair starts to grow when stimulated by developing hormones (see 'Hair anatomy' p. 102) and at the same time sebaceous and sweat glands are stimulated. Just as the growth of body hairs varies from region to region, so the development of these glands varies. The skin on the forehead, cheeks and nose, for example, is usually oily, whereas the skin on the jaws and chin is relatively greaseless. The skin on the palms of the hands and the soles of the feet has more sweat glands than the skin on the backs of hands and the tops of the feet.

The sweat glands which develop in human skin are of two types. The apocrine glands are usually associated with the hair follicles and are found mainly where there is obvious body hair. They can be found, for example, in the armpit, around the anogenital area and on the nipples. The apocrine glands produce a very small amount of fluid in comparison to the eccrine glands. The average man or women has several million eccrine glands which means that there are two or three hundred of them to the square centimetre, although the quantity on the palms and soles is much higher than the number elsewhere.

The sweat glands are an important part of the body's mechanism for controlling its own temperature. The various organs inside the body can only operate effectively within a relatively narrow temperature range and the sweat glands help to keep the temperature inside down when outside it is up. Under normal circumstances they are responsible for the loss of about half a litre of fluid a day but in hot climates this loss can be greatly increased. The rate of fluid secretion is also increased when an individual is under stress. This isn't as illogical as it may seem. Lubricating the hands and feet when the body is threatened (and the human body can't differentiate between physical and mental threats) helps to improve sensitivity and prepare the skin for action. The man who spits on his palms before starting a heavy task is simply imitating nature.

The sweat gland secretions are themselves odourless but when they are broken down by bacteria on the surface of the skin they produce a characteristic odour which many people find offensive. It may be but slight consolation if you suffer from body odour but the sweat that caused that smell was produced in a good cause.

Sweat helps lower the body temperature because when it evaporates it takes heat from the surface. This helps to keep the internal environment stable during heavy exercise and hot weather. In case this mechanism is not efficient enough there is another way in which the skin can help lower the body temperature. This involves the use of the many blood vessels which supply the skin with a far greater supply of blood than it would ever need for its own purposes. When the blood flow is at its peak there is considerable loss of body heat through the skin and the cooled blood, by returning to the hotter parts of the body to pick up more heat, turns the whole skin system into a very effective cooling radiator. Similar mechanisms work when the body temperature is raised by infection.

When the body temperature is in danger of falling both these protective mechanisms are automatically reversed with the amount of sweat lost being reduced and the amount of blood circulating through the skin being limited to the amount needed to supply the skin with oxygen and food.

As well as the sweat glands the skin contains sebaceous glands which are usually attached to hair follicles and which produce a substance called sebum, itself a mixture of fatty acids, cholesterol, waxes and broken down old cells of various kinds. The glands along the inner borders of the eyelids, which can be seen if the eyelids are pulled up and out, are sebaceous glands. Enlarging in puberty and greatest in number on the face and around the anogenital region the sebaceous glands produce what is effectively an automatic emollient designed to prevent the skin from becoming too dry.

As though all that were not impressive enough the skin has a complex lymphatic system designed to help combat infection, and a highly complicated nervous system designed to supply the brain with an enormous amount of information about the outside world. These systems operate automatically for most of the time, isolating infective sites and providing a supply of up-to-date information that makes the CIA look introspective.

LOOKING AFTER YOUR SKIN

Read the beauty pages of half a dozen magazines and the advertisements composed on behalf of an equal number of leading companies selling skin care products and you should be thoroughly confused about how best to look after your skin

To begin with you'll probably find it difficult to understand exactly how to decide what sort of skin you have. This basic confusion is then made considerably worse by the fact that different experts advocate different techniques for maintaining skin health, for dealing with skin problems and for ensuring a trouble free future. Either through simple ignorance or through a mixture of ignorance and stupidity or through a combination of ignorance, stupidity and dishonesty experts of all kinds write and talk with great conviction but little understanding about the skin's acid mantle, the properties of avocado oil and the importance of opening up the skin's pores.

For a decade I have studied and written about the claims and counter claims made by drug companies. The nonsense talked by the beauty experts and the manufacturers of skin care products makes the drug industry look like a bunch of monks. I have never in my life come across so much pseudo-scientific rubbish as I have during the months I've been investigating the cosmetics industry.

Forget everything you have read or heard about skin care and let me explain the real truth based on what we really know about human anatomy and physiology and on the known chemical properties of the products available.

First of all, of course, there is the question of skin type.

Most experts seem to divide skin into four main types: normal, combination, dry and oily. This fairly simple and straightforward classification has been tossed aside by some manufacturers, however, who prefer to add such terms as 'slightly dry' and 'sensitive', to the more familiar quartet.

Because many people find it as difficult to tell exactly what type of skin they have as they do to tell whether they are small or big boned, a number of tests have been advocated over the years. One expert suggests that if small pieces of brown paper are stuck to the face the pieces which become translucent will show up the oily areas. Other experts have suggested that tissue paper is more suitable. The Clinique company have an impressive sounding computer designed to help identify skin type (see p. 28).

In my opinion these techniques have little value since it must be remembered that human skin is not always dry or greasy any more than a nose is always clear or stuffy. Moreover, most people cannot be said to have clearly dry or greasy skin any more than they can be firmly described as tall or small. It is also important to remember that skin varies in quality from one part of the body to another and that an individual with greasy facial skin may have very dry skin on his or her legs.

The phrase 'sensitive skin' is particularly confusing. It usually seems to be applied to those people who suffer frequently from allergy reactions or who are particularly prone to suffer when environmental changes occur, but in practice we all have potentially sensitive skins, and I strongly suspect that using too many exotic skin creams is as common a cause of 'sensitive skin' as anything else.

General skin care does not depend overmuch on identifying skin type. There are certain basic rules which apply to all types of skin.

To begin with it is important to look after the skin and to protect it from unnecessary damage. You don't have to spend a great deal of money on expensive products to do this.

Diet, of course, plays an important part in all aspects of health. The human body is permanently changing and repairing itself and these natural processes depend directly on the quantity and quality of food consumed. A badly balanced diet can result in skin damage just as it can result in damage to any other organ and a surfeit or a shortage of food or drink can cause problems too.

The weather can have an important effect on the skin. Strong sunshine causes both temporary and permanent damage and is a major factor in the ageing process as it affects the skin. Cold weather has a harmful effect too since by constricting the blood vessels it limits the essential circulation to the skin. The body can be protected against too much sun by the use of sunscreening agents (see p. 230), loose-fitting clothes and wide-brimmed floppy hats, and against the cold by gloves, boots and warm coats. Modern air conditioning is theoretically designed to control the amount of moisture in the atmosphere (the humidity), the temperature, the amount of impurities and the movement of the air. If done properly air conditioning can be very beneficial, but many air conditioners are badly made or used and the air is so thoroughly dried that the skin loses much of its natural moisture. Commercial humidifiers can help solve this problem which can also be alleviated by putting a large bowl of water in an affected room or even by draping wet towels over radiators.

Most women will probably agree that they often fail to dry their hands properly after doing minor kitchen chores. This can lead to a number of skin problems but in particular it leads to a loss of natural skin oils and moisture. Keeping a good quality hand towel near to the kitchen sink and using it regularly is an important weapon in hand care. Only slightly less important is the use of rubber gloves when washing dishes and clothes in strong detergents (see p. 142). Those who argue that they can't handle dishes with their hands covered might remember that surgeons perform extremely tricky operations while wearing gloves, and although domestic gloves need to be thicker in order to be durable there are gloves available which are usable. Ridged gloves may prevent sad breakages and it is important to buy gloves which are large enough. Rubber gloves shouldn't be worn for more than fifteen or twenty minutes at a time and it will also help if the water isn't allowed to get too hot.

If these environmental hazards are avoided the skin will be far less likely to suffer damage. However, there are in addition many things that can be done in a more positive way to clean and protect the skin. Traditionally these techniques fall into the well established trio of cleansing, toning and moisurizing. I'll deal with these one by one.

Cleaning the skin is not just an essential toilet activity, it is also a vital part of cosmetic care. Queen Elizabeth I is said to have had a bath every three months whether she needed one or not. The basic aim, of course, is to remove environmental dirt and old cosmetic preparations, but it is important that any cleansing agent should be itself removable and should not irritate the skin.

The cleansing armoury is enormous and the variety of products extraordinarily confusing. Many consumers and even experts seem uncertain about the relative merits of soaps. detergents, cleansing milks, cleansing liquids, and so on, and the confusion isn't helped by the fact that manufacturers often give products with similar constituents and methods of action different names. For example, I've seen tablets of soap described as cleansing bars.

Ordinary soap is often dismissed by beauticians as unsuitable as a cleansing agent. This just is not true. The purpose of a cleansing operation is simply to remove the dirt and soap is very effective for doing this. Ursula Andress, for example, has been quoted as saying 'I attribute my glowing skin to soap and water.' However, any soap that is designed to do more than cleanse will only do harm. Moisturizing is a separate process which can only be done after the skin has been properly cleaned, so there is no point in buying a soap designed to be also used as a moisturizer.

Soap is basically made of two ingredients – fat and lye. The fats combine with hard water minerals to form an insoluble scum but they do work particularly well as cleansers. Unfortunately, by removing natural oils from the skin soaps can have a drying effect on the skin and probably make the later use of a moisturizer well worthwhile. Transparent soaps are more difficult to make and consequently cost more than others, but I have been unable to find any evidence that suggests that they work more effectively, efficiently or safely than any other kind of soap. Super-fatted soaps are sometimes advocated for use on dry skins but again I don't know of any evidence supporting this suggestion. It is important after using any soap to ensure that it is rinsed away well and that the skin is carefully dried. Skin folds, such as those in the groin and under the breasts, are often left damp and this can lead to future skin problems (see p. 224). Powdering with a little talc may help prevent dampness. Triple or hard milled soaps are simply soaps that have been processed to a very hard consistency.

In addition to their basic ingredients many soaps include added perfumes. Some major companies produce soaps which are designed to fit into their range of products by containing the same perfume as marketed colognes and deodorants. I cannot see any real point in buying a perfumed soap since the added perfume is always likely to cause skin irritation and should, if used properly, be rinsed away afterwards. If the soap perfume doesn't match your other perfumes then there is even less reason to use it.

Making your own soap is probably unnecessarily time consuming and I doubt if you could save money that way, but you can save money by melting down small bits of leftover soap in a saucepan and then shaping the resultant block when it has cooled.

Medicated soaps are an important part of the market today. The usual additives to medicated soaps are antiseptics or disinfectants and again these are unlikely to do any real good at all, whereas they can and sometimes do cause allergy reactions.

There are also many soaps which appeal largely through their packaging and shaping. A flick through the Bronnley catalogue, for example, makes it difficult to remember that soap is used only to help clean the skin!

In deference to the fact that the skin is normally slightly acid, whereas soaps are usually slightly alkaline, there are companies making soaps designed to help maintain the skin's acid *status quo*. Vichy, for example, make what they call a *Dermatological Cleansing Bar* which looks a bit like a bar of soap, while *Neutrogena* is also designed to be alkali free. I think that efforts to preserve the pH of the skin are probably unnecessary. Other products which are similarly designed to reduce the risk of allergy reactions, while providing the basic ingredients for cleansing, include *Simple Soap* (advertised as 'not perfumed, not coloured, just kind') and other similar products.

Liquid soaps are also obtainable now and indeed there are those in the industry who believe that liquid soaps have a bright future. There is no scientific reason that I know of to prefer a liquid soap to a bar of soap. Incidentally, the main difference between liquid soaps and cleansing milks is that the former foam and lather whereas members of the second group do not.

When hard water combined with soap causes the formation of an annoying scum of mineral salts, a synthetic detergent may prove more acceptable. Detergents are made of petroleum derivatives and they don't form a scum at all with hard water. They can be mild, and indeed shampoos and bubble baths are basically detergents.

The cosmetics industry being what it is, bathing and showering are considered to be rather different from ordinary washing. There are consequently a large number of special products available.

First, let us look at the equipment for the bathroom; what the computer people might call the 'hardware'.

The pumice stone is probably the oldest piece of bathroom hardware around and it is still as good as most aids for removing hard skin and superficial layers of dead cells. It is simply made of volcanic lava. Alternatives to the pumice stone include sea salt, which acts as an abrasive, the loofah (a dry, rough, vegetable gourd), the friction mitt or strap and the ordinary bath brush. For getting a good lather out of your soap you can use an old fashioned flannel or face-cloth (as long as you put it into boiling water after use to prevent it getting filthy and smelly), or a natural sponge which is also a mild natural abrasive. Helancyl make a kit which consists of a special glove, some soap and a special cream, but you can probably get a similar effect by using a loofah, a bar of soap and your ordinary moisturizing cream.

Bathroom software consists of an enormous range of products. Bubble and foam baths, which are much loved by young children and film starlets, contain surfactants, foam stabilizers and detergents which can irritate the skin and which can cause cystitis if used to excess. The detergent makes the use of soap superfluous. Bubble baths should be mixed well before getting into the bath and they should be abandoned if skin rashes occur. They are drying and shouldn't be used by those with dry skin.

Bath oils consist of two main types, there are those which disperse in the water and those which float on the surface. They can help the treatment of dry skin (see p. 202) but they are often wiped off after bathing when the skin is being dried. It is important to remember that the bath can get very slippery if you use a bath oil. Incidentally, Cleopatra was said to have been very fond of having oils in her bath. She also used fine white sand as an abrasive.

Bath essences are simply products designed to add scent to the bathwater. These are sometimes alcohol based for greasy skin and oil based for dry skin. They make the bath smell nice, but if the skin is properly rinsed and dried afterwards they probably have little lasting effect. There is also the risk of causing an allergy reaction by bringing the skin into unnecessary contact with perfumes. Bath cubes, crystals and salts perfume the water but they do dry the skin a little. They may help soften water and thereby reduce the amount of scum when soap is used.

Bath and shower gels are usually made from detergents and they are used just like soap. Radox make a product called *Showerfresh* which they point out can be used to cleanse from head to toe and to shampoo hair.

Radox, like Badedas, also make a product which contains horse-chestnut, and I wonder if the executives of these companies have read the collected works of the Marquis de Sade. Radox use horse-chestnut in their *Herbal Bath*, while Badedas use it in their *Badedas Vita Bath Gelee* which is advertised with the well known picture of the half-naked lady looking at a fully dressed man standing outside. The advertising blurb reads: 'Things happen after a *Badedas* bath. Tonight abandon yourself to the foaming caress of *Badedas*. Discover the mystery of extract of horse-chestnuts.'

If you can't wait, let me explain that the mystery of horse-chestnuts, as described so beautifully by the Marquis in one of his bawdy short stories, is that when in flower the horse-chestnut tree has a smell very strongly reminiscent of semen.

At least that gives horse-chestnut some reason for being present in bath gels and foams. I know of no reason why herbs or plant extracts of any other kind should make bathing more effective or more pleasant apart from the fact that they smell rather nice. That effect can be easily obtained by tying a muslin bag filled with herbs under the tap or by making an infusion with herbs and adding that to the bath. (To make an infusion pour boiling water on to your selected herbs and strain the result.)

The advantages of uses of mud baths, saunas and so on are discussed on p. 56 and the types of bath additives recommended for use in the treatment of dry skin are discussed on p. 202.

Cleansing lotions, oils and creams are essential for the removal of oily pollutants and make-up since these products are not soluble in water. The problem is that oily cleansers are not as thoroughly effective as straightforward soap and water and they are themselves difficult to remove from the skin. Apart from their importance in the removal of make-up special creams are particularly useful when the skin is exceptionally dry and likely to be made worse by the daily use of soap. Even then soap and water is probably the best way to clean skin on most occasions.

The original cold creams consisted of a mixture of olive oil, beeswax and water together with rosewater or some similar substance included to add fragrance. The evaporation of water from the mixture makes the skin feel cool and therefore gives the cream its name. Oil and wax cleanse by liquefying on the skin and loosening and picking up dirt and dead cells on the skin surface. Traditionally, cold creams used for cleansing have sometimes been left on the skin as moisturizers although this is no more sensible than leaving a layer of dirty lather on the skin after washing with soap. Removing cold cream requires tissues or cotton wool since the cream itself, being oily, cannot be washed away with water. In today's creams the olive oil is often replaced by mineral oil which is less likely to go rancid.

Cold cream is rather thick and heavy (an emulsion of water in oil – see p. 203) and lighter creams can be prepared by adjusting the quantities of the various constituents. Milks are an emulsion of oil in water and are simply thin versions of cold cream. Cleansing creams are available which contain fragrances, disinfectants and many other additives. The fact is that any oily mixture can be used as a cleanser and no additives improve the efficiency of the product.

This is perhaps the right place to point out that cold creams and other cleansing creams are basically the same as moisturizing creams in that they are a mixture of oil and water. Those creams with a low melting point feel particularly greasy on the skin while those with a high melting point do not feel as greasy. Vanishing creams, so called because they seem to disappear on the skin, fall into this second category. As cleansers these products help remove oils and oil products; as moisturizers they help cement a rough skin surface, help make it feel smoother and silkier and help prevent the loss of essential moisture. Emollients or softening creams, night creams or nourishing creams are just heavy cold creams. Products sold specifically as hand creams or lotions and which are designed to prevent or reduce dryness of the hands (see p. 203) are usually oil in water emulsions so that they do not leave a greasy feeling on the hands. These are the same as vanishing creams.

Because there are so many different cleansing lotions available each company usually manages to find its own particular selling point. Almay, point out that their *Almay Cleansing Lotion* is hypoallergenic; Delph say that their *Delph Cleansing Milk* is so light that it cleans really deep down and leaves no trace of stickiness: while Vichy, like Almay, produce their *Cleansing Milk* in varieties to suit different skin types. I very much doubt whether there is any reason to consider any one cleansing milk or lotion superior on scientific grounds but I do not recommend buying medicated cleansers such as *Swiss Bio-Facial* which contains chlorhexidine, since antiseptics can cause allergy reactions under certain circumstances and there does not seem to me to be any advantage to be gained to balance this additional risk, however small.

Cleansing lotions are available in special pad form, designed to make the removal of make-up simple away from home. *Quickies* are available in neat containers and are sold in three strengths, as suitable for removing make-up from nails, eyes and face.

There is one additional way that dirty skin can be cleaned and that is by using some sort of thinning or abrasive procedure. Dry, dirty skin will often have a thick, coarse, leathery outer layer with blocked pores and accumulated dead cells.

The simplest way to remove this accumulation of debris is by rubbing with a face-cloth, loofah, pumice stone, brush or coarse towel, but there are many commercial products available. These are discussed at some length in the section describing the treatment of acne (see p. 179) since clarifying, or scarifying as it is sometimes called, is an excellent method of reducing the incidence of acne. Ground almonds, orange peel, strawberries or fine oatmeal paste massaged into the skin for a minute and then rubbed off are popular 'natural' ways of doing the same thing. This procedure should not be carried out more than once a week or the skin can be damaged.

More dramatic scarification is often done to remove the build-up of old cells and pigment which develops as skin ages. Since nails and hair occasionally need trimming there is, I suppose, some sense in the argument that the skin occasionally needs a trim. More dramatic thinning in this way usually requires the services of an expert, and chemical and mechanical thinners are discussed on p. 180.

The second procedure in the traditional skin care regime consists of toning. This is a waste of time and money.

There are many different skin tonics available and as usual the industry has dignified them with a wide variety of important sounding names. Generally speaking skin toners, fresheners and astringents contain similar ingredients although astringents, which tend to make the skin tingle and feel tight contain a higher proportion of alcohol than the others. Glycerine and water are the two other most important ingredients.

The alcohol in these products acts as a mild chemical thinner and evaporates quickly to cool the skin. By irritating the skin astringents cause swelling around the skin pores so that obvious and opened pores look temporarily less obvious. It is important to realize that skin pores cannot be opened and closed at will and that enlarged pores cannot be prevented or treated. Using astringents to deal with pores is no more sensible than deliberately allowing yourself to get sunburnt so that skin swelling conceals the pores.

None of these products does anything useful but if you really want to use a toner you can make your own by mixing one part of rubbing alcohol with four parts of water or by mixing witch-hazel and rosewater to your own prescription.

The third part of the skin care trio – moisturizing – is vitally important.

The most important thing to understand about moisturizing, however, is that you cannot add moisture to the skin by using any product. A remarkable number of beauty editors don't seem to understand this simple point, so I'll explain what I mean in some detail.

The human skin contains a good deal of water and that water helps to give the skin its plump, fresh, healthy look. When the skin loses moisture (as it does if the weather is hot or if air conditioners have dried the local atmosphere) it looks dry and cracked and becomes uncomfortable.

Moisturizers help not by adding moisture to the skin but by preventing the loss of moisture which is already present. It is vitally important to remember this simple physiological fact when reading manufacturers' claims and comments on the beauty pages.

Moisturizers are of two main types. The larger group includes those products which act as occlusives; these simply form a thin protective layer on the skin surface. The skin itself uses exactly this same technique to prevent the loss of water and produces an oily material designed quite simply to help retain moisture. Some of these natural oils are removed by the cleansing process, and supporting that inbuilt defence system makes good physiological sense. *Vaseline* or simple petroleum jelly is the simplest moisturizer of this variety but there are very many more. Since the sole purpose of a moisturizer is to protect the skin from moisture loss there is no point in spending large amounts of money on a moisturizing jelly, cream, milk, or whatever, that contains any additives. Additional materials don't improve the effectiveness of the moisturizer but simply increase the possibility of there being allergy reactions.

The skin should be moisturized directly after being cleaned and special care should be taken of dry or potentially dry areas of skin. The eyebrows, knees, elbows, feet and hands are as much in need of help as is the main part of the face. Excess moisturizing cream should be wiped away with a tissue. If the moisturizing cream is added to slightly damp skin it will retain that extra amount of water.

Moisturizing cream has another function: it protects the skin from the numerous pollutants in the air. Few of us live far away from factory and traffic polluted air, and the chemicals which exist in the atmosphere can be extremely harmful to the skin. A thin layer of moisturizing cream will provide some protection.

The traditionally fine English complexion, perhaps a result of our damp climate, has suffered in recent years from air conditioning and annual travel to warmer, sunnier climates, but the careful use of a moisturizer can do a great deal to protect the quality of the skin and prevent premature ageing. There are a great many different products available as moisturizers and all of them probably work. I doubt if price plays much of a part in the effectiveness of the moisturizer you choose, but if you pay a high price you'll probably get a pleasant smell and a pretty package.

Oil of Ulay is probably one of the best known skin care products in this category although I cannot see any reason why it should 'refresh parched cells'. *Innoxa Special Formula* is free of fragrance, free of artificial colour and carefully pH balanced but then so are many other products. The Helena Rubinstein range is advertised with the slogan 'The Science of Beauty' but I don't see why their *Skin Dew*'s exclusive reinforced Milk Protein Complex should do anything to make it more effective than all other moisturizers. Estée Lauder's *Swiss Performance Extract* contains soluble protein although I don't know what evidence they have that it does any good, while Elizabeth Arden's *Visible Difference* contains active ingredients that 'penetrate 20 cell layers deep, pillowing and cushioning the skin with moisture'. The advertisements claim that only Elizabeth Arden can call a face cream *Visible Difference* and that is undoubtedly quite true, but don't be misled by the claims about twenty cell layers deep into thinking that the Elizabeth Arden scientists have found a way to get moisture further into the skin. Nor do I believe that Clinique's *Dramatically Different Moisturizing Lotion* really is dramatically different, even though it is described as a 'golden genius lotion' that 'gratifies the thirst of every skin'.

I like the advertisements from Vichy for their *Equalia* because there is a great deal of straightforward truth in them. Vichy point out that their laboratories have developed *Equalia* to help the skin retain its water and that their product does not try to put moisture into the skin. Such honesty is welcome although Vichy do rather give the impression that the idea is a new one. They do, by the way, point out that *Equalia* only needs to be applied sparingly, and this is true of all moisturizers.

There are many products which seem far more complex and Orlane's *B23* is one. The advertisements for this product claim that it contains 'precious amino acids and Colloid OR38'. This 'unique' complex is said to aid the skin's moisture retaining qualities but I have found no reason to suspect that these ingredients make Orlane's product better than everyone else's.

The Boots *17* range includes a moisturizer and their claim I like. They say that their products are special because they don't cost a fortune.

Moisturizers contain oils and greases with wax added to change the texture or water included to make the product feel lighter or less greasy. It doesn't really matter what the constituent oils are, or whether they are animal, vegetable or mineral oils. If the skin is being wrapped the source of the wrapping is irrelevant and mink oil, shark oil or whatever will do no more good than olive oil. Nor will added extra constituents such as perfumes, vitamins, hormones, placenta, honey, seaweed or even baked beans make any difference. Moisturizers work in the same way that waxed paper helps keep bread fresh – not by adding anything but by preserving what is already there.

The second group of substances in the moisturizing category are those known as humectants. These, which include such products as glycerine, work by absorbing moisture from around them. They make the skin feel smoother but they can, paradoxically, have a drying effect. One of the best known glycerine containing moisturizers is *Crème Simon*, the manufacturers of which advise that it should always be used on wet skin. *Nulon Hand Cream* also contains glycerine.

The theory is that the humectant will work by attracting moisture from the atmosphere and as long as the air contains enough moisture the theory works well enough. Problems arise when the amount of water in the air falls. Then the humectant draws water not from the atmosphere but from the skin; thereby doing damage rather than helping maintain the quality of the skin.

Those who have particularly dry skin probably need more moisturizer than people with oily skin, but it is probably fair to say that everyone should use a moisturizing cream of some kind. Only small quantities need to be used, but in summer, when bathing and perspiring may remove the protective layer, it is important to reapply it regularly. There is no reason why men shouldn't need moisturizers as much as women but so far the cosmetic companies selling products to men seem to have concentrated their efforts on less essential and more feminine fragrances and deodorants.

In conclusion, then, the two main ways to protect your skin by using toiletries are to clean it properly and to use a moisturizer.

Anyone who has so much as looked at a beauty page will realize immediately that there are many products available which are said to be able to do much more than this.

There are, for example, the nourishing creams. These are said to actually feed the skin and to add specially formulated foods to the skin's diet. There are products containing protein, vitamins and collagen, for example. These skin wonders are discussed at greater length on p. 27, but the simple fact to remember is that the inner layers of the skin derive their nourishment from the blood supply and not from the outside world. The dead cells on the skin surface need only water to remain healthy looking and plump and to give the skin a soft, smooth appearance. Without water the outside skin surface appears dry and rough and wrinkled. However, those outer cells can only take in so much water. If they were insatiable we would all blow up like balloons every time we bathed. And if our skin could absorb foreign materials we would all be full of soap wouldn't we?

Nourishing creams are a waste of money in my view.

There are also products designed to help preserve the 'acid mantle' of the skin. These wonderful creations are of equally doubtful value since although we know that the skin produces a slightly acid secretion in order to help destroy bacteria, we also know that the skin is quite capable of preserving its own 'acid mantle' without outside help. Not even when alkaline soaps are used does the skin pH change permanently or to the skin's detriment. It is important to rinse off the soap but that is all.

Exercising the facial muscles has been recommended as a way of preserving a wrinkle-free skin, but I haven't been able to find any evidence at all to suggest that exercises make any difference to the number of wrinkles around. Indeed, it is possible that by doing more exercises than usual the skin may become more wrinkled.

Face masks are often said to help rejuvenate ageing skin and to improve the complexion.

Most face masks fall into one of two categories. There are those which are rinsed off and those which are peeled off. Those which are rinsed off cleanse better while those which are peeled off do remove some dirt and dead cells but don't clean as evenly or as well. On the other hand, the peeling types of masks are soothing and can have a short-lived beneficial effect. They pinch the skin as they harden and then, as the blood vessels expand when the mask is removed, the skin's superficial wrinkles temporarily disappear.

Finally, I would like to point out that if you find washing your own face too much of a chore you can buy a *Pifco Facial Brush* which is a battery-operated device which comes complete with a cleansing brush, a massaging disc, a firm massaging brush, a soft sponge and a pumice stone to do everything from cleaning the skin through to applying make-up.

Tips on Cleansing

Soap and water are the best products for cleansing the skin. A cheap, simple soap which contains few additives is less likely to cause problems than one which contains perfumes and other inessentials. Water should be warm rather than hot and soap should be rubbed on to the skin gently in widening, circular movements. It is vitally important to then rinse off all the lather, preferably using running water.

This technique should be followed every morning and evening.

When make-up has to be removed this should be done first. Any excess make-up can be blotted away with a tissue or cotton wool (absorbent toilet rolls are cheaper than paper tissues and cotton wool can be bought in large quantities from pharmacies). A cleansing cream, oil or milk (it doesn't really matter which as long as it works) is then used to remove what is left. The cream is rubbed on to the skin gently and then removed with cotton wool or tissue. Thorough rinsing is followed by a wash with soap and water. Eye make-up should be removed with particular care since the skin around the eyes is exceptionally thin and sensitive. Mineral oil or baby oil can be used for this.

Do remember that after washing, the skin needs to be dried

thoroughly and that a good dry towel should be used – not a dirty, damp one.

Tips on Moisturizing

Choose a moisturizing cream that you find pleasant to use and that you can afford to use regularly. Apply it to exposed areas of skin whenever you go out of doors and use it to protect your hands when performing household chores.

A moisturizing cream can also be used to remove make-up, but don't leave moisturizing cream in place if it has been used for this purpose. Cleansing and moisturizing must be considered separate activities, but similar products can be used for both.

There are many products available in both commercial categories but their essential contents are similar, so sales depend upon packaging and pseudoscientific claims. It really doesn't matter what the constituents are or whether they are animal, vegetable or mineral oils. *Boots E45* is a good simple inexpensive moisturising cream as are *Nivea*, *Vaseline* and liquid paraffin.

Skin care tips

1 Drink a pint of fresh water each day.
2 Eat a sensible, varied diet. Don't try unbalanced slimming diets.
3 Wear gloves in the winter to protect the hands against cold weather.
4 If you live or work in an air-conditioned environment ensure that the air does not become too dry – open a window or keep a bowl of water in the room.
5 Learn to relax – stress causes wrinkles.
6 Clean the skin daily – removing environmental pollutants and cosmetics.
7 Wear a wide-brimmed, floppy hat in summer and use sun-screening agents.
8 Don't stay in the bath for too long, and don't have very hot baths.
9 Wear cotton-lined rubber gloves when washing up.
10 Dry hands carefully whenever they have been in water.
11 Remember that you have a total of about two square metres of skin – don't just look after your hands and face.

PURELY COSMETIC

Make-up

While writing this book I was reminded over and over again that many women regard make-up not as a luxury but as an absolute necessity. 'If I go out without make-up on I feel naked,' one young woman told me. Others pointed out that make-up helped them to deal with daily stresses and helped to give them confidence. One potential reader, suspicious of my motives in writing this book asked whether I intended to condemn all forms of make-up as potentially harmful or damaging. 'I shan't read it if you do,' she warned me. 'I'd use make-up even if you told me that it would ruin my skin.'

I assured her that I had no intention of condemning make-up products but that on the contrary I hoped to help my readers choose the best and most useful products.

There are, of course, so many individual make-up products that a comprehensive analysis of each and every one of them would be an impossible task. Since products disappear almost daily and are replaced by new ones at approximately the same rate the effort would hardly be worthwhile.

There are, however, a nember of points about make-up in general which are worth making.

First, and perhaps most important of all, I think I ought to dispel the myth that make-up must necessarily be harmful. The truth is that make-up won't damage your skin as long as the skin is cared for properly before the make-up is applied and as long as the make-up is removed completely later. All skin needs cleaning regularly and facial skin, which is exposed to the elements, needs cleaning and moisturizing. By and large it is also wise to avoid using too much make-up and to avoid using particularly greasy make-up. However, neither of these precautions is likely to adversely affect the aesthetic result. The only other point of warning which I think I ought to make is that where brushes and other pieces of equipment are used they should be kept as clean as possible and should not be shared. Infected brushes will result in infected skin, and it is difficult to look your best if your face is covered with an ugly impetigo rash.

The most fundamental make-up product is probably the foundation cream which is really just a variation on the moisturizing cream theme. Foundation creams consist of oil and water emulsions designed to spread easily on the skin. Manufacturers often produce special lines for people with dry skin and for those with greasy skin but the only difference is that the creams for use on dry skin contain a little more oil. Foundation creams are sold in a variety of colours and if you want to buy a foundation cream as well as a moisturizing cream it is obviously sensible to buy one that matches your natural skin colour. To be honest, however, you probably don't need to buy a foundation cream as well as a moisturizing cream unless your complexion is particularly bad.

Face powders, which are traditionally applied on top of a foundation cream in order to give the skin a finishing touch, were originally made of rice starch with a colouring agent included. Later, talc was substituted for the starch and insoluble pigments were introduced as colourants while other substances such as zinc oxide and titanium oxide were added to make the powder more opaque. More recently other additions were made to help make face powder adhere more firmly to the skin and to help it spread more readily. Face powder manufacturers have spent a great deal of time improving their products and today you can expect a powder to adhere well, to remain resistant to the skin's own secretions and to mask the natural shininess of human skin.

Chalk, magnesium carbonate, starch and kaolin are used to help absorb oily secretions and perspiration; talc, zinc stearate, magnesium stearate and starch are added to help make the powder spread easily and to make it feel smooth to the touch; titanium dioxide, zinc oxide, kaolin and magnesium oxide are among the substances used to give the powder covering power; magnesium or zinc stearates, together with oils or fats, are added to help the powder cling to the face, while to give a peach-like finish chalk or starch are included.

The main function of a face powder is to conceal shine and to give the skin a new, artificial surface. The smaller the size of the powder particles the better the effect since each individual particle will reflect light in different directions and reduce the risk of shine. Unfortunately, the finer the powder the greater the surface area and the quicker any perfume will be lost to the air.

If your skin is particularly dry you will be able to use what is called a 'light' powder. This does not refer to the weight of the product but to its covering power. A greasy skin, on the other hand, will need a 'heavy' powder with better covering power. Obviously, the powder for a dry skin will need more adherence than one designed for a greasy skin which can be expected to stick fairly well without much help. It should be clear now why a foundation cream is more help to an individual with a dry skin than to someone who has greasy skin if both intend to use a face powder.

Much the same effect as can be obtained with a foundation cream and a powder can be obtained with a make-up lotion which is primarily an emulsion in which have been incorporated ingredients designed to help the product spread easily on the face, dry reasonably quickly, leave a good colour effect and cover up grease and blemishes effectively. Not surprisingly the ingredients used to obtain this effect are similar to those used in the preparation of face powders.

A compact or powdered rouge, by the way, contains the same ingredients as a face powder but in addition includes extra pigment.

Lipsticks are probably the most traditional make-up products and even women who rarely use powders or lotions may feel lonely without a lipstick in their bags.

Lipsticks are a great source of worry within the cosmetics industry and I can assure you that a great deal of time and money is spent on ensuring that products spread well and do not break. Most of the major manufacturers are obsessed with ensuring that their products do not get a bad reputation, so if you do buy a 'dud' complain and you'll probably get it replaced without too much difficulty.

Most lipsticks consist of a fatty base to ensure that the product stays firm but is easily spread and colour added by dyes or pigments. A good lipstick must be soft enough to stick to the lips smoothly and with a minimum of pressure and it should stay there when the owner of the lips drinks, eats, smokes or kisses. Toxicity testing obviously has to be very thorough since the product is often ingested. Lipstick colours vary in different lights, so when you are choosing a particular colour it is best to choose it in the light that you'll be wearing it in. In other words if you are buying a lipstick that you intend to wear out of doors then have a look at it away from the store's fluorescent lights – but do make sure that you ask for the assistant's permission or else you may end up in the local magistrate's court. When a lipstick goes blue on your lips it is usually a sign that the colour has begun to wear off and the time has come to reapply it. Liquid lipsticks, by the way, are applied to the lips with a brush and some experts believe the final result is more pleasing. It's slightly more time consuming.

If you find the price of lipsticks too high to bear and you can't stand throwing out lipstick stubs, you can always get the last penny's worth by mashing up the stubs, putting the result into an eyeshadow pot and then using the result with a brush.

Incidentally, anyone, male or female, who has sore or dry lips should use an ordinary moisturizer on them.

Generally speaking make-up these days is made to high standards, and you can choose your products according to colour and price. Recently some companies have started to introduce scientific verbiage into their advertisements (Helena Rubinstein who subhead their advertisements 'The Science of Beauty' claim that their *Skin Life Make-Up* contains 'GAM – an exclusive biocomplex that matches the natural fluid present in your skin'. I think that you can safely ignore such enthusiasms.

Perfumes

It is no more possible to classify perfumes than it is to classify paintings, cities or beautiful people. Scientific judgements and harsh economic evaluations are of no value at all when there is no way to retain more than token objectivity. One can almost argue that a perfume does not properly exist until it has aroused an emotional response of some sort in one or more individual. It is the impact and the influence rather than the scent itself which gives perfume its value, and who can assess such intangibles?

Having begun with that cautionary note I intend to write a little about perfumes and the art of perfumery (surely an art and not a science, whatever scientific techniques are involved in its prosecution) because some basic understanding of the nature of perfume cannot but help the discerning customer searching for the most suitable purchase. In an earlier part of this book (p. 19) I have described some of the marketing and advertising ploys used in the promotion of perfumes; here I'll discuss a few traditions and some principles of the art.

It was in ancient Egypt several thousand years ago that perfumes were first developed and used in earnest. Standards of personal hygiene and medical care were extraordinarily high, and perfumes were used at that time for many different reasons. Egyptian labourers once went on strike after complaining that there was a shortage of perfumed ointments for them to use and Egyptian women appreciated the value of perfume for sexual attraction.

Over a hundred different perfume formulas were known, the most important constituents being ambergris, musk and civet – the first two of which were considered to have enormous erotic potential. Perfumes were used as camouflage and as lures, in public places and in the home, to soothe and to attract; and women used different perfumes for their hair, their mouths, their genitalia and general bathing. They even perfumed their food.

As traders travelled further and knowledge was carried from one country to another so the use of perfume spread around the world. By the time the Roman Empire had reached its zenith perfumery had become a truly international art with knowledge from India and Egypt helping to form the basis of a sophisticated and valued art. During the centuries following the collapse of Rome, when the use of perfumes was considered decadent and indecent by Catholic Europe, scientific work continued in Arabia where prejudice and intolerance were less pervasive. Arabic scientists made many discoveries which were incorporated by European perfume makers when the Renaissance revitalized the European scientific world.

Perfume was reintroduced into European life when the Crusaders returned from their travels and their women found themselves competing with the seductive memories that had been brought home. Perfumes may often have been used during the Middle Ages to disguise unpleasant smells rather than for their inherent sexual quality, but the art of perfumery had at least been reintroduced into Europe.

With the Renaissance the perfumer's art was revived with a vengeance. It was thought that sweet smells provided some protection against disease, but it was also acceptable once more for men and women to search openly for the erotic. Trade with the Orient provided spices and oils with which perfumes could be improved and the French court, for example, took to perfume with outrageous delight. Grasse became the world centre for flower cultivation and distillation and Paris became the fashion centre of the perfume industry, with perfumery and *haute couture* joining forces for the first time. It was even reported that the more sophisticated ladies acquired the art of scenting their farts.

Perfumes today are a blend made up from two main ingredients. First there are the essential oils which come from all over the world that are extracted from flowers, leaves, seeds, roots and barks. They can be very expensive, but when you consider that it takes an estimated 100 million rose petals to make a single pound of rose oil it is perhaps not surprising that the price of essential oils is sometimes high.

Oils can be obtained from plants in any one of several different ways. The oldest technique is simply to place sweet smelling flowers in fatty oils with the result that the oils take up the odours of the plants and can then be stored and used at leisure. This is called *enfleurage* and it is a technique usually used by home perfume makers today.

It was the Arabs who developed the technique of distilling ethyl alcohol from fermented sugar and who thereby provided a new solvent for extracting essential oils from plants. Distillation spread into Europe during the Middle Ages and medieval alchemists and pharmacists obtained oils from such raw materials as cedarwood, calamus, rosemary, incense, sage and cinnamon, materials often brought around the world along the spice routes from China, India and the West Indies. Distillation is still a favourite method of extraction and today leaves or flowers are put into sealed 1000-gallon containers with a solvent that is boiled away to leave a concentrated essential oil or essence.

Two other commonly used methods of extracting the perfume from a plant are maceration and expression. In the first, molten fat is used and in the second (used only for citrus fruits), the outer peel is squeezed in presses and then centrifuged.

The resultant essential oils vary in every way possible. Some evaporate easily while some do not, some hold their smell and some are less retentive. These variations are all used by the perfume maker. The cost of an oil depends upon the rarity of the original source and the cost of the extraction process. The cost of the oil extracted from jasmine, for example, is measured in hundreds of pounds whereas the cost of turpentine oil is measured in pence. Perfume prices obviously reflect these variations although no one would deny that the cost of raw materials makes up only a small part of the price of perfume.

In addition to the essential oils, perfumes contain fixatives. These help to slow the rate of evaporation of a perfume and to maintain the quality and character of a fragrance. The three main ones are ambergris, civet and musk – still the same as the ones used in ancient Egypt. Ambergris is extracted from the bones of the cuttlefish after they have been spat out by the sperm whale. These bony remnants float around in lumps in the Pacific Ocean, are powdered, soaked and stored for years before being used. Civet, which is said to have a rather nasty smell on its own, comes from the Abyssinian civet cat, while musk comes from the Himalayan musk deer.

And in case you may worry that these important ingredients sound limited in quantity let me reassure you that the chemists have produced synthetic reproductions of most essential oils and fixatives, although these reproductions are not necessarily cheaper than the 'real' thing.

Perfume itself (or *parfum* as the French and the francophiles call it) is the most powerful and concentrated product of this branch of the cosmetics industry. It is also, of course, the most expensive. Perfume extract (or *extrait*) may be even heavier but it is not as widely sold as perfume itself. Solid perfume is simply what the name suggests – it consists of a small box filled with perfumed heavy wax.

Lighter weight scents which need to be used more generously and which do not last as long can be obtained from such products as eau de toilette, eau de Cologne, toilet water, parfum de toilette and so on. Eau de Cologne, when first invented by Johann Maria Farina in 1709, was simply a blend of citrus oils; today it is a diluted perfume with added citrus oil base. Toilet water is usually slightly stronger than a cologne and is made by diluting the original perfume formula with alcohol. Unlike cologne it does not contain any citrus oil. Generally speaking the terms are interchangeable. Toilet waters and other lightweights are designed to be fresh on impact and to be short lived. Perfumes are longer acting and obviously more overpowering.

For the perfume industry toilet waters and other 'lightweights' are invaluable. They are cheaper to buy than perfumes and are often put on special offer so that a female customer can be tempted to buy; the manufacturer then hopes to sell the more expensive perfume to husband or boyfriend at Christmas or birthday time. Over the last ten years the perfume industry has slowly seen its market changing; cheaper travel and wider access to duty-free shops has meant that expensive, sophisticated, quality French perfumes are now taking up a larger and larger part of the annual £125 million women's fragrance market.

Although Paris is regarded as the heart of the perfume industry, New York is now its head, and today there are more perfumes marketed in the USA than in France. Marketing techniques are so well developed across the Atlantic that perfumery is dominated by the head rather than the heart.

Although many individual perfumes contain hundreds of constituents the results of the perfumer's work can be divided into olfactory families. According to an article by Peter Wörner, the senior perfumer of Haarmann & Reimer, published in *Manufacturing Chemist and Aerosol News* in 1980, there are ten main perfume families in America, each described according to the dominant notes in the perfume or by the name of a classic perfume which is a member of that family. For example, *Joy*, the expensive French perfume, is a member of the family described as having Flowery notes as is *Charlie*, the perfume which revitalized the world's perfume trade in 1973. Many classical French perfumes such as *Chanel No. 5*, *Arpège*, *Je Reviens* and *Madame Rochas*, are members of the aldehyde family. (Incidentally those four perfumes are all very well established for an industry that thrives on innovation. *Chanel No. 5* was introduced in 1921, *Arpège* in 1927, *Je Reviens* in 1932 and *Madame Rochas* in 1960.) Men's perfumes often contain strong Woody notes or Tobacco and Leather notes although *Brut* is a member of the Fougère family which takes its name from the perfume *Fougère Royale* created in 1882. *Old Spice*, introduced in 1937 when few men considered using perfume, is a member of the Oriental family and like its relatives has an intensive, long-lasting smell.

Whatever the perfume family name the more immediate, volatile odours of a perfume are usually described as the head or top notes, whereas the solid, middle-of-the-range odours are known as the middle or heart notes and the less volatile and more persistent odours are known as the base or lower notes.

When they get round to describing the individual qualities and strengths of finished perfumes the olfactophilists produce reviews which make the dreamiest ravings of oenophilists sound crude and prosaic.

For example, in a trade journal I found a perfume called *Anaïs*

Anaïs described as 'a blend of luxurious floral notes composed of natural essences underpinned with woodier notes of vetiver, patchouli, mousse de chêne from Yugoslavia and cuir de Russie' while in *CTP Marketing* a perfume called *Metal* from Paco Rabanne was described as a 'wondrous fragrance with an astonishing presence'. Revlon's copywriters say of a perfume called *Ivoire de Balmain* that 'the warm sensuous dry out is the key to this fragrance's diffusive tenacity'.

Macasser, a new fragrance from Rochas designed for men, has been described in *Cosmetic World News* as 'woody, dry, intense with a floral hint' while *Versailles Pour Homme* is described as follows: 'strong top note of black pepper, coriander and nutmeg mingles with the freshness of lemon and bergamot and then gives way to a harmonious blend of woody notes of pine tree needles and sandalwood and flowery notes of rose, jasmin and ylang-ylang'.

Worth say of *Je Reviens* that the 'fresh green top note of orange, lemon and bergamot, mysteriously mellows into the well loved and lingering warm smoky undertones'.

Despite the technical terminology, however, when it comes down to it most perfumes are bought because of their overall effect – an image created by smell, packaging and advertising. The simple truth is that for the consumer there is no way to classify perfumes other than into one of two categories: expensive and too expensive. The important thing then is to make the best of the perfume you have chosen.

Making the best of perfume When choosing perfume you should not test more than two products in one day otherwise you'll confuse your sense of smell.

To test the staying power of perfume you have tested sniff at half-hourly intervals after testing. For this reason it is wise to apply a test spray to the inside of the wrist.

The experts say that when buying a perfume you should buy it on your own; if you choose with a friend by your side you'll probably end up buying a perfume that your friend likes.

When you have chosen a brand you like don't buy too large a bottle. Perfume evaporates and may even 'turn' after a while, and that £450 bargain bottle may not turn out to be such a good buy after all. Besides, if you buy smaller bottles you may be able to build up a fragrance wardrobe to suit your needs and moods.

If you like a fragrance marketed for men there is no reason why you shouldn't wear it. Greta Garbo is said to wear *Monsieur de Givenchy*, though I couldn't check that rumour!

When using perfume apply it sparingly (toilet waters and so on can be applied more generously).

It is said that perfume should be applied to the pulse points – that is the wrists, the inside of the elbows, behind the ear and behind the knees – but I know of no real reason for this apart from the fact that it does provide some arbitrary control over the use of potentially overpowering perfume.

It is important to remember not to combine perfumes and this means that you should bathe or shower before changing perfumes and that you should use unperfumed soap, talc and deodorant or choose products perfumed with your favourite smell.

Perfume needs to be reapplied after a few hours. Few perfumes last more than four hours. Remember that the human nose 'tires' quickly, however, and that long after you can no longer smell your perfume others will be aware of it.

Keep perfume bottles fastened tightly to avoid evaporation and keep them away from the sun and the heat.

Don't hoard perfume – it will only go off.

If you find perfume a little heavy for day-time use then try using toilet water or eau de Cologne.

If you are allergic to a favourite perfume you may be able to wear it on your clothes, but do remember to wash your clothes afterwards otherwise they will retain the stale perfume. Perfume is said to develop better on natural fibres. Remember that jewellery can be spoilt if accidentally sprayed with some perfumes, so put on your perfume first.

If you keep a tablet of perfumed soap in your lingerie drawer make sure it has the same perfume you are using and is not a competing scent.

SKIN PROBLEMS

Introduction

A recent survey which involved the impressive number of 20,749 Americans showed that nearly a third of them had at least one skin condition which needed medical advice. Another study done in London was slightly more reassuring: that suggested that only one in four needed medical help for a skin disease. A family doctor has estimated that about one in every ten consultations concerns a skin problem.

There is obviously a lot of skin disease around and I'm afraid that not even the most enthusiastic advocate of modern medicine could argue that the advances made in therapeutics have done more than scratch the surface of the problem. Indeed many would argue that developments in pharmacology have caused more skin problems than they have cured since undoubtedly the incidence of iatrogenic skin disease is higher now than it ever has been.

On the other hand, there have always been natural environmental threats to the skin. The damage done by the sun is discussed on p. 227 where I have outlined some of the ways in which sun damage can be minimized, while on p. 158 I have described the importance of using an effective moisturizer to prevent the loss of water from the skin when it is exposed to the sun, wind and air conditioning. Today's moisturizer, however, has to do more than prevent water loss. The air in and around all major cities, and indeed even the countryside, is polluted by chemicals of many kinds. There are industrial waste products, insecticides, and so on lying in the air waiting to be brought to earth by the next shower. The sulphur- and nitrogen-containing compounds in the air are partly converted into acid either before or when they hit the skin's surface and the damage can be enormous. If you live in a large city you only have to look around at the eroded stone and metal of fairly new buildings to see just how powerful these airborne chemicals are. The Parthenon in Athens is being destroyed by modern pollutants. Countryfolk who have noticed that fish are less numerous than they once were may blame local factories who pump their waste products into upwater rivers, but the blame may lie with companies, and even road traffic, hundreds of miles away who allow sulphur and nitrogen gases to pollute the air, drift, and later fall as acid rain. Clean Air Acts and local by-laws are of little use since the fines imposed on those responsible are petty compared to the potential cost of preventing the pollution. So that is another problem our skins have to face.

All these pollutants make the use of moisturizers that much more important. You need your moisturizer these days not just to stop your skin losing water but also to provide some protection from the acid rain.

Some skin problems are affected by sex hormones. Male hormones make the epidermis thicker and the sebaceous glands larger while they also influence the production of sebum and the loss of scalp hair. Female hormones make the epidermis thinner, more delicate and consequently more likely to wrinkle and age, while they also influence the deposition of fat to make thighs, bottoms and breasts more noticeable. The effect of sex hormones on the development of acne is discussed on p. 176.

Despite the undoubted importance of environmental-pollutants and other damaging irritants there is no doubt that three of the biggest skin problems today are skin infections, eczema and warts although acne, allergies and psoriasis also cause a significant amount of disease. These particular problems are discussed on other pages in this book and often the careful, thoughtful patient can do more for himself, particularly in the early stages of his condition, than any medical practitioner can do.

Finally, I think it is vital to point out that skin cancer can and does occur and that it is treatable if caught at an early stage. Any lesion which is inexplicable, which bleeds or is worrying should be seen by a doctor and any mole, birthmark or similar lesion which bleeds, changes in colour or size or does anything else exceptional needs to be seen without delay.

Acne
It is too easy to underestimate the importance of acne and to forget that even aggressive modern youth can suffer mental agonies. I recently saw a young punk in my surgery who arrived with his hair dyed a variety of colours and cut to a number of different lengths, with his ears festooned with safety pins and his clothes slashed and pinned together. Like so many teenagers before him he was desperately worried by the fact that he had a mild acne condition. Fashions change but basic anxieties do not.

The manufacturers of cosmetics and toiletries are as aware of this as anyone, and the number of products sold for the treatment and prevention of acne seems to grow each month. Indeed, the market for products of this kind actually seems to be growing and one recent survey suggested that today four out of every five people in the thirteen to twenty-four age group have acne, spots or other similar problems.

The pressures on the young consumer are often tremendous. According to *Cosmetic World News* for example, one company alone, Richardson-Merrell, planned a total expenditure of £1.6 million on television advertising for their acne products. Further promotional expenditure was expected to take the total budget well over £2 million, all destined to be spent on the three products this company makes for the treatment of problem skin. These products are *Clearasil Clearguard*, *Topex* and *Biactol*.

Understanding the way in which spots form is quite naturally a vital basis for knowing how to prevent or deal with spots and how to cope with what the copywriters coyly call 'problem skin'. In the section on the anatomy of human skin I have already described (p. 148) the skin's special glands which continually produce a substance called sebum to help keep the epidermis moist and supple. When that substance is in short supply for any reason the skin becomes dry and scaly but when the sebum is available in excessive quantities then the skin becomes greasy and oily to the touch.

The production of sebum is increased by a number of factors but one of the most important influences is a rise in sex hormones. In men the hormone is the one which is responsible for the development of male patterns of hair growth and for the development of a deep voice and other secondary sexual characteristics. In women the hormone concerned is the one which helps to trigger menstrual flow. It is the relationship between the relatively sudden increase in the availability of sex hormone and the consequent increase in the amount of sebum secreted which explains the high incidence of greasy skin amongst teenagers.

An increase in the level of circulating sex hormones and the secretion of sebum are not the only changes which occur during adolescence. There are also changes in the anatomy of the skin, the outer, horny layer of which gets thicker while the skin pores tend to dilate on certain parts of the body. On the face, for example, the pores in the middle of the forehead, on the nose and the chin often dilate.

Problems arise and acne develops if the ducts through which the sebum travels from the sebaceous glands to the skin's surface become blocked. Dead skin cells are the commonest cause of a blockage and when these have been stuck for a while in a duct they turn black – producing blackheads. Later they may become infected, producing red, swollen acne spots.

The treatment of acne and of spotty skin in general has much in common with the treatment of greasy skin since, after all, the basic problems are similar. If an acne sufferer could reduce the production of sebum the chances of his skin pores being blocked would be greatly reduced.

Unfortunately, there is no simple way in which the production of skin oils can be cut back. It would, in theory, be quite possible to prevent boys developing acne by preventing the production of male hormone within their bodies but unhappily this would mean that the price for acne-free skin would be rather high: not many sufferers would be prepared to become eunuchs to avoid getting spotty skin. Simpler, more mechanical solutions have to be sought.

The obvious way to remove oil from the skin is to wipe it away but as those with greasy hair quickly discover to their cost this isn't always an effective solution. What tends to happen is that the faster you wash and wipe away the grease the faster your body struggles to replace it. Your body thinks it's doing the right thing since it is simply struggling to maintain the *status quo* and to provide the skin with an essential protective layer of moisturizing cream. Using emulsions of oil in water or water in oil to help remove the excess sebum simply inspires the sebaceous glands to pump out more oil. Similarly if you use an alcohol-based skin tonic or astringent to wash the skin the glands will simply replace what oils have been lost.

Clearly, if we regard oily skin as a problem that needs to be solved we're doomed to disappointment. There isn't going to be any simple, perfect solution because we're going to keep coming up against the human body's extraordinary ability to protect itself.

But, in fact, oily skin can, if treated properly, be a blessing rather than a problem. (Oily, greasy hair is something else and I discuss this problem on p. 132). Maintaining a thin layer of oil on the surface of the skin is an essential part of skin care and this is exactly what moisturizing creams and lotions do. The oil helps to prevent the loss of water from the skin and therefore helps to prevent the development of dryness. The fact that oily skin is prone to form spots is a hazard but not an insuperable one and the solution is perhaps not to combat the oiliness but to protect against the de-

velopment of spots. Excess oiliness can be removed temporarily
with a tissue or a premoistened packaged cleanser or with soap and
water.

Before I discuss some of the useful ways in which spots can be
prevented I'll describe some of the myths which have risen up
around the subject of acne.

It is sometimes said, for example, that diet plays an important
part in the development of spots. Fatty foods and sweet things such
as chocolate have in the past often been listed as causing acne, but
experts now seem to agree that there is no evidence at all linking
food of any kind with spotty skin. It is also said that a shortage or
surfeit of sex can make acne worse and that too is nonsense. The
development of acne is certainly linked to the quantity of sex
hormone circulating in a body and in so far as a eunuch is unlikely
to enjoy many sexual experiences there is, I suppose, a link between
sex and acne, but the relationship is between an uncontrollable
hormone level and the skin, not between satyriasis, nymphomania
or frigidity and the skin.

Another common myth is that the skin pores can be opened and
closed by specific products and that by doing this those products
control the formation of blackheads or comedones. This again is
nonsense since pores themselves cannot be opened or shut like
doors. Products which irritate the skin and which cause localized
swelling of the tissues may temporarily close the pores but that is
all. I would suggest that you ignore all advertisements which claim
that such and such a product will help you control your pores since
the irritants which can cause the necessary skin swelling may also
stimulate the formation of additional oils.

A number of manufacturers selling skin care products for spot
and acne sufferers have produced and are perpetuating myths of
their own.

There are, for example, a good many products which contain
antiseptics as main ingredients and which are promoted as being
particularly suitable for acne sufferers. I don't believe that this is
wise, realistic or fair since acne itself is not primarily an infectious
disease. Using an antiseptic cream or liquid may help partly dis-
infect the skin but it cannot possibly remove all bacteria and it will
have no effect on the accumulation of sebum and dead cells in the
ducts of sebaceous glands. It is the blocking of these glands that

causes acne and spots and antiseptics aren't going to help prevent this. For this reason I do not recommend such products as *TCP Liquid Antiseptic* which is claimed to be 'today's most used spot treatment' or *Spotoway* which is said to contain 'powerful, hospital proved antiseptics'. There are antiseptic soaps available too and I don't recommend them either. Antiseptics are unlikely in my opinion to do very much to prevent the development of blackheads but they could cause skin irritations and allergies.

As for the 'magic' remedies sold by some of the herbal specialists – I can think of nothing useful to say. Products such as *Blood Purifying Tablets* which are said to 'assist in clearing the blood of impurities in the case of boils, pimples, etc.' are of no medical value at all in my view.

So much for the myths and misconceptions. Now for some facts and for some ways in which acne can be prevented.

Spot control

1 Long hair which hangs over the skin can make acne worse. Since greasy skin is often accompanied by greasy hair and since long hair is difficult to manage and keep grease free, a shorter style is often an important prelude to healthy skin and healthy hair.
2 The evidence about sunshine (and indeed ultraviolet light in general) and acne is rather confusing. Some experts believe that sunlight makes spotty skin worse but on balance I think that the opposite is probably true. Ultraviolet light (whether from the sun or from a lamp) encourages skin peeling and that should help to clear blocked ducts.
3 If you can prevent pores being blocked by sebum and dead cells then you will prevent the development of blackheads. Do that and acne is a non-starter. The simplest way to keep the pores clear is to wash the skin regularly with a rather rough abrasive of some kind. It does not matter whether this is a rough face-cloth, a cleansing paste such as *Brasivol*, a special cleansing sponge such as *Buf-puf*, or even a fairly soft brush. You can buy an electric face cleanser such as the *Pifco Facial Brush* to do very much the same sort of job if you don't have the energy to clean your own face. (I think that electric toothbrushes can be useful since they manage movements and positions many people find difficult, but I don't believe that

electric face cleansers offer much more than novelty.) Some
with a taste for the unusual recommend using almonds ground
with milk, orange peel or strawberries as abrasives. If they
seem to work and you like them, then use them.

4 Sometimes simple abrasives don't clear out the pores
thoroughly enough. When this is the problem then a
keratolytic can be used with great success. There are a number
of useful products on the market which peel away blackheads
to unblock the pores. Resorcinol is a basic ingredient of a
number of preparations such as *Acnil, Avrogel, Clearasil
Cream Medication, DDD Lotion, Eskamel, Medac Acne
Cream, pHiso-Ac, Vanispot* and *Wigglesworth Acne Cream*.
Salicylic acid is another keratolytic which is present in
substances such as *Avrogel, Clearasil Cleansing Lotion,
Dermaclear* and *DDD Lotion*. A third keratolytic substance,
benzoyl peroxide, is obtainable as *Benoxyl 5* and *Benoxyl 10,
Dry Clear Acne Lotion, Panoxyl 5 Acne Gel* and *Panoxyl 10
Acne Gel, Quinoderm* and *Vanair*. You may be able to buy
non-branded versions of some of these products. Resorcinol is
available as *Compound Resorcinol Ointment BPC* or *Resorcinol
and Sulphur Paste BPC*. Salicylic acid is available as *Salicylic
Acid and Sulphur Cream BPC*. These fairly harmless products
should prove powerful enough for most young blackheads.
More dramatic abrasives are sometimes offered by
dermatologists, plastic surgeons and beauty specialists to those
who have particularly badly affected or scarred skin. Both
chemical and mechanical abrasives are used to remove top
layers of skin entirely but these remedies are only suitable for
extremely bad skin afflictions and my recommendation is that
they should only be used under medical supervision. I do not
approve of beauty therapists or others without medical training
using such potentially hazardous techniques. Incidentally
beauty parlours also sometimes offer electrical treatments,
vacuum suction and ozone steaming techniques to open or
cleanse the pores. I think you are wasting your money if you
spend it on short-term treatments of this kind which can at
best provide only temporary help.

5 Whether or not blackheads should be squeezed may not sound
like a major question of our time but it has probably been
asked and answered more times than many questions with

deeper philosophical meaning. I think the simple answer is that if an uninfected blackhead can be removed then it is probably better to remove it although it is important to ensure that the skin of the face and hands is washed first. If warm water is used then the blackhead will probably be easier to remove, Chemists sell comedone expressors but finger nails are, if used with care, probably just as effective and safe. Infected spots should never be squeezed, of course, since by doing so you can easily spread the infection and make things worse and comedones which are closed (and which appear as whiteheads) shouldn't be squeezed either since there is no exit through which the block of sebum and dead cells can escape.

6 Women who take the contraceptive pill may find that their spots get worse since, as I've already described, there is a real relationship between hormone levels and the condition of the skin. The hormone in the contraceptive pill that usually causes the problems is progesterone. A woman who thinks that her skin has got worse since she's started to take the pill should discuss the problem with the doctor who prescribed it for her.

7 Teenagers and those with greasy skin are best advised to avoid wearing too much make-up. Thick foundations, cream, pastes, powders and so on block pores and make the development of spots more likely. If spots do develop then the avoidance of make-up will help speed their disappearance.

8 When spots have become badly infected, then a doctor's advice should be sought. Long-term antibiotic therapy is often extremely effective in the prevention of and treatment of acne and infected skin.

Allergies

It may appear rather trite and simplistic to say that there is no substance in the world to which someone, somewhere, will not one day develop an allergy reaction. But it is, nevertheless, quite true.

Each Christmas I see a large number of people suffering from allergy reactions to presents they have been given. Mums turn up with nasty red rashes in the places where they have sprayed the new perfumes they have been given, Dads arrive embarrassed by the red raw patches under their armpits where they have sprayed their deodorants and there are always one or two patients with telltale allergy rashes caused by new items of underwear.

There are usually a few patients who have turned out to be allergic to new items of jewellery too and these are invariably the most upset. If you're allergic to a new pair of ear-rings, a necklace, or, even worse, a new ring, then the chances are high that you're going to remain allergic to it.

Naturally, allergies are not confined to the Christmas season. In the summer there are those who find that they are allergic to sun tan lotions and creams, moisturizers and artificial tanning aids. Indeed, the summer months are particularly hazardous since the sun itself can combine with many previously guiltless items to produce a rash.

I had hoped to be able to include a list of all the substances which are most likely to cause allergy reactions. I abandoned this idea for several reasons.

First, there are so many substances known to cause allergy reactions that such a list would be meaningless. It would be too long to be of practical use.

Second, products change so quickly that it would not be possible to identify more than a small proportion of potential troublemakers in a book.

Third, and most important, the vast majority of companies just will not reveal what their products contain. The reasons for this are discussed earlier in this book (p. 40), but I must repeat that this is an attitude which is so outdated that it cannot last long. I am convinced that in the near future all companies will find themselves having to make available product contents in the same way that pharmaceutical companies do now.

All major companies make some effort and test their products on animals and volunteers to ensure that the incidence of allergic reactions is kept as low as possible. No company wants to acquire a reputation for making customers blotchy. But only a relatively small proportion of companies make a real effort by limiting product constituents and then publishing the ingredients so that customers can check at a glance for potential allergens.

Those companies that do make a particular effort to reduce the risk of reactions usually describe their products as 'hypoallergenic'. Literally that just means that they are less likely to cause allergies. Some companies claim to produce non-allergenic products but this is a nonsense and I should steer clear of these companies. If they are prepared to exaggerate in this way how can you trust them at all? The fact is that no one can produce a cosmetic that is guaranteed not to cause an allergy reaction. People have even been reported as developing allergies to water and you can't imagine anything much more bland than that!

Most of the careful manufacturers of hypoallergenic products simply cut down on fragrances and colourings. Ordinary products contain 50, 100 or even more separate constituents, so it isn't difficult to produce a product with less than the average number of potential allergens. To a certain extent it is quite true that the complexity of a product is a measure of its allergenicity. If a product contains a large number of constituents there are a lot of potential irritants.

Queen Cosmetics Limited claim to have been the first company in the history of the cosmetics industry to have developed and launched on to the United Kingdom market a range of cosmetics specially designed for women needing hypoallergenic products. Work began on the first products in 1927 and the earliest hypoallergenic cosmetics available were lipsticks, face powders and skin care products.

Today there are a number of other well known companies which specialize in the production and sale of hypoallergenic products. The Albion Soap Company produce *Simple Soap* and a whole range of matching products while RoC, which claims that one woman in three has experienced an allergy to a beauty product, claims to be the top French brand of hypoallergenic make-up and skin care products.

Almay, first introduced in America in 1934, is another well known company which specializes in this field. In an attempt to drag the cosmetics industry into the twentieth century Almay have begun promoting their products to dermatologists and general practitioners, offering detailed information about manufacturing processes and product formulations so that doctors can, where necessary, recommend products which are least likely to cause trouble.

Clinique and Academie are other companies making hypoallergenic products, but this list is by no means exhaustive.

If in the past you have suffered from allergy reactions to cosmetics there are several things you can do to minimize the risk, inconvenience and potential danger.

Buy products made by companies which specialize in catering for the allergy prone individual and then stick to the products you like as much as possible. If you are buying something new then buy a small quantity to begin with and don't try it on just before a big occasion. If you use a new perfume for an important date and develop a red blotchy face you'll wish you hadn't. When testing in a store make a note of the products you've tried.

If you like you can patch test new products on yourself. Impregnate a small piece of gauze with the cosmetic you're trying out, fix it to your skin with a small piece of sticking plaster and leave it in position for forty-eight hours. It doesn't matter where you stick it as long as you can inspect the result afterwards. If you find, when you remove the plaster, that you have developed an itchy, blotchy red rash then you'd be well advised to give the rest of the bottle away to someone else although if it is perfume you're allergic to you can, if you like, try putting it on to your clothes rather than your skin. That way you might get away with using the product.

It is important when buying products described as hypoallergenic to buy in small quantities since these products sometimes do not contain preservatives and this may mean that they will not last as long without becoming infected.

If you have had allergy problems in the past then you should be particularly careful with depilatories, hair wave lotions and hair straighteners, bleaches of all kind, nail enamels, hair colourants and perfumes. It is partly because perfumes are such common causes of allergy reaction that I recommend that whenever possible unperfumed cosmetics should be selected.

Remember that you do not need to use a large quantity of any substance to which you are allergic in order to develop a reaction. A minute quantity hidden in a product with hundreds of other constituents can be quite enough to trigger off a severe reaction.

It is also vitally important to remember that once you have acquired an allergy to a particular product or chemical you are likely to retain that allergy. Once your body has acquired its antibodies it doesn't lose them. If you once develop an allergy to strawberries, penicillin or *Chanel No. 5* it means, I'm afraid, that you're probably stuck with the allergy.

Another point which many people find confusing is the fact that allergies can develop after years of trouble-free use. I've often seen patients who have acquired allergies to favourite products who have been most indignant when I've suggested that a particular deodorant might be responsible for their rash.

'But I've used it for ten years!' they'll exclaim. 'I've never had any trouble before.'

That doesn't mean a thing I'm afraid. You can develop an allergy to a product at eighty even if you've been using it all your life. It isn't likely, but you can.

Finally, you don't have to have sensitive, delicate skin to develop an allergy. I've seen hefty bricklayers with skin as thick as tanned leather who have developed skin allergies to soaps and shampoos.

Birthmarks

Most of us have one or two birthmarks hidden away somewhere. If we are fortunate only our nearest and dearest will know their precise location. The less fortunate, however, may have very obvious and disfiguring marks which can cause much distress both to the individual concerned and to his or her relatives.

Contrary to popular belief not all birthmarks are present at birth and not all remain for ever unchanged. The type of mark known to doctors as a cavernous haemangioma, for example, may only appear a week or two after a baby's birth.

The popular name for this type of birthmark is a strawberry mark and for once the name is genuinely and usefully descriptive. The mark is usually bright red or even pink and it is clearly raised above the level of the skin so that it almost looks like a strawberry struggling to emerge from captivity.

These marks can appear anywhere on the body and for the first few months of a child's life they continue to grow in size. They look quite dramatic and are, inevitably, very worrying for young parents who may never have seen such a thing before. The good news about these lesions is that they usually fade either partially or completely over the years. By the age of ten most will have disappeared completely. The natural history of these birthmarks means that they do not usually need any treatment, either surgical or cosmetic.

Another common type of mark is the capillary haemangioma and again the popular name given to the mark is descriptive. These lesions are known as port wine stains, and since they are flat and purple in colour they do look as if they have been made by the spilling of some rich red liquid. They occur most commonly on the face, usually affecting one side only.

Unlike strawberry birthmarks the port wine stains do not fade with time. The only effective remedy is to use cosmetic camouflage creams since surgical treatments are by no means always successful. My advice to anyone contemplating paying for treatment for a port wine stain is to ask for your family doctor's advice. If there has been any miraculous discovery in the last week or two that makes treatment a real possibility then he will be able to assess the evidence, even if he hasn't heard of the treatment. As I've described on p. 69 I do not recommend paying anyone for plastic surgery of any kind unless your own doctor has arranged the referral.

These two are the commonest types of birthmarks. However, there are many more possible types of marks, the most dramatic of which perhaps being the congenital pigmented naevus (known as a bathing trunk naevus). This is like a very large common mole with the skin being very thick, deeply pigmented and perhaps hairy. As the name suggests it usually covers part or all of the region of the body which used, in more modest times, to be covered by a standard bathing costume.

Birthmarks and moles can, occasionally, be dangerous. They do from time to time develop into skin cancer. Because of this admittedly slight, but nevertheless real, risk I do recommend that anyone who has a skin lesion which has either changed in size, bled or altered in any other way should see a doctor for advice without delay. By that I mean that advice should be sought that day and not in a week or ten days' time. When discovered early, skin cancer is one of the most curable of cancers. When left late, it is one of the most dangerous.

Although this section is headed 'Birthmarks' there are other types of skin mark which ought to be included here. In pregnancy, for example, some women develop brown marks on their skin. These most commonly affect brunettes and they usually affect the face and breasts although they can appear anywhere on the body. These markings are an extension of the type of skin pigmentation which usually affects the areola and vulva of pregnant women. Since women who are taking the contraceptive pill are physiologically pregnant they too are likely to get these brown marks. The marks usually fade after the birth of the baby (or after stopping taking the contraceptive pill). If they don't, it is probably worth seeing a doctor but I'm afraid he is likely to have to recommend a masking cream. The sun can make these marks worse, by the way.

There are several disorders which cause the skin to become lighter in patches. There is at the moment no effective way to treat this problem and again a masking cream is likely to provide the best cosmetic solution to the problem.

There have over the centuries been many attempts made to deal with skin blemishes effectively. Some of the remedies have involved turning the blemish into a feature. Smallpox scars were disguised, for example, by covering them with black beauty spots. Other remedies have simply involved the use of camouflage creams.

The development of these creams in recent years has been a result of cooperation between a number of different groups, but undoubtedly the efforts of the British Red Cross Society have been important. They have run a Beauty Care Service for people in hospitals and homes for a number of years and recently a member who had trained as stage make-up artist and had worked as a Red Cross beautician showed, by working with a plastic surgeon in London, that people with skin blemishes and scars can very much improve their appearance by the correct and careful use of cosmetics.

Today a number of specialist beauticians have been trained by the Red Cross Society and many work with consultant dermatologists and specialist plastic surgeons. Many have been happy to report that patients who have used their services have benefited considerably and enjoyed much greater social success. The Red Cross Society will undoubtedly give information about where their specialists are working and if your doctor would like to refer you to the correct department, but doesn't know where to send you, he can find a list of the hospitals where Red Cross cosmeticians are operating in *Health Trends, 1980*, Volume 12.

The products doctors usually prescribe to camouflage scars, birthmarks and other abnormalities include *Keromask*, *Covermark*, *Boots Cover Cream* and *Veil Cover Cream*. These are all waterproof, and a specialist can help advise how best to mix different colours to produce a cream that matches the patient's own skin most effectively. Red Cross cosmeticians are taught how to highlight good features in order to draw attention away from blemishes. Camouflage creams are, of course, used on men and children as well as on women and they can be used on tattoos, freckles, visible veins and other skin abnormalities.

The products named above can be bought without prescription of course, although they may have to be ordered specially for you by the chemist. Some beauty therapists who are not associated with the health service will have been trained in the use of these creams and they too will have access to the products.

Generally speaking, camouflage creams should be used in small quantities and should be tapped or patted into position. Once they are in place ordinary make-up can be added on top of them.

In addition to the basic camouflage creams there are products available which are said to help brown spots fade away. Boots sell a product called *Fade Out* and Frances Denney make a cream called *Fade Away*.

One of the most important active ingredients of products such as *Fade Out* is hydroquinone, a powerful chemical which can remove pigmentation from the skin. This constituent is so powerful that it can actually turn dark-skinned individuals white. The major problem with hydroquinone is that the effect is irreversible and the result not always pleasing. It is quite possible to produce 'patchy' depigmentation and that can be nothing short of a cosmetic disaster. Additional problems include the fact that the skin may become unusually sensitive to the sun and indeed to other stimulants in general.

I do not believe that any product containing hydroquinone should be bought over the counter since the effects can be very far reaching. If you want to try a permanent skin 'bleach' then you should consult a doctor first.

Body odour

The smell of a sweaty body can be pretty repulsive. A friend of mine at medical school chose to study psychiatry simply because he couldn't stand the smell of people without their socks on and psychiatry was the only speciality he knew of where he could practise without having to undress his patients.

Although it may sometimes be difficult to remember, we do sweat for a very good reason, sweating being part of the body's complex temperature control mechanism. If you doubt this just remember how much more you sweat when the weather is hot or when you have a high temperature due to an infection. Not all sweat is produced for this reason, there are sweat glands which are influenced by other factors such as worry and stress, but when the sweat is dripping off your body in rivulets the chances are high that your body is working overtime to maintain a stable internal temperature. A loss of fluid means a loss of heat. In cool weather you may lose a litre of sweat a day; on a hot day you can lose a litre an hour.

Sweat itself doesn't smell since it consists of water together with odourless waste products such as urea. The smell is produced by the breaking down of these products by the bacteria which live on the skin in vast numbers. There are, so the bacteriologists insist, something like 100,000 microbes to the square centimetre on the average stretch of skin and getting rid of all of them is impossible. Mind you, it is perhaps just as well that we cannot get rid of them without destroying the skin since they are vital members of the body's defences. It is these resident bacteria which help to fight off invading bacteria. Kill off the local bacteria and the enemy gets a clear run at the body. (This balanced symbiosis is exemplified best of all in the vagina where the resident bacteria help to make vaginal secretions acidic. These acidic secretions prevent other bacteria surviving there. The magnificence of this defence mechanism can be seen when you realize that after puberty the vaginal walls secrete glycogen which is broken down by the local bacteria to produce the acid. This means that during the body's fertile years the vagina is protected against infection. When the local bacteria are killed off by antibiotics or by local sprays, vaginal infections are common.)

Although most of us may be embarrassed by the smell produced when we perspire, scientists have recently done some work which suggests that our individual smells have a real purpose of their own. Numerous special perfumes or pheromones produced by animals and insects have been studied and it has been found that different creatures use specific pheromones to help them gather food, attract sexual partners, mark the extent of their territory, warn others of impending danger and to establish pecking orders. Anthropologist Louis Leakey has been reported as having suggested that body odour was an important human defence mechanism in the days when man was likely to be eaten on the way back from a hunting trip. The smell, he claims, put off most predators.

A psychologist at the University of Chicago has shown that

women who live together tend to acquire menstrual patterns which match, and a researcher at San Francisco State University has produced evidence which strongly suggests that the pattern of a woman's menstrual cycle is influenced by the odours of women around her.

There is even evidence that human smells do have a genuinely sexual value. For example, researchers have shown that secretions from the vagina of a non-ovulating woman were rated as neutral or mildly unpleasant whereas secretions from the vagina of ovulating women were rated as pleasant by men and bland by women.

The first antiperspirants were dilute alcoholic solutions of aluminium chlorhydrate. These solutions were applied first with a sponge and then later they were made available in cream and stick form. Aluminium products and their derivatives are still considered to be the safest and most effective antiperspirants. Although the evidence is not conclusive, they seem to work by blocking the sweat ducts and shouldn't be used in very hot climates since if a blocked gland continues to secrete sweat, the duct may rupture, spilling sweat into the surrounding tissues and causing inflammation. It is also important not to use an antiperspirant over too large an area of the body. The unfortunate heroine in the film *Goldfinger* died because her skin was denied the opportunity to lose any sweat at all. Incidentally, since antiperspirants work by blocking sweat pores there is no point in using an antiperspirant directly after bathing – the pores of the skin are closed then and the effectiveness of the product will be greatly reduced.

Deodorants contain a mild germicide which is designed to interfere with the bacterial activity in sweat. In addition to the germicide most deodorants also contain a perfume which is simply added to disguise whatever body smell does develop.

Most of the sprays and roll-ball applicators on the market today contain an antiperspirant to help cut down the production of sweat, a deodorant to reduce the odour produced by the sweat that does appear on the skin and a perfume to disguise whatever smell is made.

Manufacturers believe strongly in the importance of an added perfume and they claim that customers usually unfasten and sniff doedorants before buying them. Consequently they tend to add strong-smelling perfume to their deodorants although it seems just as likely to an innocent observer that women are sniffing deodorants to make sure that they don't have a powerful aroma of their own which is going to compete with that of their favourite perfume. Whatever the truth, it is now a fact that some deodorants are made without added perfume to avoid this unpleasant clash of smells. *Arrid Extra Dry* is, for example, advertised as smelling of your favourite perfume – it is unscented. The companies which specialize in hypoallergenic products tend to make unscented deodorants too.

The deodorant market is said to be worth something like £50 million a year so it is hardly surprising that there are a good many different products on the market.

In the early 1970s aerosols were particularly popular but roll-on deodorants have taken over for four reasons. First, aerosols are costly. Second, roll-ons are more effective since the deodorant is applied directly to the skin rather than being squirted over the bathroom. Third, it has become widely known that aerosols can pollute the atmosphere. Fourth, aerosols are more likely to sting and burn when applied. Today, *Mum* is said to be the biggest-selling deodorant on the market with *Sure* and *Right Guard* in second and third places, and all three are available as roll-ons. Men are said to prefer aerosols and stick deodorants, while women prefer the roll-on products.

There are of course other ways to prevent body odour in addition to the use of antiperspirants and deodorants.

Talcs and dusting powders may help and if they include a germicide they will have a deodorant affect as well as an antiperspirant action. *Arrid Light Powder*, for example, is said to puff a light absorbent talc on to the skin.

Some top-selling soaps contain deodorizing agents, although I don't see that these products offer any great advantage over washing well with an ordinary soap.

If you do sweat a lot remember that natural fabrics such as silk and cotton are cooler than synthetics which restrict the evaporation of perspiration and which therefore inhibit the body's own cooling mechanisms, while loose sleeves and loose-fitting clothes are much more comfortable and much cooler than tight-fitting clothes. Drinking the right type of fluids can help too; very hot or very cold drinks can make you sweat more but cool drinks, without ice, seem to be just right.

When feet are the major problem there are a number of suitable products on the market. Scholl make a *Foot Refresher Spray* and a *Dry Powder Spray* which covers the skin with a layer of powder. Deodorant sprays and insoles help by killing some bacteria and absorbing sweat.

The most effective remedy for a perspiration problem, however, is not to use any special deodorant or antiperspirant. It is simply to wash regularly with a plain soap, to dry carefully and thoroughly and to change clothes as often as possible.

Final Note Sweating may be an embarrassment and an irritation to all of us but to some people it is more than that. In a condition known as hyperhidrosis the amount of sweat produced (usually by the glands which are present in large numbers and in the armpits) is so great that ordinary deodorants and antiperspirants are quite ineffective. The production of sweat has been measured as high as 12 g per hour per armpit. Doctors can help this condition in several ways. First, and most simply, they may prescribe a product such as *Anhydrol Forte*, a roll-on which allows the application of a very thin layer of concentrated aluminium chloride hexahydrate to the skin in the armpit. Cosmetic preparations contain a very diluted version of this product which is so powerful that it can cause skin irritation. Second, an operation can be performed to remove the sweat glands.

Breast improvers

Since the number of women seeking breast augmentation is probably larger than the number whose complaint is of a surfeit of tissue, I'll start with the alleged remedies available for these consumers. But first let me start with some common fears and myths.

Few women seem to realize that breasts, like all paired organs, tend to vary slightly in shape and size but that this is not in itself medically or even cosmetically abnormal or undesirable unless the difference is extreme. Activity contributes to the variation, and it has been suggested that whereas professional right-handed women tennis players will usually develop larger right breasts, professional typists will usually develop larger left breasts since the left hand is usually used to control the carriage lever.

Next, I think that it is important that all women should understand that it is quite natural for the well developed female breast to droop a little under the influence of gravity. The teenage bosom, as seen on the pages of men's magazines and some newspapers, will usually have begun to sag before its owner sees another decade out, and older models with no apparent droop usually owe some slight debt to silicone or Sellotape.

Finally, before I go back to discussing the remedies available for breast augmentation, I must just mention that any woman who notices a specific abnormality (whether it is an additional nipple, a lump, a pain, a discharge from a nipple, or anything else that concerns her) should visit her doctor without delay for an examination. Most breast lumps are harmless and most breast cancers are treatable if found early on.

Over the years there have, of course, been very many different treatments offered to women hoping to increase the size of their breasts. Today, despite the fact that the British Code of Advertising Practice specifically forbids the advertising of bust developers there is no shortage of manufacturers anxious to take advantage of this sizeable market.

Aquamaid recommend a course based on the *Aquamaid* hydrotherapy appliance which they claim will 'tone the breast muscles and draw the tissues together to give more pronounced breast contours' but they also recommend the use of specific food supplements and of special massage creams. Their food supplements contain such magical aids as lecithin, vitamin E and vitamin F and their massage creams contain vitamin E and vitamin F.

The *Aquamaid* hydrotherapy appliance is perhaps worth discussing in a little more detail since it is widely advertised. The brochure describes two simple arm exercises which should, it is said, be done in preparation for the *Aquamaid* treatment. These involve arm stretching and swinging which may well help develop the chest muscles. The *Aquamaid* device itself enables the user to squirt cold water on to each breast in turn.

I cannot see that this device does anything that couldn't be obtained quite simply by splashing the breasts with cold water, and I don't honestly believe that a woman who does that is going to notice any appreciable permanent difference in the size or shape of her breasts. The exercises which are recommended may well help but you don't have to spend any money to do them. For anyone who is interested, the first exercise involves swinging the arms backwards and pushing out the chest forwards while the second exercise involves standing up with the arms held out to the side and then swinging the arms round in wide circles for a minute or two.

Those who feel that I've been too harsh about this device (and the manufacturers have collected many admiring comments from beauty editors) might like to reflect on the fact that the *Aquamaid* device is said to tone the breast muscles.

According to every anatomy textbook I can find the human breast does not contain a single muscle. It is a gland.

Apart from the hydrotherapy device *Aquamaid* also promote pills and creams for breast improvement. As far as I know there is absolutely no evidence at all to support the suggestion that rubbing vitamin cream on the breasts or taking pills containing vitamins or anything else will make any difference to the size of the breasts. If Aquamaid can produce any real scientific evidence to support the use of their tablets and creams I'll be delighted to report it.

Aquamaid aren't the only people making bust-improving creams. Clarins, who claim to produce 'pure natural beauty products' and who also make the remarkable *Evian* facial mist spray recommend an 'ideal care program for a beautiful bosom' which involves the use of a selection from their seven special products. They claim that their treatment course helps to maintain good skin tension, stimulates and vitalizes the tissues which support the bust and contributes to the delay of the ageing process by cell regeneration. These claims are so promising and important that I think they merit careful study.

Their *Tenseur Bust* product contains a number of constituents and is sold in a twelve-day course of separate phials. Each morning the contents of one phial are to be patted on to the whole of the upper part of the bust, between the breasts, on the neck and the beginning of the shoulders. In a delightfully prepared scientific introduction to this treatment Clarins state five facts. They point out that the breast does not contain any muscle (quite right), that the breast is not solidly fixed to the chest (remarkable observation that, but I don't think anyone is likely to dispute it), that the breast is only hanging from a fan of skin which extends downwards from the neck and forms a natural brassière, that the muscle tone of this natural brassière is endangered by the bust being kept immobile (that's right in so far as it is quite true that if muscles are not exercised they lose their tone and strength although, as we've seen, the breasts contain no muscles) and finally that before Clarins introduced their range, all beauty products for the bust were only concerned with the skin of the breast itself Those are the introductory facts upon which the treatment is based.

The constituents of *Tenseur Bust*, which are said to combat the first signs of premature sagging and to help tighten the envelope of skin which forms the natural brassière, include collagen, aloes, Filatov tissular extracts, horse tail juice extracts, arnica and witch-hazel. Let me discuss these contents one by one.

Collagen is, Clarins say, a structured complex of amino acids and it is certainly an essential constituent of the dermis. It is collagen which helps provide support and shape for any part of the body. But the company claims that their collagen, when rubbed on to the breasts, will help strengthen the superficial supporting skin of the breasts and prevent a premature slackening and loss of firmness. I dispute this claim since to my knowledge there is no evidence that collagen applied externally has any really useful effect whatsoever on the skin or the tissues beneath it.

Aloes and the Filatov tissular extracts are included in the remedy to accelerate the cell renewal process. Now aloes is best known as a purgative and I cannot find any scientific evidence whatsoever that it has any effect when rubbed on to the skin. If there is any evidence to support the claim I would be delighted to see it. As for the Filatov tissular extracts I have to confess that I have been totally unable to trace this substance in any medical or pharmaceutical textbook.

Horse tail juice extract is also said to improve the skin regeneration but the only effect I have been able to associate with this product is diuresis, and as far as I know you have to take it internally to get this effect.

Arnica and witch-hazel are included as astringents to strengthen skin tension, according to Clarins, and indeed both do have astringent properties. In my opinion, however, this effect is likely to produce only temporary changes and I doubt if the changes (some tingling and tightening of the skin) will make an appreciable difference to the shape of the breast. I do not recommend the use of astringents since they can cause skin reactions.

My conclusion has to be that the *Tenseur Bust* is a waste of money. Clarins do, however, make other products. Let's look at them.

First there is the *Tonic Bust* which is sold to stabilize and maintain the results obtained with *Tenseur Bust*. This is said to be a highly stimulating lotion which contains, among other things, the strengthening properties of bilberries and strawberry trees.

Then there are the three types of *Laits aux plantes* which contain mixtures of such ingredients as 'hawthorn, wild lemon, sage, arnica and the active Filatov principles' which are said to help balance the fat metabolism and skin tissue functions while protecting, softening and strengthening the epidermis.

The *Tonic Oil* which is made by this company is said to help prevent stretch marks and to help firm up tissues after pregnancy, and with some relief I'm delighted to say that since this product contains oils it might help. Clarins also make a device which looks rather similar to the *Aquamaid* hydrotherapy tool. Called the *Super-Active Model Bust* it is said to help tone and firm the cutaneous envelope right from the formation of the breasts and to give a balanced and harmonious contour.

The best thing I can say about any of these products is that the *Super-Active Model Bust* is said to be made of special material that 'should not wear out, rust or become furred up'. They do not actually claim that it won't wear out, rust or become furred up.

There are other products which are sold to help boost breast size, but I suspect that by now you're as tired of all this as I am. It is extremely unlikely that any company will ever produce a cream, tablet or device which genuinely boosts breast size without your being aware of it. Such a product would not need advertising since it would merit yards of space in newspapers and magazines all over the world. My advice is to save your money.

The only genuine way to increase the size of a pair of breasts is by a surgical operation, and the number of plastic surgeons driving around in expensive cars is ample proof of the fact that there are a great many ladies prepared to risk pain, expense and even worse in order to improve their shape. This section of the book does not include any account of the plastic surgery done for women who have had breast removal (mastectomy) for cancer or any other reason since breast replacement or augmentation under those circumstances is not, in my opinion, simply cosmetic. The fact that many medical insurance companies are happy to pay for their clients to have such surgery done under health care policies supports this view.

I have discussed elsewhere (p. 68) the general advantages and disadvantages of plastic surgery and the best way to ensure that a competent operator is found. Here I'm just going to describe some of the techniques used and the specific problems associated with breast augmentation surgery.

The improvement in breast size which can be obtained by an operation is usually limited by other physical factors, and most surgeons will make specific recommendations about the amount of additional boost they feel would be most suitable.

Apart from physical limitations on surgery there are psychological factors to be taken into consideration as well. Psychiatrists claim that a considerable number of women seeking surgery to improve the size of their breasts have sexual or marital problems and are seeking a surgical solution. There is evidence that many women have personality problems or suffer from depression. And, of course, there are those who are reluctantly seeking larger breasts with which to satisfy the requirements of lovers or husbands. When the operation is done for these reasons there is little chance of it proving a permanent success since an improvement in breast size is unlikely to be enough to stabilize a relationship so weak as to need such strengthening.

That said, there are undoubtedly a large number of women who simply want larger breasts and who honestly feel that they themselves will be happier and have more social and sexual confidence once such an operation has been done. The evidence suggests that many such women do benefit and are happier.

Several types of operation can be done today. The classical technique is of course to use silicone to help boost breast size. It is vitally important that silicone should never be injected freely into the breast (as has happened in the past) since the silicone can cause permanent injury or even death. Today surgeons only use silicone when it is enclosed within an inflatable envelope and cannot irritate the tissues or spread away from the site of implantation.

The inflatable envelope of silicone rubber can also be filled with dextran or indeed with any suitable solution which will feel normal and give a good contour. These envelopes are fairly easy to insert but if too large an implant is used the skin can be stretched too far and the strain on local blood vessels can be too much, with the result that the skin and the breast tissue may be permanently damaged. The silicone envelope is usually put into position behind the breast tissue, simply pushing the breast out from the chest wall, and so there should not be any problems with breast feeding in the future.

The patient having such an operation will usually need to stay in hospital for a few days and will need to wear a firm bra and take things gently for a month or so afterwards. Some bruising and swelling is almost inevitable, but the long-term effect is likely to be good with the breast feeling and looking natural. Problems usually only occur after injuries to the chest although inevitably there are some disasters due to infection or failure of the wounds to heal. The scars will be almost invisible if the operation is done properly.

Breasts can also be augmented by using lipodermal grafts. The surgeon takes some fat from the buttocks and transplants it into the area between the breast tissue and the chest wall. The amount of fat that can be transplanted naturally depends on the amount of buttock that there is to start with, and there is a failure rate with this operation – sometimes, for example, the transplanted fat is simply absorbed and gradually disappears. This type of operation takes slightly longer than envelope augmentation. Both types of operation are costly and, as with any type of plastic surgery, the total cost may well run into four figures.

Operations to reduce the size of female breasts are commonly done on quite young girls. Those women whose breasts are small may feel like most men do that any breast reduction operation is a type of sacrilege, but women who have over large breasts complain bitterly that they have difficulty in sleeping, that they get backache, that they cannot find suitable clothes, that they suffer from recurrent intertrigo (see p. 224) and that they have pains in their breasts all the time. They also complain that they have difficulty in forming heterosexual relationships which are not dominated by the size of their breasts. Indeed, breast reduction operations are often extremely successful in that the patients concerned are often happy and grateful.

The type of operation used will depend upon several factors, including the amount of tissue to be removed, the likelihood that the patient may want to breast feed and the surgeon's personal preference, but there will inevitably be some scarring and some reduction in nipple sensitivity. The breasts may not end up entirely level or equal in size either.

The other common type of cosmetic operation done on the breasts involves a tightening of the skin and is similar to the type of operation done to remove wrinkles. It is, if you like, a face-lift for the breasts. In this operation the excess skin is simply trimmed away and the hang of the breasts readjusted.

Finally, I should mention that it is true that some contraceptive pills can make some women's breasts larger, that there is no evidence that I know of that rubbing ice on the breasts improves their size or appearance, that swimming does develop the pectoral muscles and may therefore improve the shape of the chest, that manual massage may possibly increase breast size and that cosmetic highlighting techniques can be used to accentuate cleavage.

Cellulite

To begin with I'll try to define precisely what cellulite is and what it is not. First of all, I must point out what it isn't; the word has nothing at all to do with the medical term 'cellulitis' which refers to an inflammation of the skin.

Nicole Ronsard, who is famous as one of the experts to introduce the fight against cellulite to the Americans, describes it simply as 'those lumps, bumps and bulges you couldn't lose before' and she says that it consists of lumps of fat, water and toxic substances that have lodged in the skin and which persist despite normal dieting routines. She claims that eight out of ten women of all weights and ages are cursed with it and in a book entitled *Cellulite* she describes how it was first analysed by Swedish doctors at the end of the last century and then made fashionable by the French.

The main point about cellulite, according to Ms Ronsard and others who believe in its existence, is that it cannot be got rid of by normal dieting techniques since cellulite isn't burnt up like ordinary fat. There are, however, other differences. Cellulite isn't found everywhere on the body but is confined to certain areas – notably the thighs and the buttocks. It is also unusual in that it is extremely rare amongst men.

The orange peel test is a commonly practised trick to tell whether those fatty areas are made up of ordinary fat or of cellulite. It is said by those who believe in cellulite that when the skin and tissues are squeezed between thumb and index finger the skin will ripple and look like orange peel if the condition is caused by cellulite. The disbelievers argue that the orange peel effect is due to the hair follicles in the skin. Real experts differentiate between soft and solid cellulite but here the arguments become rather tenuous and the scientific sense rather stretched to my mind.

The causes of cellulite are, according to the believers, many and varied. Stress, exhaustion, poor eating habits, too little exercise, air pollution and too little fresh air and water are all described as definitive causes. It is also claimed that such poisons as food additives, alcohol, animal fat, chocolate and tea and coffee are responsible for the cellulite phenomenon.

The treatment, as you've probably guessed, is to reverse all these factors and to cut down on bad eating habits, to learn to relax, to take more exercise and to get a good supply of fresh air and water.

It is said that if you do all these things your body will lose the toxic wastes it has stored and will rid itself of those unwanted patches of cellulite. There are, claim the believers, specific diets and exercises which must be followed as an extra aid to cleaner, fresher living.

I began to drift towards disbelief when I found that the diet advocated by the believers was said to be designed not as a weight-reducing diet but to help the body burn up wastes. The diet, however, consists of vegetables, fruit, salad, yoghurt, low fat products and lean meat. That is exactly the sort of diet I would recommend to anyone looking for a weight-reducing regime.

And the more one looks into the cellulite phenomenon the more one finds that the carefully created programme for cellulite elimination begins to look like an ordinary programme for weight loss. The exercises that are recommended are sensible enough but they do not involved anything special. The advice to drink plenty of water is sensible enough as is the advice about coping with stress and learning to relax.

But none of these elements in the cellulite control programme, either individually or collectively, seem to offer any unique system of body purification. The advice is all good, but I believe that anyone who follows the recommended programme would inevitably lose weight, look fitter and feel better. Stored fat, whether stored as ordinary fatty lumps or as toxic rich cellulite, would be eliminated in due course.

The argument put forward by the believers, that cellulite only disappears when the strict regime is followed and that since the regime isn't designed to deal with ordinary fat the lumps lost must be special – and must therefore be cellulite – is a very loose argument in harsh scientific terms.

To really prove that cellulite exists, that it is different in form and content to ordinary fat and that it needs a special regime to clear it, the believers would have to conduct some simple but strictly organized clinical trials. They would, for example, have to show that individuals with ordinary fatty lumps on their thighs and buttocks didn't benefit from the regime. And they would have to show that individuals with cellulite had genuinely failed to benefit from other strict weight-reducing programmes.

It really isn't enough to base claims for the cellulite phenomenon on non-scientific evidence that people with cellulite have failed to shed their fatty lumps when undertaking ordinary diet and exercise programmes unless those ordinary diet and exercise programmes are strictly defined and then compared to the cellulite regime.

From the evidence I've been able to find I'm certainly not convinced that cellulite exists at all. In my opinion it is nothing more than stored fat that is difficult to get rid of. If a sufficiently severe diet and exercise programme is followed then the fat, cellulite or whatever will disappear. I'm certain that cellulite believers like Nicole Ronsard are genuine in their beliefs, but as a professionally open-minded sceptic I would need to see much more hard scientific evidence before I became a believer.

Having jumped firmly down from the fence let me now describe an anti-cellulite regime. It is, after all, an excellent route to general good health.

1 Review your eating habits. Cut out foods that are stuffed with chemicals and other additives, avoid stimulants (such as caffeine and alcohol) and foods that are high in animal fats. Eat plenty of fresh fruit, green vegetables and lean meat and drink plenty of fresh water each day.
2 Take up gentle exercise. Walking is the best exercise you can do and you should plan to walk more than you have in the past. You don't have to set off across Europe, but try leaving the car at home or missing the bus occasionally.
3 Get plenty of fresh air. If you take your exercise in a big city you won't be getting fresh air, so try and get out into the countryside occasionally. The cellulite believers don't always

seem to differentiate between city air and country air when recommending fresh air as a part of the regime but this seems to me to be vitally important.

4 Learn to relax both physically and mentally and be prepared to take time off occasionally. My book *Stress Control* contains a great deal of information on how best to relax.

Dry Skin

When the skin's superficial layer of cells is well supplied with water the surface feels soft and smooth and looks pink and well preserved. When those same cells are short of water, however, things are very different and the skin's surface feels hard and rough and looks cracked and parched like the muddy bottom of a dried-up river bed. Dry skin is exactly what it sounds like.

There are a number of reasons why this state of affairs can occur. A loss of water from the cells can be triggered by the removal of grease and natural oil from the skin or by the removal of water from the atmosphere. In either case the end result is the same – the skin's surface cells lose water.

The remedy for dry skin obviously depends to a certain extent upon the cause. In the Positive Plan Dry Skin Programme (see p. 204) I have detailed some of the ways in which the loss of water or oils can be prevented and many of these remedies depend upon the avoidance of harmful activities.

The cosmetics industry on the other hand seems determined to convince the world at large that dry skin can only be remedied by the use of exotic concoctions which are intended to add water to the skin or which provide the skin with some special type of nourishment. These remedies are discussed on p. 27, but here I want only to deal with the simple, well established truth.

The fact is that there are no remedies which can reliably add water to the skin. All you can do is to stop water from being lost; and the one way to do that is to use a straightforward moisturizing cream or lotion which helps to oil the skin's surface and thereby prevent the loss of natural moisture. It is, after all, the skin's natural fats and sebum which help to control the loss of water from the surface cells. The loss of that fat and sebum is what so often leads to dryness.

Moisturizing creams usually consist of an oil in water emulsion trom which the water quickly evaporates leaving a layer of oil behind. If the layer of oil is thick enough then the cream can do its job effectively. If, however, the moisturizing product contained little oil then there may not be enough oil left on the skin to do an effective job.

More effective than these oil in water emulsions are the water in oil emulsions which are sometimes sold as protective creams or ointments. Traditionally these are known as cold creams when sold for the face and barrier creams when sold for the hands. These products are extremely effective moisturizers and they are the ones that dry skin sufferers are likely to find most effective.

Don't be misled by the advertisements for special creams for dry skin. They are often very appealing. For example, Helena Rubinstein make a product called *Skin Life* which is said to contain GAM, 'an exclusive bio-complex that closely resembles the natural fluid surrounding your skin cells. And it's this natural fluid that helps to maintain the skin's moisture.' Orlane say that their *Ligne Intégrale Crème Sport Antideshydratante* is part of their 'extensive research into the problems associated with dry skin' and that being 'rich in moisturizing ingredients, it shields the epidermis in any weather'. Bowman Beauty Products say that their *Nutrivena B25* 'softly permeates every pore, replenishing moisture, restoring the skin's natural balance and providing gentle, natural nourishment'.

Read these claims carefully and you'll see what the manufacturers *seem* to be claiming is that if skin is moisturized it won't get dry.

They are quite right, of course, but you don't have to spend money on their products to keep your skin soft and supple. Any oily product will do a similar job, and I suggest that you choose a simpler, and probably cheaper, product.

A bath oil is a simple way to grease the skin and the oil can either be added directly to the bath water or else rubbed on to the skin after bathing. *Oilatum emollient* is recommended by some dermatologists as is *Aveeno Oilated*.

Creams which can be used vary a great deal in price and I suggest that you choose the cheapest non-scented moisturizer you can find.

In the past few years many products have been advertised as containing such wonderful extras as hormones, placenta extracts and embryo extracts. Many of these additional constituents make no difference to the quality of the skin and those that may, such as hormones, also prove hazardous. I don't recommend any of them.

Positive Plan Dry Skin Programme

1 Do keep in the shade in sunny weather unless you are protected with sunscreen creams (see p. 230). The sun is a major cause of skin dryness.

2 Do not soak in the bath or shower for more than fifteen minutes. Prolonged or repeated bathing causes damage to the skin and results in a loss of natural oils and water – that produces dry skin. Use an alarm clock to remind you when your time is up.

3 Do avoid daily baths. You do not need to bath daily to preserve personal hygiene if you learn to bathe with a sponge or flannel. A bidet is a useful addition to the bathroom and probably contributes greatly to the average French complexion since it means that bathing is done infrequently.

4 Do avoid chlorinated swimming pools.

5 Do use a pair of rubber gloves when doing kitchen chores.

6 Do make sure that the air in your home or office is not too dry. Air conditioning often dries out the air and this causes the skin to lose moisture. Open a window or keep a bowl full of water in the room to help maintain the amount of moisture in the air. A humidifier may help but is rather an expensive solution.

7 Do not use bubble baths and avoid excessive use of soap since both detergents and soap dry the skin if used excessively.

8 Do use a moisturizing cream or lotion regularly. The brand you choose is irrelevant but it is important that you use the product regularly each day. If the cream is applied while the skin is slightly moist it will be particularly effective. Keep your moisturizing cream by the kitchen sink and use it often.

9 Do not waste money on moisturizers with added substances. These can do harm and are unlikely to be any more effective than simple moisturizers.

10 Bath oils that disperse in the bathwater and which then adhere to the skin are easy to use and are useful for the dry skin sufferer who doesn't have the patience to apply a moisturizing cream.

Eczema

The two words 'eczema' and 'dermatitis' confuse a lot of people who feel that there must be some difference between them but are not quite sure what the difference is. There is no need for confusion for the two words are interchangeable as far as we non-specialists are concerned. Dermatologists may be able to produce minor pedantic differences, arguing that a dermatitis has a known cause whereas an eczema does not, but in practical terms we can use the two words as if they referred to but one condition. I'll use the word 'eczema' here.

The cosmetic problems associated with eczema are often immense since the condition usually involves unsightly changes in the skin's appearance. Red, angry looking rashes are common and often there is some weeping from blistered, raw looking skin. The whole area may itch, get scratched, and thereby become infected.

Eczema can be caused by many different triggers. Women who wear brassières with nickel buckles or clips and those of either sex who wear nickel watch straps are common victims, since allergic reactions to nickel often cause eczematous reactions. Other potent allergens include such varied substances as rubber, detergents and flowers.

Allergens are not the only causes of eczema. Sometimes the condition is caused by the repeated application of irritant substances which damage and dry out the skin surface. Powerful cleansing solvents are a common cause of eczema among housewives and even water can cause eczema in this way. It is important to remember that irritants may collect under rings thereby causing eczema and erroneously suggesting an allergy to the ring itself. Remove rings before immersing hands in any potentially irritant substance so that rinsing can be thorough and complete. Excessive scrubbing with a harsh brush is another possible cause; in this case the superficial layer of skin is scrubbed away leaving newer cells naked and vulnerable.

The occupation of an individual with eczema is often an important clue to the cause. I long ago lost count of the number of young hairdressers who have come to me suffering from eczema. It seems that the more junior the hairdresser the more often she has to put her hands in damaging lotions, shampoos and detergents. It is important to realize that not all industrial eczemas are caused by an allergy and that in many cases the individual can continue to come into contact with the substance which seems to be responsible just as long as the contact is controlled and limited. For example, the housewife who suffers from eczema when her hands are in regular contact with bleaches and detergents may be able to control her condition and prevent further outbreaks by wearing rubber gloves whenever possible when doing household chores.

Sometimes there is no known reason for the development of eczema and not even Sherlock Holmes could discover a link between the skin condition and any outside factor. When this happens there is usually a history of the skin being rather dry and prone to cracking and of it tending to become itchy after being subjected to quite minor insults.

Eczema is a fairly common problem among young babies and children where the face may be the first part of the body to be affected. The skin is invariably dry and rather coarse with cracks appearing regularly over bends and joints. This type of eczema often improves a great deal as the years pass by and young mothers should ignore the threats and warnings of well meaning friends and relatives.

The treatment of eczema obviously depends to a very large extent upon the cause (if any can be found) and the natural history of the individual disease.

Where the skin has been obviously irritated or where there is any possible history of an allergic reaction being responsible, then the solution is fairly obvious. The skin must simply be protected from the irritant or allergen.

When there is a history of the skin being particularly dry the best solution may not be the use of powerful medicaments but rather the careful use of simple moisturizers intended to protect and preserve the quality and integrity of the skin surface. The various ways in which dry skin can be protected are dealt with on p. 204. Some of the branded products available for the treatment of eczema rely to a large extent on the fact that a simple cream will provide relief. *Eczederm Cream*, for example, contains nothing more active than calamine and starch in a cooling cream.

Where eczema does not respond to simpler treatments physicians will often prescribe more powerful products. It is important not to use these products without the attention and supervision of a doctor since the skin's barriers are damaged in eczema and the absorption of medicaments can be greatly increased. This fact can be useful and can help in the treatment of an eczematous reaction but it can also lead to the deterioration of an already bad situation. Eczema can be made worse by the injudicial use of prescribed and non-prescribed creams.

Is your eczema preventable? If you are an eczema sufferer you can tell whether or not your condition has been caused or been made worse by an irritant or allergen by answering these questions.

1 Has your condition only started recently?
2 Have you noticed a deterioration in your condition since taking a new job or changing your duties at an old one?
3 Have you noticed a deterioration since changing the type of detergent, washing powder, bleach, shampoo or soap you use?
4 Is the condition localized to a specific area of your body while other areas of skin seem quite normal?
5 Are any colleagues at work similarly affected?
6 Have you recently started using any new skin cream – either prescribed or bought over the counter?
7 Does your condition clear up when you are on holiday or away from work for any other reason?
8 Have any other members of your family begun to suffer recently?

If you have answered 'yes' to any of these questions then you should suspect a specific cause for your eczema.

If you suffer from or are susceptible to eczema:
1 You should avoid using powerful detergents or solutions of any kind.
2 You should not wear clothing that is irritating or too tight. Woollen clothing often causes problems.
3 You should avoid extremes of temperature by wearing warm clothes, scarves and gloves in winter and by keeping in the shade during the hotter months.
4 You should take care to rinse hands carefully whenever they have been in contact with soap or any other potential irritant and you should take care to dry them thoroughly immediately afterwards. Moisturizing creams should be applied regularly during the day.

Foot problems

Most of us start off our lives with well shaped, flawless feet. The problems which develop and which cause so much discomfort in later life are largely due to poor foot care in childhood. Yesterday's parents can hardly be blamed for the high incidence of foot pathology among today's adult population since information and advice about foot care and footwear was not widely available a decade or two ago. Today, however, there is no shortage of good advice about foot care, and modern parents can hardly plead ignorance if their children grow up with damaged or deformed feet.

Good foot care needs to begin shortly after birth. It is important to be aware of the damage that can be done by the wearing of shoes, socks or stretch suits that do not leave room for growth and movement. Babies shouldn't wear shoes at all until they are walking around by themselves; until then they should be allowed to remain barefoot or should wear only socks that are plenty big enough. Stretch suits often constrict the feet when they are comfortable elsewhere.

As the child grows it is the choice of footwear which plays as important a role as anything in the development of healthy feet. I've made a list of some points to watch out for when buying shoes for children. The list applies to adults, too, except that it obviously isn't necessary to leave room for growth when buying shoes for an adult.

1 Always buy shoes from a shop where the assistants have the time and knowledge to measure your child's feet properly. Good shoes are made in several widths and fittings to each half size. Both feet should be measured every time when shoes are bought and they should be measured with the child standing up straight. Some shops display a certificate stating that they are on the Children's Foot Health Register and in these establishments experienced staff should be available.

2 Buy shoes that are big enough. There should be ¾ inch at the front of the foot between the longest toe and the front of the shoe. A quick way to check that a shoe is big enough is to ask the child to push his toes right to the front of the shoe. You should then be able to get your finger down between the back of the heel and the heel of the shoe. Adults' shoes need less room but there should be some space between the heel of the

foot and the heel of the shoe when the toes are pushed right to the front of the shoe. You should be able to wriggle your toes in your shoes. Try on both shoes and walk about in them.

3 Don't buy stacked heels, high heels or pointed toe shoes except for wearing at parties. Everyday shoes need to be comfortable and well fitting.

4 If possible, buy shoes in the afternoon rather than the morning. Feet are slightly larger then.

5 Children shouldn't have Sunday Best shoes. If shoes are kept for special occasions they will be too small long before they have been worn out. Shoes are an expensive item and it pays to buy one pair of good shoes, to look after them and to replace them when they are worn out or too small. If shoes are bought with space available they will usually wear out at about the same time that they become too small.

6 Shoes with laces or adjustable straps are best because they hold the foot firmly in position even though there may be space available.

7 Good shoes are firm but supple. They provide support but bend with the foot.

8 Pumps, trainers or plimsolls are not usually sensible shoes for regular use. They are rarely available in a full range of sizes and they often make the feet sweat. They should be kept for use when playing sport.

9 Rubber and synthetic shoes often make sweating worse. Leather shoes are in my opinion usually the best buy and need not necessarily be more expensive in the long run.

Buying the right shoes and replacing them when necessary is the most important part of foot care. There are, however, other ways in which the feet can be protected from damage. One obvious point is to wear socks which are not too tight. Socks or stockings which are too small or which accommodate the foot only when stretched can severely damage a growing foot. Socks and stockings should be changed and washed daily whenever possible.

It helps to wash feet daily but it is vitally important to ensure that they are dried carefully afterwards. The area between the toes is often left damp and this can easily lead to the growth of fungal infections. It's much easier to contract foot infections than it is to get rid of them. Most women put a moisturizing cream on their hands at least once a day but very few put moisturizers on their feet. It's a sensible habit which can help prevent the development of dry, cracked skin. Toe nail care is also important. Indeed the toe nails are more important than the finger nails in many ways, but few people spend a fraction of the time on their toe nails that they spend on their finger nails. Here is a programme which might be worth following once a week.

1 Soap the feet in warm soapy water for a few minutes.
2 Scrub them with a pumice stone and nail brush to remove ingrained dirt and loose, dead, surface skin cells. Dry carefully.
3 Cut the toe nails straight across if they need cutting. Toe nails don't grow as quickly as finger nails and you won't need to cut them every week.
4 Use a fine emery board to remove the rough edges.
5 Apply a cuticle cream (see p. 138).
6 Ease the cuticles back carefully with an orange stick or cotton bud.
7 Remove hard skin on corns or calluses with a special cream or file (see p. 211).
8 Apply a moisturizing cream to both feet. This should be a daily ritual.
9 Check for any signs of foot infection.

This short routine will do a great deal to help maintain your feet in good condition.

It is worth remembering that most of us walk an average of five miles a day (if you think you walk less than that just count how many times you go up the stairs, down the garden and out to the shops) and that is nearly 2,000 miles a year. In a lifetime of three score years and ten that means that most of us will walk 140,000 miles on one pair of feet.

Think how many sets of tyres your car would use up in travelling that far and just imagine how many times you'd have to have leather-soled shoes repaired to walk that distance! I recently read a report which suggested that shoe makers now only expect new shoes to last a matter of weeks if used for regular walking.

There are a number of products designed to help soothe and relax tired and aching feet but I do not recommend any of them. Scholl, for example, make a *Creme Foot Bath* which is described as having a special moisturizer with skin softener. I'm in favour of applying a moisturizer to the feet but I feel that ideally it should be applied after the feet have been washed and dried.

Antiseptic or medicated sprays, balms and creams are of little or no value in the care of the feet in my opinion. The use of deodorants and antiperspirants is discussed on p. 190.

Tired and aching feet can usually be soothed with a warm bath, it is true (though it is important not to allow the feet to soak for too long), but prevention is, as always, better than cure, and good walking shoes and general foot care will prevent the development of these symptoms in many cases. Swollen, aching feet can often be relieved if they are placed above the level of the legs. That helps fluid to drain away from the feet.

The specific problems associated with the feet are inevitably varied but a few problems do occur with great regularity and can to some extent be treated successfully at home.

Dry skin is a perpetual problem and can be treated in one of two ways. It can be soothed and softened with a moisturizing cream or it can be rubbed away. You don't have to buy any special cream to soothe and soften the skin since any moisturizing cream will do just as well (see p. 202) but it probably is worth while buying a hard skin remover if you intend to tackle your problem that way. There are many products on the market (Scholl make a *Hard Skin Stone*, and there is a *Miracle Stone* which is also said to be impregnated with special cleansers which make it suitable for removing stains), but a good old-fashioned pumice stone is probably as good as anything. You should be able to buy one from your local pharmacist. Moisturize after using the skin remover.

Calluses and corns are both caused by a thickening of the skin's horny layer. In a corn the thickening is shaped like a cone with the apex pointing inwards, into the foot. A callus is simply a flat hard piece of thickened skin. Both are commonly caused by badly fitting shoes and both can be dealt with successfully at home.

To deal with a corn or callus it helps if the affected skin is first soaked in warm water for a few minutes. It should then be rubbed with a rough towel, soapstone, pumice stone, emery board or one of the branded hard skin removers such as *Miracle Stone*, *Newtons Chiropody Sponge*, or *Scholl Hard Skin Reducer*. Don't try cutting any corn or callus with a knife because you might make it infected.

There are a number of creams and ointments available which are recommended for use on calluses and corns. A number of these contain salicylic acid and you can choose from: *Ayrtons Corn and Wart Paint*, *Boots Corn Paint*, *Carnation Corn Paint*, *Diamond Corn Solvent*, *Dispello Corn Cure*, *Freezone*, *Hiker Corn Salve*, *Pickles Ointment for Hard Skin*, *Scholl Corn and Callous Salve*, *Three Flasks Corn and Wart Solvent* and *Union Jack Corn Plasters*.

Special corn plasters which are impregnated with salicylic acid include *Amovon Corn Caps*, *Carnation Corn Caps*, *Scholl Zino Corn Pads* and *Union Jack Corn Plasters*. You can also buy *Salicylic Collodion BPC* and *Salicylic Acid Paint*.

If you have sore feet and think you are developing a corn or a patch of hard skin you can try using *Scholl Air Pillo Insoles*, *Scholl Cosy Sole Insoles* or *Omniped Foot Cushions*, all of which might help prevent the development of these problems.

Bunions usually result from the wearing of narrow, pointed shoes or wearing high-heeled shoes which forces the toes down into the front of the shoe. Commonly, the big toe is pushed out of shape and ends up pointing inwards with the inevitable result that its joint points outwards. They are invariably larger, usually more painful and always more permanent than corns or callouses and may need surgical removal. The long-term solution is simply to choose roomy, comfortable shoes.

Ingrowing toe nails can cause a great deal of pain. The best prevention is to ensure that the toe nails are cut regularly and straight but not too short. Scholl make an *Ingrown Toenail Treatment* and a whole range of cushions and pads to help shield painful parts of the feet, but if this problem persists or recurs then I recommend that you seek medical advice.

Athlete's foot is a phrase which was said to have been coined by an advertising man promoting a foot product! It is certainly colourful enough and inaccurate enough to have that pedigree, since I doubt if more than a small percentage of the total number of sufferers from athlete's foot do in fact engage in any exercise more daunting than pushing a shopping trolley or pressing a lift button. Sweaty feet develop this infection, and it isn't just athletes who sweat.

Athlete's foot is in fact a fungal infection, the symptoms of which usually include moist, red, split skin. Good foot hygiene helps to keep the infection away, and anyone whose feet sweat a lot may be helped by wearing cotton socks which tend to cause less sweating than any other kind. It's important to clean and dry the feet carefully and thoroughly every day and to wear shoes which enable the feet to breathe. Leather shoes and sandals are the most suitable footwear and when pumps have to be worn they should be the aerated type with little holes designed to enable air to circulate around the feet. There are a number of products available over the counter to help deal with the infection.

Balto Athlete's Foot Lotion, *Mycil Ointment*, *Mycil Powder*, *Scholl Athlete's Foot Powder* and *Scholl S1 Athlete's Foot Liquid* should all be effective, but treatment should be continued for several days after the symptoms have subsided.

Athletes should remember that the infection can be picked up off the floor of changing rooms, swimming baths and public showers.

The general measures I've described as being suitable for the treatment and care of athlete's foot are perfectly suited for the treatment and care of feet which sweat a good deal and cause either physical discomfort or social embarrassment. There are products available which are designed to absorb sweaty smells (*Odour Eaters* contain charcoal), but many people will find careful bathing and changing hosiery regularly a satisfactory solution. Those that find that this regime is totally inadequate should consult their doctor, since hyperhidrosis (the medical term for a condition which involves excessive sweating) can be treated surgically in extreme cases.

It is important to remember that the feet can sometimes show early signs of impending disease processes. Small ulcers, or black patches or skin problems which do not heal up need expert attention and should be seen either by a qualified chiropodist or by a doctor. I have described the work of chiropodists on p. 50. The elderly and the disabled who may not be able to look after their own feet should be regularly attended by a chiropodist, and a home service is usually available through family doctors. Those suffering from poor circulation and hormone disorders such as diabetes mellitus (sugar diabetes) should have their feet examined regularly.

Infections
Every year millions of healthy people splash and smear themselves with thousands of gallons of antiseptic liquids and tons of antiseptic

creams. They do this because they are under the impression that by using such products it is possible to clear the skin of nasty, evil bacteria which may have settled there temporarily.

They are wrong, and they are wasting their energy and their money.

Human skin is permanently inhabited by millions of invisible creatures and however much the skin is scrubbed and washed with antiseptics there will still be millions of those tiny creatures left. You have about as much chance of clearing all the bacteria from your skin by using an antiseptic as you have of clearing the sand from the Sahara with an old broom. Indeed the unselected, non-specific use of antiseptics can be dangerous since allergy and sensitivity rashes to antiseptics can and do occur.

Antiseptics are also frequently used for the treatment of cuts, scratches, scalds and abrasions and two out of three British households stock an antiseptic of one sort or another for just this purpose.

The human body, however, is really very good at coping with minor problems of this kind without any such help. When you cut yourself the flow of blood helps to wash dirt and germs away from the wound and within a few minutes the clotting blood will form a hard protective scab which seals the wound from the rest of the world. Any bugs underneath the scab will usually be cleared away by scavenging white blood cells.

The best way to help your body heal itself and deal with any potential infection is simply to wash any damaged area with clean, running cold water. Gentle scrubbing with or without an ordinary unperfumed soap will help remove any dirt, hair, dead cells and some bacteria and will prepare the area for the natural healing processes. Washing with a salt solution may also help.

I realize that this simple regime will sound very unsatisfactory to a lot of readers who will feel that if they don't do something more they are not being thorough enough. So if you feel that you must use an antiseptic let me suggest that you use a liquid antiseptic such as *Dettol*, *Savlon Antiseptic Liquid* or *TCP Liquid Antiseptic*. These products don't leave a greasy smear behind as the creams and ointments do. If you want to carry some sort of medicated product with you in the car or on picnics and you don't want to carry a bottle of liquid antiseptic then take antiseptic wipes of some sort with you. There are a number of different products available in-

cluding one which comes in a pull-through canister which defeated
me entirely when I tried it out. I ended up with about fifty soggy,
uncontrollable antiseptic wipes in my lap.

I do not recommend antiseptic sprays or antiseptic creams of any
kind.

Obesity

A huge industry has grown up in recent years specifically intended
to satisfy the demands of the many millions of women who want
help with their slimming programmes. The very fact that there are
so many different diets, slimming aids, and volumes of conflicting
advice on the market is fairly ample proof that there is no single,
superior, totally effective solution to the problem of excess weight.

The commercial products which are available vary in their use-
fulness, and before I describe some of the basic principles of effective dieting I'll discuss the various categories on sale.

The product most slimmers would like to find is one in pill shape
that can be simply swallowed once a day without any change in
eating habits being necessary. In an attempt to satisfy this Utopian
demand there are a number of tablets and pills on the market.
These products can be divided into two categories.

First, there are the pills which are only available on prescription.
Products in this category include *Apisate*, *Duromine*, *Durophet*,
Filon, *Ionamin*, *Ponderax*, *Tenuate*, *Tenuate Dospan*, and *Teronac*.
Despite the enormous amount of evidence which has been produced
in recent years which shows that amphetamines are addictive, the
company making *Durophet* (which consists of amphetamine and
dexamphetamine) still recommends its product for the treatment of
obesity, I am not satisfied that the products available only on
prescription are useful, effective and entirely safe, although I know
that some doctors would disagree with me about this.

Second, there are the pills which can be obtained either on
prescription or over the chemist's counter without a prescription.
The products in this category are often described as appetite re-
ducers and they frequently consist of nothing more mysterious
than roughage. They include such non-digestible, bulky materials
as bran, methylcellulose, carregeenan, guar gum, gelatin and agar.
Products available in this category include *Bisks*, *Celevac*, *Diabisc*,
Methylcellulose Biscs, *Pastils 808*, *Prefil*, *Simbix*, *Simbix 14 day*

Bran Plan, Slim Disks, Slim Disks for Men, Slim-Maid tablets, 10 day Slimmer Treatment, Test Sixty, and *Trihextin G Weight Reducing Plan.* Some of these products come with dietary advice and extra ingredients.

These products certainly help a number of slimmers but they are sometimes expensive (even on prescription), and you can get very much the same sort of result by sticking to a high residue diet. Apples, celery, raw carrots, salads, plenty of vegetables and coarse breakfast cereals and bread are all useful. These make the slimmer feel full and take the edge off the over hearty appetite.

Many of the products available are foodstuffs rather than medicinal aids. Meal replacements and products described as 'meals in a glass' are carefully balanced mixtures of food, which often include added vitamins and minerals and which are designed to be used as part of a calorie-controlled diet. Products such as *Carnation Slender, Nutriplan, Simbix Meal in a Glass, Slim Gard* and the *Unicliffe High Protein Diet* fall into this category. My opinion is that anyone who is capable of counting calories and who eats a balanced diet is wasting money by buying these often extremely expensive products. Similarly low-calorie foods and calorie-counted meals are to my mind nothing more than expensive gimmicks.

Artificial sweeteners on the other hand are a great boon to the slimmer and they can result in money saving. Saccharin is available as *Bisks Sweetener, Hermesetas Solution* and *Hermesetas Tablets, Mini Sax, Saccharin Tablets BPC, Saxin Solution, Saxin Tablets, Sucron Mini Lumps, Supasac, Sweetex Liquid* and *Sweetex Pellets.*

Some people find that saccharin has a rather bitter taste and for them there are such products as *Sucron* on the market, which contains a mixture of saccharin and sugar.

The slimming toffee called *Ayds* doesn't fit into any specific category but it is well worth mentioning. It contains liquid glucose, together with the apparently obligatory mixture of vitamins and minerals, and the theory is that by raising your blood sugar before a meal you won't want to eat as much as usual. There is some sense in this theory and many Mums who have warned their children not to eat sweets before meals because they'll ruin their appetites will already have proved that it can work.

I'm less convinced of the effectiveness of *PLJ.* The advertisements for this lemon drink claim that 'If you train your taste buds to enjoy foods that are less sweet you'll find it easier to say "no" to some of the fattening things that can ruin your diet – and your figure' and they say that if you drink a glass of *PLJ* before a meal 'that clean, sharp tang of lemons helps melt away your taste for sweet things'. Hmph.

The number of herbal slimming products available has increased at a phenomenal rate in recent years. Many of the herbal products which are sold contain laxatives and diuretics despite the fact that the British Code of Advertising Practice rules quite specifically that diuretic or laxative slimming products are not acceptable because their effectiveness has not been demonstrated. I have yet to come across a herbal slimming product that I can recommend and there is no reason that I know of why such substances as kelp should make dieting more effective or safer, while the apparent obsession that health food manufacturers have with vitamins and minerals seems positively *unhealthy* to me.

In addition to pills and diet foods there are, of course, many items of equipment and machinery sold to slimmers. The simplest products are those which are just designed to encourage the over-weight individual to undertake a little exercise. Cycling and rowing machines and exercise bars fall into this category but I don't really recommend any of them. Exercise can help you lose a little weight and it can certainly help to tone up muscles, but you don't need to buy anything more expensive than comfortable shoes in order to enjoy the advantages of exercise.

During the last year or two a number of electronic muscle exercisers have come on to the market and many of these are sold to slimmers.

Slendertone is probably the best known of the products in this category and its advertisements claim that it is 'specifically designed to lift, tighten and firm your figure by giving concentrated exercise to just those muscles that most control your shape. As muscle tone improves, sagging, bulging and flabbiness simply disappear.' For slimmers there is also a personal nutrition programme with dietary advice. In one of their brochures Slendertone specifically point out that effortless exercise won't cause weight loss, but they say 'If you don't lose pounds and inches we will refund pounds and pence.'

The *Figuretrim* electronic muscle exerciser is advertised with the heading 'A beautiful figure can be yours', and in one advertisement I've seen it is said to 'slim and tone up the whole body'.

These machines can be bought for home use or they can be used in a clinic or beauty parlour. I doubt if they can do any harm, if used sensibly and according to the manufacturers' instructions, but I'm not sure they are particularly valuable either. I rather feel that a good daily walk would do more good.

Among the other slimming treatments available only in beauty parlours and clinics is *Kwik Slim*, described as a 'unique reducing treatment that produces results within hours' and 'comfortably and effortlessly trims away unwanted inches from the areas causing shape problems'. This promising treatment involves the use of a herb-based gel solution which is applied to the areas to be trimmed. Special non-absorbent body wraps are then bound round the body and for ninety minutes the client is kept warm, dry and relaxed on the clinic couch. When the wraps are removed the client is measured.

The idea, according to the promoters of this product, is that the special gel acts upon excess body fluids, cellulite and tissue weaknesses producing most benefit in the intra-cellular fluids of the fat tissues. There is also, according to the company's brochure, an improvement in bladder function. Surprisingly, perhaps, the company says that virtually no weight is lost but that 'the inner body response and tissue strengthening are the factors through which the dimensional methods are achieved'.

I'm not sure that I can recommend this treatment to slimmers but I certainly do recommend it to anyone thinking of setting up a beauty business. The special slimming gel apparently costs the operator £1 per treatment while the holding company charges just over £100 for a day's training, a diploma, thirty body tapes, body charts, explanation sheets, posters, mirror stickers and so on. The recommended charge per client is said to be between £10 and £20, and the company point out that twelve treatments will cover the initial outlay. 'From then on,' they say, 'you will have a very healthy profit margin.'

The *Quickslim* product sounds rather similar and also consists of a special gel and some bodywrap bandages. A quote on the company literature suggests that inch loss continues for a day or so after treatment, so I suppose that if you want to look slimmer for a special event a visit to a *Quickslim* clinic might be worthwhile. I found the finances more interesting than the scientific claims, however. Beauty clinic operators are advised that 'one trained operator could increase your turnover £360 per week'.

Then there is the *Maillecrin Massage Glove* which is said by its British distributors to 'get rid of dead cells' and which is also described as 'an effective slimming aid for local areas of fat'. I'll accept the first claim but I'm sceptical about the second.

Whatever you spend on slimming products the majority of independent experts agree that there is only one really effective way to lose weight: that is to eat less calories. You can either do that by eating less generally or by eating less of the sort of things that are rich in calories.

To slim effectively, there are some basic rules which are worth following.

1 Acquire a calorie list and become familiar with the calorie values of different foods. Many dieters do not realize, for example, that alcoholic drinks are often very rich in calories. A pint of beer or a gin and orange can ruin a day's careful eating habits.

2 Do not try to lose too much weight too quickly. A slow steady loss is easier to manage and easier to maintain. Many slimmers suffer from what I call the Pendulum Problem. They lose weight rapidly, get tired with their boring diet of lettuce and yoghurt and then go on an eating binge again. That means that they put all their weight back on in a day or two and need to diet again. If you retrain yourself to eat sensibly then you'll have a slimmer figure for ever.

3 Remember that dieting is nothing more than organized eating and that losing weight simply means choosing to eat less. To give yourself the necessary willpower you must have a vision of your slimmer self. You must choose to eat less because you want to be slimmer – either to be more attractive or to be healthier.

4 Be positive when dieting. Don't make lists of all the foods you can't eat but make lists instead of all the foods you can eat. Try and prepare imaginative menus containing low-calorie foods. *Cuisine Minceur* by Michel Guérard contains excellent slimming recipes, and there are a number of other cook books for the slimming chef.

5 Identify your bad eating habits and try to eliminate one each

week. If you nibble biscuits with your mid-afternoon coffee, nibble fruit or raw vegetables instead. Better still, train yourself to eat less between meals and eventually to just have the coffee by itself.

6 Don't allow yourself to be tempted. Refusing the first chocolate is easier than refusing the second. And don't reward yourself with fattening foods. That just makes dieting harder and may reinforce the old belief that fattening foods are associated with good times.

7 Learn to listen to your own body when it tells you that you have had enough to eat. We all have automatic appetite control centres designed to regulate the intake of food. That isn't just science fiction – it's an established fact. A study published in the *American Journal of Diseases of Children* showed that when newly weaned infants just a few months old were allowed to choose what they ate from a range of simple, natural foods, they selected balanced diets which were just as good in nutritional value as the carefully balanced ideal diets worked out by nutritional experts. The infants not only chose a perfect diet but they also automatically limited their intake of food. Another study published in the *Journal of the American Dental Association* showed that young children automatically chose foods that enable them to avoid digestive upsets and constipation, while a third study, done on soldiers during the 1939–45 war, showed that when allowed access to unlimited supplies of food troops ate what their bodies needed according to the outside temperature and that they automatically chose an ideal mixture of protein, fat and carbohydrate.

Most of us have lost the art of listening to our own bodies and we eat three times a day whether we're hungry or not, stuffing ourselves with food not because we need it but because the clock says it is time to eat. If we get hungry between meals we eat then as well. The human body does not adapt well to huge meals at lengthy intervals. It can cope far more effectively with smaller meals taken at shorter intervals. Eating a large meal encourages the storage of excess food as fat.

We also make the mistake of finishing all the food on our plates because we've been trained that it is wrong to waste food. Again the appetite control centre is ignored and food eaten in the mistaken belief that unwanted food is better off inside the body than in the dustbin.

To re-establish control of your own appetite control centre nibble smaller meals rather than stuff yourself with large meals. People who eat by inclination rather than habit put on less extra weight. Eat when you feel hungry and stop when you feel full. And concentrate when you're eating. If you eat while watching television then you won't be able to hear your body when it talks to you.

It is also important to remember that if you teach your children to listen to and take notice of their appetite control centres then they will be far less likely to put on excess weight in later life. To help children, don't force them to clear their plates – let them leave what they don't want and give them smaller portions next time. Don't reward children with food or use it as a punishment. If you do, the child will associate food with emotional as well as physical needs.

8 Eat a large breakfast rather than a large evening meal. Food eaten in the morning is burnt up during the day. Food eaten late at night, just before going to bed, is far more likely to be stored as fat.

9 Don't be ashamed of tricking yourself in such simple ways as using a smaller plate, buying smaller quantities of food and so on.

10 A mum who has a new baby can help it to a slimmer life by breast feeding it. There is strong evidence to support the theory that breast-fed babies are far less likely to put on extra weight than bottle-fed babies. Something like 80 per cent of bottle-fed babies have been reported to gain weight faster than their breast-fed contemporaries. The reason is simple: when the breast-fed baby has had enough, he stops sucking. The feeding mother has no way of knowing just how much the baby has drunk and therefore she doesn't push the last few drops on to the satisfied baby. Human breast milk actually contains its own appetite control trigger – the composition of the food changing during a feed and becoming four to five times richer in fat at the end than at the beginning. This change in fat content seems to be a reminder to nudge the control centre.

A baby's habits are particularly important because there

seems to be a strong possibility that a fat baby will have more fat cells than a normal weight baby. In the future, the baby with more fat cells will have more capacity for fat storage and will therefore find staying slim more difficult. In addition, the baby whose appetite control centre has been overridden by a mum with a half-empty bottle will be less likely to listen to his body when it talks to him.

Psoriasis

A patient of mine once complained that she had dandruff of the elbow. What she really had was psoriasis, but her description was perfectly accurate: psoriasis of the skin really does look like dandruff. The skin is usually white and flaky and small dusty scales tend to come off the skin's surface layer at the slightest touch. Underneath the superficial layer of flaky white cells the skin is usually red and rather raw.

Under normal circumstances the human skin is continually producing new cells to replace the ones that are being worn away. In the condition called psoriasis the skin produces new cells far too quickly with the result that older cells are pushed off the skin's surface at an unusually rapid rate. Underneath the scaly, white cells is the pink layer of newly formed replacement cells.

Psoriasis is one of the vast number of diseases about which we know very little. What we *do* know is that it often seems to be triggered off by such incidents as a severe infection, an accident, or a period of stress. It isn't catching but it can be inherited, and whereas the chances of a child having psoriasis if one parent is a sufferer are probably one in ten, the chances of a child with both parents having psoriasis are more likely to be evens. It's an extremely common disease affecting something like two people in every hundred; some of those having quite severe symptoms with flaky, white patches over large areas of skin and others having very small patches of affected skin.

Because scientists don't really know what causes psoriasis they don't really know how to treat it. They have found out, however, that the condition tends to improve when the sufferer has a holiday or learns to relax. And it also seems that whereas psoriasis is made worse by extremes of heat and cold it can be dramatically improved by some pleasant sunshine.

There are a wide variety of products available for doctors to prescribe for this condition and some of them help considerably in the short term. So far there still isn't a permanent cure available. Up-to-date information about remedies and research appears in the journal published by the Psoriasis Association. I recommend that any sufferer join this group – the address can be obtained either through a public library or family doctor.

Inevitably there are a number of proprietary preparations available for psoriasis. I do not recommend these remedies.

I have seen the condition many hundreds of times and I'm not always certain of the diagnosis at first, so I don't see how any individual who has never seen the condition before can be expected to make his own diagnosis with any degree of conviction. There are other skin diseases which resemble psoriasis and the treatments sometimes vary.

Anyone who has a skin condition which they think could be psoriasis should see their own family doctor. If he is in any doubt he'll arrange an appointment with a dermatologist. And only then, when the diagnosis has been made, should a treatment be tried. Whatever treatment it is, I doubt if it will be one of the remedies sold over the counter or through the post.

Rashes

Any attempt to include in this book a comprehensive study of the types of skin rashes which can occur would prove a failure unless the printers could work out a way to bind a volume of several thousand pages.

There are many, many reasons why skin rashes develop, and not even the most arrogant dermatologist would claim that he can always identify the natural history of a specific rash. It is obviously impossible, therefore, to attempt any classification in just a few lines.

There are, however, some general rules which are worth while following. To begin with I would suggest that if you develop a rash that you haven't seen before while taking a drug of any kind, then you should consider that the rash has been caused by the drug. It has been said that if a patient has two diseases then the chances are high that the second disease was caused by the treatment for the first and in no area of medicine is this truer than it is in dermatology. The skin is in many ways a window for the body's internal state. If you're angry you skin will go red, if you are frightened your skin will go white and if you are allergic to something your skin will become itchy and blotchy.

A rash that accompanies a fever is likely to be due to one of the Big Three infectious diseases: chickenpox, measles and German measles (or rubella). Chickenpox spots are like blisters and the measles rash tends to be rather blotchier than the rash of rubella, but if you're in doubt then ask for advice.

The skin rash that can most safely and effectively be treated at home is the one known as intertrigo. The rash is always red, sometimes wet and may be itchy and uncomfortable. It is caused by two areas of skin rubbing together and is usually associated with localized sweating.

Intertrigo most commonly affects those who are overweight and it is frequently seen underneath pendulous breasts during the summer months. It may also occur between the thighs and anywhere where there are two areas of skin gathered in together. Men get it around the scrotum.

To prevent intertrigo developing the skin should be kept clean and dry. Talcum powder usually seems to help. The area between pendulous breasts and the chest wall can usually be protected by the wearing of a strong and adequate bra, and if the scrotum is particularly badly affected a scrotal support may be needed. If the condition doesn't resolve itself within a few days when this is done, then a medical practitioner should be consulted, since intertrigo can often become infected by a fungus which needs treating with a special type of cream or ointment.

Stretch marks

When you were born you probably weighed around seven pounds. Today you probably weigh twenty times as much.

In the intervening years, as your body has slowly grown to its present size, your skin has gradually stretched and adapted to contain the additional mass of bones and flesh. If it had not stretched your body would long ago have burst its way out of your skin.

The human skin can accommodate this gradual change in shape and weight very successfully, but when changes are more rapid it does not adapt anywhere nearly as successfully. The fibres which lie in the dermis of the skin and which help provide the skin's elasticity are stretched and strained by any sudden change in total body weight, with stretch marks becoming clearly visible after the accumulation or loss of weight. The marks show where the elastic fibres were put under exceptional stress and their number and size will be more or less proportional to the rate of weight change.

In purely mechanical terms what happens during a massive weight gain is that the skin is stretched too quickly with the stretching permanently damaging the elastic fibres.

However, apart from this simple mechanical explanation for the formation of stretch marks there are thought to be other reasons for their development. It has been argued that hormonal changes can result in the development of stretch marks and since in a condition known as Addison's disease a hormone called cortisone is produced in exceptionally large quantities by the suprarenal glands and is accompanied by the development of striae (stretch marks), this additional argument seems irrefutable. It is also established that the use of steroid injections and creams may be associated with the development of stretch marks.

It seems possible that the hormones weaken and rupture the elastic fibres in the dermis while mechanical forces subsequently decide the extent, length, site and direction of the striae.

Stretch marks usually first appear during adolescence when there is often a change in hormone levels in the body, associated with a rapid increase in body weight. The marks affect about a third of all teenagers although girls are twice as likely to suffer from these as boys. Varying in length, stretch marks are usually pink or purple to begin with although they invariably fade to white scars as the months and years go by. They can be elevated or depressed, but with time the skin tends to become wrinkled and to feel and look rather like tissue paper. Adolescent boys usually notice striae on the back, buttocks and abdomen, while girls usually find them appearing on their breasts as well as the abdomen.

Stretch marks can be caused by any sudden and excessive weight gain but there is of course one condition peculiar to women that is particularly closely associated with this problem.

During the nine months of pregnancy an ordinary female abdomen has to stretch considerably to cope with the growing foetus and the result is often a legacy of extremely visible stretch marks.

Indeed, four out of five pregnant women will usually have stretch marks (called striae gravidarum) as a permanent reminder of their motherhood.

Since the breasts often swell, too, with the accumulation of milk, stretch marks also often affect the pregnant woman's chest. Subsequent pregnancies tend to make any striae more obvious.

There is no certain way of preventing the development of stretch marks (apart from maintaining a steady weight, avoiding pregnancy and controlling the output of your suprarenal glands), but some doctors do claim that women have minimized the formation of stretch marks by keeping their muscles in trim and their skin moist. It may be that the gentle massage used to apply moisturizing cream does as much good as anything else. There are special creams available (such as *Maws' Supple Ante Natal Cream* and *PreNatol*) which are said to help prevent the formation of stretch marks, but I am not really convinced that these products are more effective than ordinary moisturizing creams and lotions (see p. 158). These should be massaged gently into the skin each day.

The breasts seem to be helped by the wearing of good supporting maternity bras, while intertrigo (another consequence of mammary hypertrophy in pregnancy) can be prevented by careful cleansing and drying and by the judicious use of talcum powder after bathing (see also p. 152).

When stretch marks have developed and are a real burden, the most effective solution is probably the careful use of cosmetic camouflage. There are many useful camouflage creams available and these are described in some detail on p. 187. It is only fair to point out that stretch marks never disappear altogether, although they may fade and become less obvious as the years go by.

Women who have suffered particularly badly during pregnancy or weight gain and who have been left with exceptionally visible stretch marks are sometimes tempted to try plastic surgery as a therapeutic solution. It is sometimes claimed that when the stretch marks are being removed any excess fat can also be taken away – thereby leaving the fortunate woman with a flat, smooth stomach.

I'm afraid that many realistic plastic surgeons are a little less hopeful. It is very often difficult, if not impossible, to remove all stretch marks from the abdomen and where the marks have affected the thighs as well there are often very visible residual scars after an operation. Generally speaking, the woman looking for plastic surgery to adapt the appearance of her abdomen should be prepared to settle for a better shape. In other words, after surgery she may well have a flatter abdomen but she may also have scars which make bikini-wearing unwise.

Incidentally, stretch marks are not the only cosmetic problem pregnant women need to face. Pregnancy usually results in an increase in the secretions from oil and sweat glands in the skin with the result that the hair and the skin may become oilier, while body odours become more pronounced. Some pregnant women notice an increase in the amount of body and facial hair, and nails may become more brittle. Puffiness and thickness of the skin is common, and many pregnant women notice the deposition of a brown pigment in the skin. Where this brown pigment is confined to the area around the nipples (the areolas) and the vulva there is no cosmetic problem, but where the pigmentation affects the face and the skin on the rest of the body cosmetic camouflage creams may be required (see p. 187). Visible veins and capillaries may be a problem for the first time during pregnancy, and again cosmetic camouflage creams are probably the best solution.

Sunburn

Sunbathing is a relatively new fashion which has risen in popularity as a result of a number of social developments. First, there was the upsurge in popularity of seaside holidays which made sea bathing acceptable and bathing costumes essential. Then came the introduction of briefer and more daring bathing costumes which enabled holidaymakers to expose larger areas of skin to the elements. And third came the increase in international travel which enabled those of us normally denied a chance to expose ourselves to more than an occasional glimpse of sunshine to indulge ourselves in a positive orgy of bright light.

The social developments of the last few decades have naturally not been accompanied by any appropriate genetic adaptations. Fair-skinned individuals whose ancestors were largely confined to the temperate climates of Northern Europe are poorly prepared to cope with all this exposure to sunlight. Celtic, Nordic and Anglo-Saxon skins are easily damaged, and the bluer the eyes, the redder the hair and the lighter the complexion, the greater is the risk of temporary and permanent damage.

The dangers, however, have been poorly reported and as a huge industry has grown up to satisfy the demands of sunseekers and holiday-makers anxious to acquire suntans, so the facts about sun-bathing have been eclipsed by the claims, counter-claims and ex-hortations of the companies encouraging the sunworshipping cult.

The truth is that lying in the sun acquiring a suntan may be the fashionable thing to do but it isn't sensible. The sun damages more human skin more effectively than any other single external factor. Those are the simple facts, and since I realize that there is too large an industry dependent upon the universal Caucasian ambition to acquire a deep, all-over tan for sunbathing to become *passé*, I state them not in any expectation that pallor will once again become fashionable but in the hope that those who worship the sun might in future do so with a little more caution, respect and preparation.

What is often forgotten is that when the skin turns brown it is trying to protect itself from the effects of the sun, since the ultra-violet light emitted by the sun can cause changes in the structure, chemistry and function of the skin's tissues.

Sunshine is partly responsible for the ageing process that affects the skin and this is why the hands and face are usually wrinkled, dry and papery before other parts of the body. Most of us expose our hands and faces to more sun than, say, our upper arms and thighs.

When white or pink skin is exposed to the sun a number of things happen. To begin with skin cells are injured and they release a histamine type of substance which produces reddening and itching of the skin. After a period of time, which may vary from hours to days, cells deep inside the skin start to release a substance called melanin which slowly migrates towards the surface. Melanin is the pigment which gives the skin its tan and its purpose is to provide some protection against further damage. Dark-skinned people already have a protective layer of melanin on the outer skin surface and they can sunbathe with relative impunity, although of course few do!

Those are not the only effects which the sun has on human skin. There is also a drying effect, and the skin becomes thicker and tougher too. The thickening blocks the skin's pores and the drying up leads to a shedding of powdery white particles made up of dead cells. Blood vessels dilate as a result of the heat and fluid may leak out into the tissues giving the skin an overall tight feeling. Blisters and peeling are common sequels. All these are harmful changes which can at best lead to temporary burning or premature ageing and at worst to the development of skin cancer.

The damage the sun can cause to the skin depends on a number of factors.

The skin type is obviously important since darker skinned folk are obviously already protected to an extent which relates directly to the colour of their skin. Fair-haired or red-haired people with light blue eyes and pale, freckled skin are most susceptible and most likely to develop skin cancer.

The intensity of exposure and the duration of exposure are also important factors. Latitude, altitude, season, time of day and the surrounding environment all affect the type of exposure. The sun is more dangerous when high in the sky, when the sunbather is near the equator or when the air is thin and relatively unpolluted as it is on mountain ski slopes. Snow, water, sand and white buildings all reflect the sun's rays and can all make sunbathing that much more hazardous. And, of course, you don't have to deliberately sunbathe to be exposed to the sun. Sportsmen and sportswomen usually age more quickly than night-club people simply because they tend to spend more time out in the sunshine. Outdoor living ought to be a healthier existence, and in general it may be, but as far as the skin is concerned it isn't. Finally, it is important to realize that many white-skinned people of European extraction now live permanently in climates for which they are genetically quite unsuited. White Australians, for example, commonly suffer from ageing skin and skin cancers.

It is no coincidence that skin beauty is traditionally associated with the pale-skinned women of Northern Europe.

There are, of course, a great many ways in which you can protect yourself from the sun.

The most obvious way to avoid sun damage is to keep out of the sun when it is at its most dangerous. This may sound very obvious, but it is always surprising just how many tourists forget that the sun is much hotter and potentially more dangerous in holiday areas. While the locals keep to the shade at midday and stick to the shady side of the street in early afternoon, the tourists will be out there with Noël Coward's mad dogs, mopping their brows and peeling.

Even when keeping out of the sun is impossible there are many purely physical ways in which to obtain protection. A broad-brimmed hat is the most obvious form of protection and those Mexican bandits didn't just wear them because they looked romantic. Long sleeved, loose-fitting cotton clothes can provide a considerable amount of protection too. Sunshades and umbrellas are slightly old-fashioned now unless they're fixed in position on the beach but they do provide good protection.

But it is the creams and lotions which most people turn to when sunbathing, either because they want to get a suntan quickly and safely or because they have had some experience of the discomfort that may be associated with too much sun.

The simplest products with which to obtain protection are those which do nothing but provide a screen, protecting the skin against the ultraviolet light of the sun. Moisturizing creams (and within this category I include everything from cleansing milks, which provide relatively little protection, to cold creams which provide much more protection) will help without their containing any added ingredient. Moisturizing creams should be applied after sunbathing, too, since they help to keep moisture in potentially dry skin. Your ordinary moisturizer will do just as well for use after sunbathing as any product sold specifically for this purpose.

It is important to remember that whatever protective cream is used it must be applied to every piece of skin which may be exposed. The neck and lips are often forgotten when the face is being protected, but they are easily burnt. It is also important to replace creams every few hours since they are easily rubbed or washed off by clothes, perspiration or seawater.

Much more useful than simple, ordinary moisturizers, however, are those products which contain a sunscreening agent. These products won't help you get a tan but they will help stop burning occurring and they may help you acquire a tan more safely. As usual with cosmetic products the problem is trying to differentiate between the rival claims of different manufacturers.

The most effective total sunscreens are those which contain substances like zinc oxide. These products, usually known as sun barrier creams, do not let any sun through if applied properly and are most useful for those with very sensitive skin who want to go out into the sunshine but who are worried about the effect it can have. *Zinc Cream BP* or *Zinc Ointment BP* are cheap ways to buy this type of total protection. A heavy foundation cream can also prove helpful.

For most people, however, a sunscreen cream should provide some protection from the sun but should not prevent tanning taking place. This desire to have the best of both worlds isn't entirely outrageous since there are a number of creams available which provide protection but which allow the skin to acquire a tan.

Sunscreen creams depend for their effectiveness on the fact that ultraviolet light comes in various sizes. Short wavelength ultraviolet light tends to produce a lot of redness but not much tanning, while long wavelength ultraviolet light does the opposite, stimulating the migration of melanin cells but doing a minimum of damage to the skin.

Ideal sunscreen protection should, therefore, screen out some of the short wavelength ultraviolet rays while letting through the longer rays. The ideal preparation should, in addition, be packaged so that it is compact and easy to use.

Chemicals which filter out the shorter length rays include para-aminobenzoic acid, the benzophenone derivatives, and a number of other substances These compounds vary in their efficiency, their tendency to stain clothing and irritate the skin and their ability to remain on the skin when wet, although most of them when sold in an oily or greasy base are more resistant to water.

The sunscreen manufacturers often claim that their products provide protection according to some sort of scale and that this system enables the consumer to choose a product suited to his or her skin. This is very neat theoretically but the only problem is that there doesn't seem to be any generally accepted scale and so manufacturers' claims vary.

Generally speaking, however, the higher the number on a product the greater the protection provided and the more suitable the product is to a pale, sensitive skin. The theory is that a product with a factor of 6 will delay burning for six times as long as usual. So if you would burn after being in the sun for fifteen minutes without a sunscreen cream, you shouldn't burn in the sun with a cream of factor 6 until you've been there for ninety minutes.

The difficulty in comparing products becomes obvious when you compare the range of protection offered. *Coppertone*, said to be the world's No. 1 sun-tan range, has a product with sun protection factor 6 for redheads and light-skinned people who burn very easily. The same factor number is given to Vichy's product *Extra Protection*, and Lancome's *Hydra Bronz* for the fair skinned also has a factor of 6. *Piz Buin*'s product for skin that easily burns is given a skin protection factor of 8 as is Clinique's *Sun Block*, while the *Delial* range, said by its manufacturers to be Europe's top-selling sun-tan products, has a product with a protection factor of 10. Now I really don't know how far these figures are truly reliable, and as far as I know it is possible that one company's higher numbered product might provide less protection than another company's lower numbered product. And, of course, since there are so many other factors involved, ranging from individual skin type to the intensity of the sun and the amount of reflected light, truly objective assessments of products are impossible to make. Still, the number system should help a little when you're choosing a product.

Incidentally, some products are given extraordinarily high protection factors – I've seen products said to have sun protection factors of 23.

These simple sunscreen compounds are effective and useful. They provide some protection but they don't completely prevent tanning. However, today these basic ingredients are not considered to be enough by many sun lovers who expect their sunscreen agent not only to provide them with some protection but also to help them get a sun-tan quicker than they might otherwise have got one. To do this, creams have to contain an accelerator – a substance which temporarily increases the sensitivity of the skin to the types of ultraviolet light which produce tanning.

One of the first companies to produce a compound containing an accelerator was Bergasol. They make oils, gels, lotions and creams designed for those who tan easily and for those who burn at the tenderest touch of a solar ray. There are, however, a number of other products on the market. Helena Rubinstein make *Golden Beauty*, for example, which contains an accelerator.

A number of companies make ranges of products said to be designed to suit the tanning individual. The theory is that as the days go by and your tan gets darker you need less protection and can afford to use more accelerator. BioBronze, for example, make two tubes of cream: one contains a larger amount of sunscreen and a relatively small amount of accelerator while the second, designed to be used in the latter part of a holiday in the sun, contains both a mixture of oils and more accelerator. The cleverest packaging, however, has to be from Concept Pharmaceuticals whose product *Sun by Sun* is packed in a tube with a dial-type nozzle.

When the dial is put in position 1 and the tube is squeezed a white moisturizing cream comes out. This is a sunscreen agent which is suitable for the fair-skinned sunbathing novice. When the dial is put in position 2 the resultant cream contains a mixture of sunscreen together with a natural accelerator which turns the cream slightly brown and which consists mainly of the enhancer obtained from the bergamot fruit. A third dial position increases the amount of enhancer and is said to be most suitable for those individuals who already have a tan.

The advantage of this product is obviously that only one tube has to be carried down on to the beach.

Roche claim to have spent five years developing their *Eversun* product which, they promise, will help the skin go browner and the tan go deeper than ever before.

Roche were kind enough to ask Dr Gustav Erlemann, their Director of Cosmetic Research and Development in Basle and the President of the Swiss Society of Cosmetic Chemists, to let me see some of the background information on the product and its active substance guanine.

The reports seem to me to be undramatic, however, and the only conclusion I could draw is that *Eversun* contains a new sunscreen agent.

Roche also make a range of products described as *Aquasun* which are said to be water resistant. This may well be (there are a number of water-resistant sunscreens), but however resistant to water a product may be, it can still be rubbed off, and so I still recommend that sunscreens need reapplying after bathing and after a couple of hours on the beach.

The cosmetic companies have, of course, made it possible for all of us to acquire a tan without ever leaving the bathroom by using one of the artificial sun-tan products. These are variously described as quick tans, indoor tans and bronzers, and although many people find them useful, they can occasionally cause problems. Some people find that they turn a nasty shade of orange and others have discovered that artificial tans have a nasty habit of settling in skin creases and staining their hands a rather unnatural looking mahogany brown. The first problem can to a certain extent be avoided by doing a patch test on a small area of skin before applying the product to a wider area, and the second problem can be avoided by applying the product with great care and washing the hands thoroughly afterwards. If the skin really does look a mess, most fake tans can be removed with a rough flannel or loofah. Another problem is that artificial tanners containing dihydroxyacetone may produce a patchy appearance.

Generally speaking, artificial suntan products are safe and effective but it is most important to realize and to remember that a fake tan does not provide any protection against the sun.

You can, by the way, purchase products which contain a fake tanning agent as well as a sunscreen. I don't recommend these products at all since a sunscreen (even if it is described as waterproof) needs to be reapplied regularly and if you do that with a product that contains a tanning agent you may end up darker than you wanted to be.

Despite the availability of these products and the dissemination of good advice about how to avoid getting sunburnt there will always be those who through ill fortune or poor judgement do suffer from sunburn.

At the first signs of burning (usually a reddening of the skin and a feeling of tightness which may or may not be accompanied by swelling and blistering) it is vital to get out of the sun completely. It is also important to stay out of it for several days since any more sun on the damaged skin will only make things worse. Blisters should not be burst, and fluids lost in sweat need to be replaced as cool drinks.

Mild discomfort is best treated with a moisturizing cream of some kind and *Nivea* and *Boots E45* are as good as anything else for this purpose, while *Calamine Lotion BP* or *Calamine Ointment BPC* can be used if the skin is also hot and itchy. Generally speaking, your favourite unperfumed moisturizing cream is probably the best product to use. There is little point in buying anything special.

More severe burning needs to be treated in the same way as any other type of burn. Cold water, followed by a dry, non-stick dressing, is the best first-aid treatment for burns that don't exceed more than two or three square inches or which are not accompanied by general symptoms or more severe skin damage.

Sunbathers sometimes discover that they develop brown, blotchy patches. What has happened is that the skin has been made more sensitive to the sun and that tanning has continued at a faster than usual pace. Unfortunately, the faster pace isn't uniform, hence the development of darker patches. The really bad news is that the patches of browner skin sometimes don't fade at all but stand out year after year, often darkening more rapidly again when re-exposed to the sun.

There are various products which cause this peculiar sensitivity. A number of cosmetics and perfumes can be responsible, and, in particular, perfumes which contain oil of bergamot seem to cause the condition. The secrecy which surrounds the composition of many perfumes means that it is more or less impossible to prepare a list of potentially troublesome perfumes, and the best advice I can give is to avoid perfume altogether when sunbathing. If you must use it, then make sure you apply it evenly over the areas which will be exposed to the sun. A variety of prescribed medicines can cause skin blotches and rashes, too, but since drugs which have been found responsible vary from antibiotics to diuretics and from contraceptives to tranquillizers, it is again difficult to offer specific advice. In general, I think it is probably best to simply be aware of the potential hazard and to stay out of the sun and seek medical advice if you develop a skin blemish or rash while taking a prescribed product. Don't be tempted to leave off prescribed pills unless your doctor has given you permission to do so, since modern drugs can cause unpleasant reactions if stopped suddenly.

So far I've dealt only with natural sun-tans and with the problems associated with outdoor sun bathing. Today, however, sunlamps and sunbeds are becoming more popular both in beauty clinics and at home. The claims for these products often seem to be wildly enthusiastic, and the advertisements rarely include the sort of warnings which I think they ought to carry.

To begin with, it is only reasonable to point out that sunlamps and beds which are designed to give you a sun-tan can usually damage the skin in just the same way that the sun can. In my opinion, it is no exaggeration to describe sunlamps as electric wrinkle machines.

It is also important to point out that the same sort of precautions need to be taken when using a lamp as when sunbathing out of doors. In other words, a strict time limit should be applied until a tan appears, a screening agent should be used if the skin is sensitive and a moisturizer used afterwards to help prevent dryness developing. It's also a good idea to protect the eyes and hair too.

During the months I spent researching for this book I collected a whole armful of brochures and leaflets about sunbeds, sunlamps and solariums, and the warnings given about the dangers of too much exposure are either non-existent or inadequate. One manufacturer coyly dodges the issue by including at the back of its brochure a note which says that 'persons using cosmetics, medicines, drugs or receiving medical attention should consult their doctor before using a sunbed'. This sort of warning really is not fair since it effectively enables the manufacturer to pass the buck on to the customer and his doctor. How many people never use cosmetics of any kind, and how many doctors could or would be happy to advise their patients on using or not using a sunbed?

The products sold which provide artificial ultraviolet light fall into three main categories: sunlamps, sunbeds and solariums. The difference between them is simple: you sit in front of a sunlamp, lie on a sunbed and under a solarium.

You undoubtedly can get sun-tanned by using any of these products, but I don't agree with the claims from some manufacturers' that their products are 'safe' and that the rays they give out are 'harmless'. These pieces of equipment are all potentially dangerous if not used properly and in general I don't recommend any of them, although psoriasis sufferers may well benefit from occasional bouts of artificial sunshine obtained in this way. It is known that psoriasis can be relieved by a warm, dry climate, and it may well be that using a lamp, sunbed or solarium could help improve the condition of a sufferer's skin.

Safety in the sun

1 If you have fair or red hair, pale eyes and particularly pale skin you must be very careful in the sun.

2 Whatever your hair and skin colour, don't sunbathe for more than fifteen minutes if you haven't previously been in the sun for the last few months. If you sunbathe at midday you should limit that period to ten minutes, since midday sun is more dangerous than afternoon or morning sunshine. Locals in hot countries take a siesta for good reason.

3 Remember that you can burn even when wet since ultraviolet

light is not filtered out by water. Sun can burn through clouds for the same reason.

4 If you lie down when sunbathing or if you think you're likely to go to sleep, use an alarm clock or borrow a watch with a timer on it.

5 Don't be tempted to use an aluminium reflector to increase the speed at which you tan. It's an easy way to acquire localized burns.

6 Remember to apply sunscreen creams liberally and generally and to reapply them every few hours and particularly after bathing.

7 Sunglasses and sunhats provide good protection, as do parasols and beach umbrellas.

8 Remember that some pills and perfumes can sensitize you to the sun.

9 When applying sunscreen creams don't forget your shoulders, shins and the tops of the feet. The skin there is easily burnt.

10 Always use a moisturizer after you've been in the sun.

11 If you've partly tanned and you're then exposed to more sun, remember that the newly exposed area needs to be introduced slowly to the sun. Women who pluck up courage to go topless after four or five days on the beach can suffer nasty burns on sensitive parts.

12 Remember that these rules apply to sunlamps and sunbeds as well as to the sun itself.

Vaginal problems

'Feminine' odours and secretions, as they are coyly called by the pharmaceutical and cosmetic industries, are not necessarily unnatural or unacceptable. Like all animals, humans produce their own individual secretions as a result of chemical, psychological and hormonal pathways. Those secretions are physiologically essential in the vaginal area where they lubricate the inner walls and maintain the vaginal environment in the best possible condition. The precise chemical composition of those secretions varies from one individual to another with resultant differences in the odours.

Always ready and willing to exploit new commercial opportunities, the combined drug and cosmetic industries have come up with a variety of products designed to cope with real or imaginary perineal problems, often basing their marketing strategies on the undeniable anxiety of women taught to regard any personal odour as potentially offensive.

The problem is, of course, that any deodorant that is to be even marginally effective must contain pharmacologically active ingredients – constituents which, by their very nature, must be liable to produce reactions on the sensitive skin around the outer vaginal area.

Femfresh, for example, formulated and sold as a vulval deodorant, contains, among other things, a perfume and an antiseptic called chlorhexidine hydrochloride which is known to cause unpleasant reactions in some users.

Most doctors do not recommend the use of any product designed to deal with odours in this way but do, instead, suggest that where vaginal odours are unacceptable, an explanation should be sought.

The commonest cause of problem smells is probably simply the accumulation of sebum and sweat as a result of inadequate cleansing. Using a deodorant to deal with this problem is quite inappropriate since the problem can be far more effectively dealt with by daily bathing and by changing underwear regularly. The continental bidet, which makes washing the perineal region simple without a full bath or shower being taken, should perhaps be a more common fixture in the British bathroom. The use of powders and sprays can cause soreness and allergies and is unlikely to have any useful effect on the basic problem.

It is certainly worth while mentioning, incidentally, that tights and panty hose, which stop the flow of air around the perineum, ensure that the vaginal area remains exceptionally warm and moist – making the local environment particularly suitable for the growth of micro-organisms. The woman who finds the wearing of stockings too uncomfortable to bear can ease potential problems by choosing cotton underwear rather than nylon.

Really offensive odours are usually caused by the collection of semen or old blood or by the development of some severe infection which will usually be associated with a heavier than usual discharge and probably some local irritation. Retained and forgotten tampons are a common cause of odour, discharge and irritation, while less common objects removed from the vagina have included a set of dentures, a gear lever and a glass eye.

A heavy, clear discharge may, incidentally, occur quite normally and is a particularly common problem among young girls, pregnant women and contraceptive pill users. There is no real solution to this problem and the only wise course is to bathe and change frequently and, if necessary, to wear protective pads.

As a cautionary note I should add that any woman who has an offensive discharge, an unusually unpleasant vaginal odour or any unusual bleeding should see a doctor for an examination and not resort to cosmetic camouflage. Similarly, I would advise any woman who suffers from rashes or itching around the vagina to see a doctor. There are products available for this type of condition, but I do not recommend that they are used without a medical examination having been performed.

The other important problem associated with this area is dryness, and where this problem exists alone it can be relieved by the use of a lubricant. The product most widely recommended by doctors seems to be *K-Y Jelly*, which is greaseless, non-irritant and inexpensive. This is, incidentally, the product many doctors choose to lubricate examining gloves. It is equally suitable for women who find that their vaginal dryness makes intercourse uncomfortable.

Veins

There are some habits which are bound to make the development of varicose veins more likely. Anyone, for example, who spends the day standing up is going to put a greater than average strain on his or her leg veins and consequently stands a high chance of developing varicose veins. Dentists and shop assistants are common sufferers for this reason.

In addition, however, there are some other factors which cause varicose veins. Female hormones, for example, seem to have an influence over the development of varicosities, and we know that for every man with varicose veins there will be five women. Pregnancy is another important influence, and many of the women who develop varicose veins during pregnancy find that the veins don't go down again afterwards.

Finally, there are many people who aren't female, who aren't pregnant and who don't spend much time standing up who develop varicose veins. It seems that many sufferers have just inherited them, and there isn't much you can do about that.

Understanding the way that varicose veins develop is an important step towards understanding the ways in which they can be prevented or controlled.

Obviously, the simplest thing you can do if you find that you are developing varicose veins is to try and sit down with your feet up for a few minutes every hour. If you do that then the blood in the veins in your legs will not have such a job fighting its way back to the heart and the varicose veins in your legs won't swell up quite as much.

Unfortunately that isn't always practicable, and I don't suppose there are many shop assistants whose employers would happily allow them to lie down every hour.

There is, fortunately, another simple remedy which does work and which depends upon the fact that the veins are squeezed empty and the blood helped back to the heart by the action of the muscles in the legs. When the muscles contract they compress the veins and squirt the blood upwards. Normally, of course, muscles contract when the owner of them is walking, but there is no reason why someone standing still should not tense his leg muscles. If you can learn to do that every hour you can help prevent the development of varicose veins.

Many people do find that an altogether more suitable remedy is to wear some sort of support or elastic hose. The supporting stockings or tights prevent blood pooling in the veins and help its return upwards.

Unfortunately, I find that many people refuse to wear any sort of elastic stockings. Men are reluctant, for fairly obvious reasons, to wear them, and women usually seem convinced that elastic stockings have to be unsightly, thick and very obvious.

This is a pity, since elastic stockings don't have to look like jumble-sale remnants and they can do a great deal to help prevent varicose veins getting any worse. There are a number of firms making elastic stockings and tights which look more or less like ordinary stockings when worn.

Some distinction is usually made between support hose and elastic hosiery, the former usually being recommended for use by individuals with mild varicose veins or by people who seem likely to develop varicose veins if they aren't careful (pregnant women for example). Support hosiery is usually available either as stockings or tights. Elastic hosiery is much thicker, more powerful and more suitable for existing varicose veins, and it is usually only sold as stockings and not as tights.

If varicose veins are ignored and no effort is made to control them they can cause many problems. The legs can swell, they can ache and the skin can break down to produce eczema and even ulcers. These problems can be difficult to treat. If veins get so bad that elastic stockings don't help at all there are two types of operation available. If the veins are isolated and small they can be closed off by injections which cause the blood to clot in them; if, however, they are long and spreading, surgical removal may be necessary.

The treatment of skin disorders around varicose veins and, in particular, the treatment of varicose ulcers needs medical attention.

Veins that swell and which become obviously varicose are not the only cause of cosmetic problems associated with the circulatory system. Broken veins, obvious capillaries and permanently dilated vessels can, and often do, cause problems at any age and on any part of the body. Often the face is involved since excessive exposure to the sun is a common cause of this type of problem. Tight garters, girdles and other items of underwear can cause problems, as can ill-fitting spectacle frames.

Beauty specialists and electrolysists sometimes claim that they can treat these minor circulatory problems with electricity, but I really do not recommend such a remedy. I am sometimes amazed at the things that medically unqualified specialists are prepared to do to other people's bodies. I suspect they do it because they don't always realize just what harm they can do. If they were just half as ignorant, many would be twice as careful.

Nor do I recommend that you take any notice of people who tell you that broken veins can be treated by special creams containing vitamins or any other magical remedies. I do not think that is possible to repair broken capillaries or reduce the size of swollen veins with any cream or ointment.

The best way to cover up small broken veins or capillaries is to use a cover-up or camouflage cream. Slightly green foundation creams seem to work best at disguising red surface capillaries. More obvious blemishes can be disguised by using masking or camouflage creams (see p. 187).

To prevent the development of damaged veins and capillaries, use a moisturizing cream regularly, avoid astringents and skin tonics and protect your skin from the sun.

Warts

Before discussing warts and their treatment I must include a short warning.

If you have any skin blemish which bleeds, grows, changes in size or colour or alters in any way, then you should seek medical advice straight away. Warty growths can become malignant, but if attended to at an early stage they can be completely and successfully removed.

Having said that I must also point out that it is difficult to assess the efficiency of wart removal techniques since a good many warts disappear by themselves in time.

Many warts are viral in origin and are consequently contagious. The warts that grow on the backs of the hands and on the feet (where they are known as verrucae) are particularly common among children and young adults since immunity develops with time. This immunity not only leads to the disappearance of existing warts in many cases but also provides some protection for the future.

Salicylic acid is a fairly effective wart remover and it is available in *Avrogel, Ayrtons Corn and Wart Paint, Compound W, Duofilm, Salactol, Verrugon* and *Wartex Ointment. Salicylic Acid Collodion BPC* can be bought, but the branded preparations usually have instructions with them which may be very useful. *Cupa Wart Solvent* contains glacial acetic acid which can be used with similar effect.

These preparations will need to be applied to the warts for several weeks at a time and may need to be used for two months or more. They should not be used for warts on the face or genitalia or, of course, for warts which have bled or become infected.

Only treat a wart as such if you are sure it is a wart. There are many other types of skin condition which have a similar appearance and which may need different types of treatment.

Wrinkles

Most of the organs of the human body age without our being unduly aware of any change. We may not be able to run as fast as we once could or to eat as much without developing pains of protest, but unless the symptoms of old age become severe or easily apparent we aren't likely to do anything about them.

There is, however, one organ which does age very conspicuously and which is the target of most of those who would seek to sell us products designed to defy and delay the process of ageing. That organ is the skin.

As we grow older there is a superficial build-up of dead cells which tend to stick together on the skin surface and cause roughness and dryness. There is also an increase in skin pigmentation, but instead of being even and regular the pigmentation tends to be rather blotchy, with the result that freckle-like patches called liver spots (which are nothing at all to do with the liver) are formed.

Changes in sex hormone levels which accompany ageing affect the skin very noticeably. A reduction in the level of circulating male hormones (which occurs in both men and women) causes a decrease in the production of oil from the glands in the skin, and a reduction in the level of female hormones produces a reversal of some of the secondary sexual characteristics so that the older woman, whose production of sex hormones has dropped considerably, will have slack breasts, flatter, sexually less responsive nipples and sparser pubic hair. The connective tissue which lies underneath the skin loses its firmness and becomes lumpy, while the elastic fibres break with the result that the structure of the skin collapses. The wrinkles in the dermis, the lower layer of skin, cause wrinkles in the epidermis, the outer skin layer, since the latter is connected to and dependent on the former. The lack of elasticity in the elastic fibres of older skin can easily be shown by picking up a patch of skin and watching it retain its new shape for several seconds. Pick up a patch of skin on a teenager and it will quickly return to its original shape.

Blood vessels within the skin sometimes expand and may break so that the skin develops a ruddy look with occasional red spots.

All these inevitable results of ageing can be hastened by any one of a number of environmental changes. The most important ageing factor is the sun and this, together with drying winds, can cause a rapid increase in the rate at which the skin ages.

Sunlight affects skin in several ways. The immediate effect is to produce an increase in the amount of skin pigmentation, a build-up of cells and a dilatation of blood vessels. These changes are designed to protect the skin and to cool the body but they may be cumulative and can become permanent, with pigment remaining in the outer skin layer and with rough red spots, which may eventually become skin cancers, developing in the epidermis. The sun is also responsible for permanent changes in the elastic fibres of the dermis.

The importance of these changes can be easily measured by studying a group of old-aged pensioners and a similar group of middle-aged people. The older folk will, if they have been exposed to sunshine as much as most of us, be easily distinguishable from the younger ones by the texture of their facial skins. If, however, both groups are then encouraged to undress and expose their usually protected areas, it will be seen that the changes affecting the older people are far less dramatic on the parts of the body that have not been exposed to the sun.

All in all, the ability of the skin to remain tightly, smoothly and neatly wrapped around the underlying tissues like a latex body stocking depends on a number of factors, but the important point is that the physiological changes which result in the development of dry, wrinkled skin are themselves irreversible. Preventive programmes and treatments designed to limit the effects of ageing and the development of wrinkles must be considered with that fact in mind.

Preventing the development of wrinkles, although in the end always an impossible task, is obviously easier than trying to deal with existing wrinkles. I'll begin, therefore, with an account of the ways in which the development of wrinkles can be delayed.

It will by now be clear that one of the most effective ways to slow down the development of signs of ageing on the skin is to keep out of the sun or to use effective sunscreen creams whenever possible. If your sunbathing is confined to a fortnight each summer then you're unlikely to do yourself much harm, but if you spend much more time than that in the sun then you really are likely to accelerate all the signs of old age. You must make up your mind whether you're prepared to pay the price a suntan costs. Suntan creams and screens are discussed on p. 230.

Using a moisturizing cream regularly is an excellent way to protect the skin from the elements and from the pollutants which are present all around. A good, simple moisturizing cream is the most effective product you can buy to help prevent the development of wrinkles. These creams are discussed on p. 158.

Exercise is often promoted as an effective way to prevent the development of wrinkles, and a number of beauty experts have thought up complicated routines designed to strengthen the facial muscles. The fact is that it is the collapse, disappearance and break-down of elastin and collagen in the dermis which determines the formation of wrinkles, and these two proteins aren't affected by exercise. Whether or not exercising the muscles helps the appearance of the skin is debatable but I must point out that there are those who claim that developing the muscles actually causes wrinkles and that those who frown and smile more than the rest of us develop more wrinkles. It is certainly said that thespians, who use their facial muscles more than most, are more likely to suffer from wrinkles than non-thespians.

Massage is another well recommended technique for the prevention of wrinkles, but again I don't know of any evidence which suggests that massage has any effect at all, although vigorous massage may cause localized swelling in the skin tissues and may in that way help temporarily disguise wrinkles that already exist. Incidentally it is often said that moisturizing cream should be applied in certain directions so as not to damage the skin and that it should be massaged into the skin along specific lines. I don't think this claim has any basis in scientific fact but I think it sensible to apply moisturizing creams gently, rubbing them on to the skin without too much aggression. On the whole I rather suspect that enthusiastic massage is more likely to accelerate the development of wrinkles than to prevent them. The skin on your buttocks doesn't get massaged too often, but if you're good at gymnastics you'll be able to see that it isn't too badly affected by wrinkles. It's the use of moisturizing cream which provides a protective layer on otherwise naked skin that makes facial massage effective, not the massage itself.

A commonly used pollutant now thought to be associated with the development of wrinkles is tobacco. There are those who claim that tobacco damages the skin and causes wrinkles through physiological changes, but I prefer to believe that the association is much simpler: cigarette smokers often screw up their eyes because of the smoke they produce, and screwing up the eyes can cause wrinkles. The answer to this particular problem is either to give up smoking or to buy a cigarette holder.

Since bright sunlight usually makes most of us screw up our eyes, wearing sunglasses can also be an important and effective wrinkle preventive.

There are many products and techniques available for the treatment of wrinkles. A simple trick is to use a headband to provide a temporary face lift by pulling up and tightening the skin. This can be very effective in the short term but it can cause headaches if left in place for too long. More suitable for longer term use are the camouflage creams which are available. If the wrinkles aren't too bad then you simply put a good foundation cream over a moisturizer, but for more prominent wrinkles a masking cream may be needed.

Cosmeticians sometimes offer electric treatments for wrinkles. They apply electric currents to the skin and claim that this helps. I don't know whether or not the treatment works but I don't recommend it since it seems to me a potentially dangerous form of treatment.

Plastic surgery is the only really effective way to deal with existing wrinkles, but before you read any further I do recommend that you read my basic notes about plastic surgery on p. 68 if you're contemplating a surgical solution to your wrinkle problem. Plastic surgery can have a tremendous effect on your life, but so can the physical, psychological and financial complications which may accompany it. It is better to minimize those complications and to be aware of them than to discover them too late and then to regret ever having considered surgery as a treatment. There are beauticians offering some of the treatments done by plastic surgeons, but I would no more dream of allowing a beautician or cosmetician to try some of these techniques on me than I would dream of allowing a petrol pump attendant to fiddle around with the engine of my car.

The classical way for a plastic surgeon to deal with wrinkles is simply to tighten the skin. This works just as effectively as tightening a piece of cloth will remove surface wrinkles.

A standard face-lift intended to deal with sagging skin, deep creases, flabby neck and so on is major corrective surgery, which will often take several hours and require a fit patient and surgeon. Mini face-lifts are sometimes done but they probably aren't worth considering since the advantages they offer seem to match the cost and the name. A full face-lift is usually said to knock five or ten years off the patient's face, but since it doesn't stop the ageing process it usually needs re-doing after five years.

Using either a local or a general anaesthetic, the surgeon makes small cuts in front of the ears, cuts the facial skin free from the face and then literally pulls it tight before cutting off the excess. It sounds simple and in theory it is. In practice, of course, there are many nerves to be missed and small blood vessels to be sealed and the operation is not as easy as I've made it sound.

The risks associated with face-lift surgery are numerous, but most importantly if the circulation is badly impaired the skin can slough off entirely, while if the facial nerve is cut permanent paralysis may result. Very oily or dry skin reacts to the operation least successfully. Most patients spend two or three days in hospital, then have their stitches out a few days after that. Bruising and so on can take another two or three weeks to subside, while remaining scars around the ears can usually be disguised by wearing the hair long. A full face-lift which leaves no scar is rare.

The other extremely popular operation done to eliminate wrinkles involves the eyelids. This operation is long lasting, heals very quickly and is usually very effective. An eyelid operation is not always done automatically with a face-lift, although the two operations are usually complementary in that a patient who has had one done usually needs and wants to have the other done. Patients who have this operation may have temporary black eyes, but there are usually no visible scars.

Neither of these operations will necessarily remove forehead creases, and a separate operation is available (called a frontal ridectomy) which does just that. The snag is that afterwards the patient won't necessarily be able to produce the sort of expressions most of us expect to see.

Surgeons can effectively deal with wrinkles on other parts of the body too. Indeed, the only part of the body that they really don't seem able to smooth out is the inside of the thighs. Crafty beach observers who suspect all around them of buying their youthful appearances can spot the fakers by looking at the inside of the thighs.

As always, it is important that anyone who has a family history of keloid development (see p. 71) should not undergo plastic surgery unless it is absolute unavoidable. Keloid scars usually prove more of a problem than the original flaw.

Plastic surgeons sometimes offer other remedies for wrinkles. In the past, for example, some have injected silicone into the skin in an attempt to smooth the skin surface. This technique is now considered unacceptable by most reputable surgeons since the silicone doesn't always stay where it is put and the risks of it migrating round the body are high.

Dermal abrasion and chemosurgery are two other techniques sometimes offered for small wrinkles (as well as for acne scars and tattoos). In dermabrasion the surface layer of the skin is removed mechanically, rather as though the skin has been rubbed very fiercely by a strong man with a tough brush. In chemosurgery the skin's top surface is removed chemically in much the same way that the skin can be burnt away if acid is splashed on to it. Both techniques are as potentially dangerous as they sound and there are those who do not recommend them under any circumstances. Both of these are sometimes done by beauticians, but because of the risks involved I strongly recommend that anyone contemplating such treatment consult a dermatologist or a plastic surgeon. I'm sure that some beauticians are competent and careful but I know of no certain way that readers can be sure of consulting such a beautician. Moreover, if something goes wrong through ignorance or carelessness the individual who has consulted a registered medical practitioner is more or less guaranteed some form of compensation by the fact that most doctors are members of legal defence societies.

Since there are a large number of people who would very much like to delay or reverse the onset of the signs of old age, there are inevitably a large number of entrepreneurs ready and very willing to sell them products said to do just that. There has always been a good market for magical remedies designed to delay old age, and for centuries there have been men making money from the sale of bottles containing the Elixir of Life. During the Renaissance, when science was waking from a lengthy hibernation, alchemists spent much of their time and energy searching for that magic remedy and their efforts were always encouraged by those who paid their bills.

Today, the products available fall into two general categories: those said to work from the inside and those which are designed to work directly on the skin. I do not believe that any of them work, but the claims made by their manufacturers are too dramatic to be dismissed in a single paragraph.

I'll begin with the products which are said to delay the ageing process by acting on the body as a whole. Many of these remedies do involve dieting and exercise programmes which will certainly have a beneficial effect on the human body. But if you eat the wrong things, take too little exercise and do too many of the things which damage your body then you will benefit simply by changing your habits according to standard medical advice, rather than by spending money on any regime. You do not have to spend any money to protect your health, and anything you pay for pills or potions designed to delay the ageing process is, in my opinion, money wasted unless you consider the advice that accompanies the product worth the price. Hormone treatment prescribed by a doctor for menopausal symptoms is the only exception to this rule.

A number of the products available contain ginseng and garlic – two products which are widely used but about which relatively little is known. Pharmacological research has certainly been done and there is undoubtedly some evidence that one or both of these products might have useful effects on the human body, but clinical testing which satisfies all known criteria has not, as far as I've been able to find out, proved that either substance has undeniable value.

Vitamins are also popular constituents of many products sold to help preserve vitality or delay ageing processes. This really is nonsense, and trying to get fitter or stay younger by eating extra vitamins is like trying to get fitter or younger by breathing faster. By the way, those who advocate the use of large quantities of vitamins to prevent illness and preserve youth should be aware that there is now evidence which suggests that taking too much vitamin C may harm the body. It has long been likely that this would be the case, and those of us who have opposed the indiscriminate use of vitamins on the basis that there is no evidence that such use is safe can now point to evidence which suggests that the vitamin can indeed be harmful in large doses. So there is now no evidence that conclusively proves that taking large doses of vitamin C does any good, but there is evidence which suggests that it does harm. If you eat a good, varied diet you don't need extra vitamins.

There have recently been a number of vitamin creams introduced on to the market. Some of these are said to protect the skin from wrinkles. The vitamins most commonly used for these products are vitamin E and vitamin F, but I know of no scientific evidence which supports the claims made for products containing these vitamins.

Some skin products which are sold sound truly mysterious and sensational. *2nd Debut with Cellular Expansion Factor* is said to 'concentrate moisture in the epidermal layers of your skin to make it more supple, more attractive' and it is said to help feed moisture back into the skin's cells. *Esthetic Formula ZB142 Lotion* is said to dramatically banish telltale lines and crow's feet for several hours. *Georgina Blake's Honeypak Skin Rejuvenator and Moisturizer* is said to be particularly useful in preserving a good skin or re-vital-izing an ageing one, while *Line Remover* is said to help you 'look younger in 3 minutes'.

I don't believe that any of these products are more effective at preventing wrinkles than ordinary moisturizing creams or more effective at masking existing wrinkles than cosmetic masking creams.

Creams are sometimes sold which are said to provide the skin with fresh supplies of collagen or elastic fibres or which are said to help restore the effectiveness of these skin constituents. There is no evidence that I know of which supports these claims. Hormone creams used to be popularly advocated for the treatment of ageing skin, but there is no convincing evidence that these work, while there is evidence that they may cause damage if used in sufficiently high concentrations. Hormone creams on sale sometimes contain too little hormone to do anything useful or damaging.

Wrinkle tips

1 Use a moisturizing cream regularly to protect and preserve the texture of your skin.
2 Use a sunscreen cream and wear a sunhat and sunglasses if you're out in the sun a good deal. Wrinkles tomorrow are the price you pay for a suntan today.
3 If you smoke, use a cigarette holder.
4 Don't spend money on any product designed to prevent skin wrinkling or to deal with it once it has wrinkled. There are no magic remedies.
5 Once wrinkles have appeared, you can do one of two things. You can cover them up with masking creams, or you can have them smoothed out by a plastic surgeon.

TEETH

Bid them wash their faces,
And keep their teeth clean.

Coriolanus by William Shakespeare

ANATOMY
I can't help feeling that when designing our teeth the Good Lord did so with a resigned and rather benevolent smile on his face. The fact that we all have two sets of natural teeth, one for our childhood years and one for the rest of our lives, suggests that it was apparent right from the beginning that children would develop an affection for sweet things and a tendency to forget to clean their teeth.

Of course, it may simply be that we have to wait for our permanent teeth until our mouths have grown large enough to accommodate a full complement of thirty-two enamel-coated incisors, canines, molars and premolars. But that is a very dull and uninspiring explanation.

Those first milk teeth or deciduous teeth which are greeted by loving parents with such joy and wonder usually last for the worst of the sweet-eating era. They are gradually replaced between the ages of 7 and 12 by the permanent teeth and adult dentition is usually completed at the age of 20 or so by the eruption of the third permanent molars, usually described with mixed accuracy as the wisdom teeth.

There are twenty deciduous teeth in all, with each jaw having four incisors, two canines and four molars. The canines and incisors, which each have one root, are designed for cutting food, while the molars, which are intended for crushing and grinding, are equipped with two or three roots to help them withstand the sideways pressures to which they will be subjected.

When the permanent teeth erupt, the spaces previously occupied by the molars are filled by the premolars, and twelve extra teeth, known as the permanent molars, appear. If you have got all your teeth and they have all erupted you should have two incisors, one canine, two premolars and three molars in each half of each jaw.

Each tooth has a root which is attached to the bone beneath by fibrous bands called periodontal ligaments, a crown which is the piece of the tooth which is in view in the mouth, and a neck which connects the two. The crown of every tooth is covered with an outer layer of enamel, a very hard and dense substance which is, in fact, the hardest material in the body and which bears little or no resemblance to the substance which used to cover stoves. Underneath the enamel is a substance called dentine which is not quite so hard but similar in composition to bone. Inside the dentine is the pulp which provides the tooth with nourishment from blood vessels and which, as many people will readily confirm, is equipped with a nerve.

Enamel can't be replaced, and if you damage or wear away the enamel on your teeth then you're likely to be in trouble. Dentine, on the other hand, is continuously replaced if it gets damaged.

LOOKING AFTER YOUR TEETH

Nearly a third of all British adults have lost all their teeth and two-thirds of the children of school age in Britain have decayed teeth. Dentists, it is said, remove a total of several tons of teeth per year. It is hardly surprising, therefore, that dental decay is said to be one of the commonest diseases in the Western world.

The level of decay is not only responsible for poor eating habits but it is also a cause of much distress and embarrassment. The woman who spends hours on her hair and make-up will not look her best if her teeth are discoloured or missing and her gums swollen and bleeding.

It is now well established that dietary habits are largely responsible for this epidemic of dental decay. It was in the seventeenth century that people in Britain first began to eat sugar in relatively large quantities and it was at that same time that they began to suffer from rotting teeth. Medical historians and statisticians have carefully traced and related the increase in dental decay to the increase in the consumption of sugar. More recently it has been shown that tooth decay among the Eskimos has risen as they have adopted the American junk diet with its heavy sugar component.

With this connection well established, it is easy to see that one simple way to reduce the rate of dental decay is to reduce the consumption of sugar-rich foods. Since the worst offending foods are those which are sucked and sipped, so bathing the teeth in a destructive solution, it is sweets and sugar-rich drinks which are best avoided. Since it has been estimated that we eat approximately two pounds of sugar a week each, there must be plenty of room for cutting back. Incidentally, a sugar-eating binge, especially if you brush your teeth afterwards, is better for your teeth than a steady, slow consumption which means that the teeth are regularly bathed in this destructive solution.

On a more positive note, there are foods which help maintain the teeth in good condition. Sugar-free foods that need a great deal of chewing help to clean the teeth in a purely mechanical fashion and, by aiding the production of large quantities of saliva, help to keep the teeth clean. To prevent children acquiring a harmful taste for sweet foods it's a good idea to encourage them to chew and nibble fresh fruit, washed raw vegetables and so on. Milk is an excellent source of calcium and phosphorus, both of which are needed by developing teeth.

In recent years there has been a great deal of publicity about the importance of fluoride in the protection of teeth, and it is perhaps not widely realized that it was in the nineteenth century that doctors and dentists first recommended that fluoride be used to help maintain healthy teeth.

It was in 1892 that it was suggested that the high incidence of dental caries or tooth decay in England might be due to a deficiency of fluoride in the diet. Tooth enamel contains a substance called hydroxyapatite which, with the addition of fluoride, is converted to a harder and more decay-resistant substance called fluorapatite.

There is now strong evidence that in geographical regions where the water supply contains less than 0.5 parts per million, the addition of small amounts of fluoride to the drinking water or the local application of fluoride to the teeth will reduce the incidence of caries in growing children. Although, however, it is recognized that if added to the drinking water at a level of between 0.5 and 1 part per million fluoride will have a beneficial effect on teeth, it is known that if quantities ten times that are reached the fluoride can cause mottling of the teeth and may even result in the development of rheumatism.

The addition of fluoride to drinking water supplies has, not unexpectedly, aroused a great deal of controversy and stimulated much heated discussion. That is as it should be; although I am convinced that adding fluoride to drinking water supplies probably does help prevent tooth decay, I can't help feeling that this could be the thin end of a rather large wedge. Who knows what else could be added to our drinking water if we let those with the necessary authority add fluoride?

The social and ethical argument is partly unnecessary since it is relatively simple to provide protection at home. A three-year study conducted in schools in seventeen American communities that did not have fluoride in the water showed that a weekly fluoride mouthwash programme was an easy, effective and cheap way to reduce cavities. Preliminary results of the study by scientists at the National Institute of Dental Research in Washington showed an average reduction in tooth decay of 35 per cent among 75,000 children for an annual cost equivalent to a single small bag of sweets. Fluoride toothpaste can, of course, do the same job as a mouthwash.

Adding fluoride in one of these ways helps provide some additional dental protection and should, it seems, reduce the number of cavities later in life. To maintain the beneficial effect fluoride toothpaste has to be used regularly throughout adult life in order to keep the concentration of fluoride in the surface enamel at a high level. One cautionary note: young children who haven't learnt to spit out toothpaste but who are cleaning their teeth should be given an ordinary non-fluoride toothpaste to use.

Although fluoride will help prevent some decay, it naturally cannot provide protection against all indiscretions, nor can it replace good cleansing habits.

We normally clean our teeth without thinking, and because of this it is often done badly. Proper teeth-cleaning habits need to be started in early childhood and continued regularly if teeth are to be protected against plaque (the sticky, colourless film which is continuously being formed on human teeth and which is made up of a mixture of saliva, food debris and bacteria). When sugary substances come into contact with bacteria found in the plaque they form acids which start the decaying process. Proper tooth hygiene, therefore, involves cleaning away the plaque and this involves a little preparation and some thought.

The first problem that has to be conquered is the fact that plaque is invisible. If you can't see it, you can't really tell where it is, when it's there, and whether it's gone after you've cleaned. So the special so-called 'disclosing tablets' and solutions that can be bought (see p. 256) are a vital first step in home tooth care. The tablets are chewed and then discarded and they leave behind a pink stain on the plaque. That stain will remain until the teeth have been properly cleaned.

There are two vital weapons in the battle against plaque: dental floss and the toothbrush. Dental floss, which is simply thin thread which can be used to clean between the teeth where a toothbrush cannot reach, has only recently acquired any sort of real popularity. It is nevertheless an essential toilet requisite. Various brands are described on p. 256. When using floss it is important to be gentle and not to cut into the gums. If used carelessly, floss can cut into the gums like a cheesewire into a fresh cheddar.

Toothbrushing is often done with a battered implement better retired to cleaning typewriter keys. On p. 257 I have described some of the attributes of a good toothbrush. If a disclosing tablet has been used, then it is fairly easy to tell when the teeth have been properly cleaned; if it hasn't, then it helps to remember that each tooth has to be cleaned. If the brushing process is designed to clean each surface of each tooth then you won't go far wrong.

Choosing a toothpaste shouldn't be too difficult but the competing claims of the many different firms involved in this commercial area have perhaps made it so. On p. 258 I have described the advantages of some of the best-known brands, but as a general rule it is wise not to choose too abrasive a paste or powder. It is possible to damage the surface of the teeth if brushing is done too violently with a stiff brush and an abrasive paste, with the result that the teeth are literally worn away leaving them very sensitive to particularly cold or sweet products. A non-abrasive paste used with a soft brush twice a day is enough. Whatever the name of the paste you choose, the brush is more important, and cleaning the teeth will probably take three or four minutes if done properly. Many dentists suggest that one good clean done every evening will help far more than several half-hearted, hurried attempts during the daytime.

There is one other thing that you can do to help preserve your teeth and that is, of course, to visit a dentist.

Many of us are frightened of dentists, and it is probably wise to start young children off at the dentist's at an early age before they are likely to need much in the way of treatment. That way they'll grow up without acquiring an actual fear of the dentist.

It is generally thought that twice-yearly dental visits are vital, but more recently there has been some opposition to this well accepted routine. There is no real evidence to suggest that such frequent visits are necessary, and at least one expert has advised that intervals of between a year and eighteen months are more reasonable – particularly if the teeth are well looked after at home. For young children, more frequent visits are probably justifiable.

Dental floss

Although it is important to clean properly between the teeth, for many people this is not an easy task. The teeth are often so close together that it is impossible to get toothbrush bristles into the space. Dental floss is designed to do this instead of the brush. A number of companies make dental floss, but *Johnson's Dental Floss* (which is available waxed or unwaxed) is said to have 80 per cent of the rapidly growing £1 million market for this new product. Incidentally it doesn't matter whether you choose waxed or unwaxed.

Using floss is fairly easy. All you have to do is break off a length of the thin, cotton-like substance and wind both ends round the fingers of your two hands. Then you insert the taut strand of floss between the two teeth and pull it up and down to clean away the plaque. It is important not to damage the gums. You can buy a device called a *Floss-amatic* dental flosser and you can also buy a product called *Flik*, which consists of a stretch of multi-stranded floss mounted on a plastic holder. These offer no technical advantage but may make floss easier to use.

Disclosing tablets

I doubt if there were many people who had even heard of disclosing tablets a few years ago. Today there seems little doubt that these tablets will be big sellers in the future. They contain harmless food additive colourings which stain the teeth red where there is any plaque, and the advantage is that by using them an individual can see whether or not he or she has cleaned his or her teeth properly and whether or not any further cleaning is necessary.

A number of companies make these tablets, and I don't know of any criterion other than price that is worth following. Most tablets are simply chewed and allowed to dissolve in the saliva. The saliva is then swished round the mouth and rinsed away lightly with ordinary water. The red stain that shows up the plaque can then be brushed away.

There is, incidentally, at least one product which is said to show up 48-hour plaque in blue and 12- to 24-hour plaque in pink. I really can't see any great advantage in using this two-tone system, which I'm afraid I would find rather too much to cope with early in the morning or even late at night.

Toothbrushes

If you've always thought of a toothbrush as just a handle with bristles on the end you've obviously not been reading the manufacturers' advertisements. Judging by some of the material I've been looking at you'd think that toothbrush technology was up there with space travel and the silicone chip.

According to the British Standard for Toothbrushes there are four official stiffness grades (extra soft, soft, medium and hard) and three standard sizes of brush (adult, youth and child). The medium grade is twice as stiff as the soft and the soft is twice as stiff as the extra soft, while the hard is twice as stiff as the medium. Manufacturers are not allowed to make hard brushes in the size for youths and children.

That, you may think, is all fairly straightforward and helpful. It is, until you realize that not all manufacturers follow the British Standard and that some manufacturers make brushes which comply with the specification and brushes which don't.

So we're back to the advertisements, and the question of whether a pure natural bristle is better than a nylon bristle, whether the number of tufts matters, whether the tufts should be shaped or even and the question of just what size of the individual bristles means in terms of tooth care. And, finally, of course, whether an electric toothbrush is better than an old-fashioned one. Toothbrushes have come a long way since William Addis first invented the modern brush 200 years ago, and in the *Kent* catalogue alone there are at least twenty-five different shapes and types of tooth-brush. Other companies make brushes with handles shaped like cartoon characters or naked women.

I'm not going to attempt to compare different companies' brushes since one company's hard brush may be softer than another company's soft brush, but I have formulated some simple rules to follow when buying a new toothbrush.

1 Buy a brush with bristles which feel soft to the touch. It does not matter whether the bristles are nylon or natural. Nor does it matter much whether or not the ends of the individual bristles are rounded.
2 Buy a brush with a flat surface, not one with different lengths of bristle or with contoured heads.
3 Buy an electric toothbrush if you are disabled or if you have difficulty in holding or using an ordinary toothbrush.
4 Buy a new brush when the old one is worn and the bristles are bent. If the bristles fell out of the brand you bought last time, try a different product. To test your brush, press the bristles down with your finger. If they don't spring back into position then the brush should be retired. Most people need a new brush every three months.

Toothpastes

People have been using toothpaste for a long time now. *Euthymol* toothpaste, which is still on sale today, was first introduced in Britain in 1898. Today, a whole industry has grown up with the sole aim of providing people with enough toothpaste to help them keep their teeth clean and, to give you an idea of the size of the industry, one leading brand, *Colgate Dental Cream*, was said to have been the subject of a £4.5 million advertising campaign in 1980.

The evidence does suggest that regular tooth brushing certainly helps combat tooth and gum problems and that using a toothpaste can make tooth cleaning more effective. Cleaning with water alone helps remove much plaque, but the process isn't as pleasant as when a good tasting paste is used, and consequently cleaning is not likely to be as thorough.

Traditional toothpastes worked because in addition to flavouring and a detergent they included an abrasive which literally helped to scrub plaque away. There are now known to be risks of damaging the teeth if pastes or powders which are too abrasive are used, but most of the big-selling creams and pastes seem safe enough. Powders are possibly too abrasive for regular use.

The biggest question to be answered about toothpaste is, of course, whether or not a fluoride toothpaste is worth buying. The simple answer is that in my opinion it is. The British Dental Association grants endorsement to toothpastes containing fluoride, provided that they satisfy certain basic criteria, and as I write there are four toothpastes with their endorsement. These are *Macleans* (made by Beecham), *Crest* (made by Proctor and Gamble), *Signal* (made by Elida Gibbs) and *Colgate with MFP fluoride* (made by Colgate). I don't endorse toothpastes or anything else, but the evidence in favour of these particular products does seem strong. It is important to realize that including fluoride in a toothpaste is not as simple as it might sound, since the mixture needs to be carefully formulated in order to preserve the effectiveness of the fluoride compound.

Beecham Products, who make *Macleans* and *Aquafresh*, have now produced evidence which suggests that both of these products may actually control the formation of plaque as a result of their chemical constitution.

In the past some toothpaste manufacturers acquired, and deserved, bad reputations for becoming too excited and enthusiastic about toothpaste ingredients. The claims seemed to owe more to the copywriter's taste for hyperbole than the scientist's devotion to truth. Major modern toothpaste manufacturers can justifiably claim to have won a better reputation.

Finally, I feel that I must mention *Zohar Fluoride Kosher Toothpaste*. This is the only toothpaste I know of which conforms with Jewish dietary laws.

Other tooth cleaning equipment

In addition to toothbrushes and dental floss you can now buy many other pieces of equipment designed to help in tooth cleaning. You can, for example, buy a battery-operated tooth polisher or you can buy equipment (known as forced irrigation devices) designed to clean your teeth by squirting jets of water on to and between them.

I do not recommend any of these products. The World Health Organization technical report on irrigation devices points out that these are 'insufficient for the control of periodontal disease' and that 'they also give rise to a risk of local trauma and bacteraemia'.

Toothpicks, made usually of wood but occasionally of quills or even ivory, are useful for removing chunks of food from between the teeth, but they must be used carefully. If not handled with care they can damage the gums badly. You can also buy wooden sticks described as gum massage sticks or interdental cleansers, but again these need to be used carefully if the gums are not to be damaged.

Finally, you can even buy an antiseptic mouthrinse which contains granules said to react with the saliva to release oxygen. The force of the oxygen is said to flush food debris from between the teeth. I find that a little hard to swallow. The World Health Organization's technical report entitled 'Epidemiology, etiology and prevention of periodontal diseases' says that 'there is no evidence that rinsing of the mouth is effective in removing microbial plaque mechanically from tooth surfaces. Studies have shown that commercially available mouthwashes may give a pleasant taste but do not clean teeth'.

PURELY COSMETIC

There are no cosmetic products which I recommend for use on the teeth or gums although there are products such as *Pearlie* (an enamel designed to give teeth a natural sparkling white finish) and *Pearl drops* ('the first ever home tooth polish').

The best way to keep your teeth looking white and strong and your gums looking pink and healthy is to clean them carefully and regularly. If you have false teeth there are several products which you can buy to help ensure that your appearance is enhanced. These are discussed on p. 264.

Teeth which are damaged, chipped or uneven can be restored to good shape by capping or crowning. This often expensive work involves filing down the tooth to a narrow point and then covering the sharpened tip of natural tooth with a porcelain substitute.

TOOTH PROBLEMS

Introduction

The two commonest tooth problems are gingivitis (an infection and inflammation of the gum) and dental caries (a decay of the teeth). These are indeed the commonest diseases in the world today.

Gingivitis usually starts between the teeth or at the margin between tooth and gum. The main early symptom is bleeding, but the real risk is that with the decay of the gums the teeth will be loosened and will eventually fall out. Factors which may make gingivitis more likely include a lack of vitamin C and badly fitting braces, but the most common cause is simply poor oral hygiene.

Tooth decay occurs due to the destruction of the tooth's enamel or dentine by the acids produced within the mouth. Those acids are formed by the bacterial fermentation of sugar and starchy food debris. Caries starts on tooth enamel, particularly between the teeth, and may spread first to the underlying dentine and finally into the pulp.

The important early signs of dental trouble are:

1 Bleeding gums
2 Persistent bad breath
3 Swollen gums
4 Loose teeth

These signs need to be taken seriously and are a warning that a dentist's attention is needed.

A third common problem that affects many people is toothbrush abrasion. If the teeth are brushed too fiercely with too stiff a brush and an abrasive paste the teeth can literally be worn away so that they become very sensitive to cold and sweet things. To avoid this problem a soft brush and a non-abrasive paste should be used, and to alleviate the condition a paste such as *Sensodyne* (which contains strontium chloride) can be used. The Council on Therapeutics of the American Dental Association is reported to have said that it has not seen adequate evidence to justify claims for dentifrices sold to provide relief from hypersensitive teeth. I don't know whether or not they have included products containing strontium in their studies but I certainly have had some relief from a sensitive tooth by using *Sensodyne*. I don't offer this as scientific evidence but as a totally subjective experience.

Bad breath

Bad breath or halitosis can be caused by any one of a number of disorders. Catarrh, sinusitis and indigestion are but three of the more general disorders likely to be responsible for a persistently unpleasant oral odour. Obviously, treatment for these conditions will be of longer lasting benefit than simply disguising the bad breath with a mouth freshener of some kind.

The local causes of bad breath include gum infections, dirty teeth and infected teeth, and again treating the cause is much more sensible and much more effective than simply trying to disguise the symptom. If you suffer from bad breath, therefore, and you look after your mouth and gums, then you need to see a dentist.

While you are waiting for your appointment you can try using a mouthwash such as *Listerine Antiseptic Mouthwash* or a special aerosol such as *Gold Spot*. Most of the mouthwashes sold contain a mixture of antiseptics, while the breath fresheners on sale usually consist of a mixture of alcohol, water and artificial sweeteners. If you don't want to buy a special mouthwash you can save money by making up your own. Simply put half a teaspoonful of salt into a glass of warm water and use it to swill round your mouth. If you want to really produce a commercial type product, add a quarter of a teaspoonful of sodium bicarbonate and a drop of peppermint oil to the glass of water.

Regularly using a product of any kind to disguise bad breath is as sensible as repapering the bedroom ceiling every morning because there is a leak in the roof.

Bleeding gums

The commonest type of mouth trouble doesn't involve the teeth but the gums. Gingivitis is a well known destructive disorder which is responsible for the loss of many millions of teeth each year. Bleeding gums are an early sign of gingivitis and require the attention of a dentist.

Discoloured teeth

The teeth can be discoloured by many of the things we put into our mouths. Cigarettes are probably the commonest cause of yellow teeth.

Abrasive toothpastes can be used to help remove stains but these can damage the teeth if used too regularly. Stained teeth are best cleaned by a dentist, although a product called *Clinomyn Smokers Toothpaste* is said to be specially formulated to remove tobacco and tar stains and to prevent the return of stains, and it may be worth trying.

Toothache

The best way to treat toothache is by taking aspirin or paracetamol and making an appointment to see your dentist. If you don't have any aspirin or paracetamol, then a glass of whisky will often provide some relief. I have conducted a considerable amount of research into the various properties of available malt whiskies but I have reached no conclusions about their comparative values in the treatment of toothache.

There are a number of commercial products available for the treatment of toothache and many of them contain clove oil as an important constituent. Those in this category which I know of include *Boots Tooth Tincture*, *Kilpain Toothache Tincture*, *Three Flasks Tooth-Ache Solution* and *Touch and Go Toothache Solution*. Alternatively, a plug of cotton wool can simply be soaked in clove oil and inserted into or on to the cavity of the pain-giving tooth.

It is worth remembering, of course, that pains which appear to be caused by bad teeth can in fact be caused by problems in other parts of the head. Earache and sinusitis are two common disorders which may mimic toothache. You'll usually need a doctor or dentist to help you decide precisely what is causing your pain if you are unsure.

Finally, I should perhaps mention the problem of sensitive teeth. Many people find that one or more of their teeth are particularly sensitive to heat, cold or very sweet things. This condition can be caused or exacerbated by too much harsh brushing with an abrasive paste and it can be relieved by the use of a special toothpaste such as *Sensodyne* which contains strontium.

Tooth removal

Removing teeth is the last thing most dentists want to do. Any fool can rip out teeth that are causing pain or discomfort or which are partly decayed. It takes skill and care to protect and preserve human teeth from the carelessness and positive stupidity of their owners.

In an attempt to preserve existing natural teeth dentists will undertake many difficult restorative tasks. They'll use curettage to scrape plaque from underneath gum margins, perform gingivectomies to remove diseased gum and drill and fill diseased teeth. They'll use splints to attach weak teeth to rock-like neighbours and they'll sometimes build bridges between neighbouring teeth and use them to hold artificial teeth in place.

But however careful and skilled a dentist may be, there will always came a time when removal is necessary. Over a quarter of all adults have no natural teeth at all.

Artificial replacement teeth have been used for centuries to fill the cosmetic gaps and to make eating easier. In recent decades many new techniques have been tried. Tooth transplantation has, for example, been the subject of a good deal of experimentation, although the problems of rejection are difficult to overcome without killing the patient. Planting and fixing artificial teeth directly into the sockets from which decayed teeth have been taken has also been tried with mixed success, as has a painful sounding trick of building teeth up on metal pins stuck directly into the jaw bone.

But these imaginative restorative techniques are still as unreal as space travel for most people. By false teeth most of us mean dentures which can be taken out to be cleaned and which, if not attended to carefully, can have an embarrassing habit of slipping out of place in the middle of a good joke or a juicy steak.

Cleaning dentures is obviously rather different to cleaning natural teeth, although for cosmetic reasons it is just as important. Your false teeth may not rot and fall out if ignored but they quickly look dirty and taste nasty. Dentures that aren't kept clean are a common cause of bad breath too.

There are a number of denture cleansers on the market, and as long as the dentures are rinsed thoroughly before being put back into place, price and efficacy are the only criteria to be considered. Whether you buy a paste or you soak your teeth in a special liquid is largely a matter of taste. There is nothing wrong with ordinary toothpaste for cleaning dentures.

For false teeth that don't fit as well as they might there are a number of useful products available. Whether you choose a fixative powder such as *Super Wernet's* or a denture cushion such as *Cush-*

ion Grip or *Snug* is largely a matter of personal preference, although I would point out that if your false teeth do not fit properly because your mouth has changed shape (all mouths change shape as we grow older) then you really need to have new false teeth made rather than just buy a fixative of any kind. Poorly fitting dentures result in bad eating habits as well as social disasters.

For dentures that break there are products which are designed to help you repair cracked or broken dentures. Products such as the *Dentifix Emergency Repair Unit* are undoubtedly a useful addition to the travel kit of anyone with false teeth.

INDEX

articial tanning agents 234; bath
essences 154; bleaches,
detergents 205, 206; deodorants
181, 185, 238; depilatories 129,
184; eye make-up 94, 96–7;
flowers 205; hair dyes 111, 131,
184; jewellery 182; medicated
cleansers 156; moisturizers 158;
nickel 205; perfumes 40, 173,
181, 183–4; rubber 205;
shampoos 106, 185, 205, 207;
soaps 152–3, 185, 207; sun 18,
182; tanning lotions 182;
underwear 182
 patch tests for 17, 40, 111, 113,
115, 129–31, 184, 234; product
contents and 182
Almay 156, 183
Almay Cleansing Lotion 156
almonds 157, 180
aloes 195
alopecia 81, 117–19 *passim*, 120
alpine lady's mantle 38
aluminium 81; chlorhydrate 190;
chloride hexahydrate 192;
silicate 87
Amazone 21
ambergris 168, 170
amblyopia 99
American Dental Association,
Council on Therapeutics of 261
American Heart Journal 112
*American Journal of Diseases of
Children* 220
aminacrine hydrochloride 90
amino acids 107, 160, 195
Amovon Corn Caps 212
amphetamines 215
anaemia 140
anaesthesia 68, 70
Anaïs Anaïs 171–2
anatomy 53, 149
Andrew Jergens Company 18
angelica root 7

anhidrosis 81
Anhydral Forte 192
antibiotics 189, 235
antiperspirants 14, 81, 190, 191,
192; for feet 211
antiseptics 68, 81, 83, 90, 97, 124,
152, 178–9, 213–15 *passim*, 262;
allergies and 153, 156, 179, 214;
wipes 214–15
anxiety 117, 118, 144, 164, 189,
200, 222, 238
Apisate 215
apronectomy 72
Aquafresh 259
Aquamaid hydrotherapy appliance
193–4, 196
Aquamaid Ltd 193–4
Aquasun 233
Arabia 168, 169
areola 186, 227
Ariane 26
Aristophanes 126
armpits (axilla) 82, 102, 125;
glands 147; hair 102, 125;
hyperhidrosis and 192
arnica 38, 195, 196
aromatherapy 55, 81
Aromatic Oil Company 55
Around the Eyes (range) 90
Arpège 171
Arpège Eau de Toilette 21
Arpège Extrait 22
Arrid Extra Dry 191
Arrid Light Powder 191
arsenic poisoning 141
aspirin 263
Association of Beauty Teachers 48
Assyrians 4, 121
Astral soap 8
astringents 81, 126, 128, 195;
lotions 157, 177, 241
Athens 174
Atlantic Ocean 17
Australia 229